SEXUAL AGGRESSION: ISSUES IN ETIOLOGY, ASSESSMENT, AND TREATMENT

Edited by

Gordon C. Nagayama Hall
Richard Hirschman
John R. Graham
Maira S. Zaragoza
Kent State University
Kent, Ohio

 Taylor & Francis

USA	Publishing Office:	Taylor & Francis 1101 Vermont Avenue, N.W., Suite 200 Washington, DC 20005-3521 Tel: (202) 289-2174 Fax: (202) 289-3665
	Distribution Center:	Taylor & Francis 1900 Frost Road, Suite 101 Bristol, PA 19007-1598 Tel: (215) 785-5800 Fax: (215) 785-5515
UK		Taylor & Francis Ltd. 4 John Street London WC1N 2ET Tel: 071 405 2237 Fax: 071 831 2035

SEXUAL AGGRESSION: Issues in Etiology, Assessment, and Treatment

1 2 3 4 5 6 7 8 9 0   B R B R   9 8 7 6 5 4 3

This book was set in Times Roman by Taylor & Francis. The editors were Heather Jefferson and Ellen K. Grover; the production supervisor was Peggy M. Rote; and the typesetter was Shirley J. McNett. Cover design by Michelle Fleitz.
Printing and binding by Braun-Brumfield, Inc.

A CIP catalog record for this book is available from the British Library.

♾ The paper in this publication meets the requirements of the ANSI Standard Z39.48-1984 (Permanence of Paper)

Library of Congress Cataloging-in-Publication Data

Sexual aggression: issues in etiology, assessment, and treatment / edited by Gordon C. Nagayama Hall . . . [et al.].
    p. cm.
    1. Sex offenders—United States. 2. Rape—United States. 3. Sex offenders—Rehabilitation—United States. I. Hall, Gordon C. Nagayama.
HV6592.S48   1993
364.1′53—dc20   92-47269
                                                                             CIP

ISBN 1-56032-268-3
ISSN 1048-8146

To Uni and Zomi

CONTENTS

CONTRIBUTORS

HOWARD E. BARBAREE, Department of Psychology, Queen's University, Kingston, Ontario, Canada K7L 3N6

JUDITH V. BECKER, Department of Psychiatry, Arizona Health Sciences Center, 1501 N. Campbell Avenue, Tucson, AZ 85724

ANDREA FOX BOARDMAN, Department of Psychology, Kent State University, Kent, OH 44242-0001

KAREN CHAMBERS, Department of Psychology, Kent State University, Kent, OH 44242-0001

VICTORIA CODISPOTI, Selson Clinics Inc., 2725 Abington Ct., Akron, OH 44313

DAVID M. DAY, California State Department of Mental Health, 1600 9th Street, Sacramento, CA 95814

LEE ELLIS, Division of Social Science, Minot State University, Minot, ND 58701

GORDON C. NAGAYAMA HALL, Department of Psychology, Kent State University, Kent, OH 44242-0001

CATHI D. HARRIS, Psychology Department, University of Arizona, Tucson, AZ 85721

GERALD HEINBAUGH, Forensic Psychiatric Center, 50 Westchester, Youngstown, OH 44515

CHRISTOPHER L. HEAVEY, Department of Psychology, University of Nevada, Reno, NV 89557-0062

RICHARD HIRSCHMAN, Department of Psychology, Kent State University, Kent, OH 44242-0001

RAYMOND A. KNIGHT, Department of Psychology, Brandeis University, Waltham, MA 02254

DAVID KRENRICK, The Forensic Diagnostic Center, 228 Park Avenue West, Mansfield, OH 44902

DANIEL LINZ, Department of Communication, University of California at Santa Barbara, Santa Barbara, CA 93106

NEIL M. MALAMUTH, Department of Communication, University of Michigan, Ann Arbor, MI 48109-1285

JANICE K. MARQUES, California State Department of Mental Health, 1600 9th Street, Sacramento, CA 95814

W. L. MARSHALL, Department of Psychology, Queen's University, Kingston, Ontario, Canada K7L 3N6

CRAIG NELSON, P.O. Box 7001, Atascadero State Hospital, Atascadero, CA 93423

STEVEN NEUHAUS, Cuyahoga Juvenile Court, 2163 East 22nd Street, Cleveland, OH 44115

LORI L. OLIVER, Department of Psychology, Kent State University, Kent, OH 44242-0001

WILLIAM D. PITHERS, Center for the Prevention and Treatment of Sexual Abuse, Vermont Department of Corrections, Waterbury, VT 05676

ROBERT A. PRENTKY, Research Department, Massachusetts Treatment Center, Bridgewater, MA 02324

BRUCE D. SALES, Psychology Department, University of Arizona, Tucson, AZ 85721

RALPH C. SERIN, Correctional Services of Canada, Joyceville Institution, Box 880, Kingston, Ontario, Canada K7L 4X9

DENISE D. SHONDRICK, Department of Psychology, Kent State University, Kent, OH 44242-0001

KATHLEEN P. STAFFORD, Psycho-Diagnostic Clinic, 209 S. High Street, Akron, OH 44308

MARY ANN WEST, P.O. Box 7001, Atascadero State Hospital, Atascadero, CA 93423

LORI BOONE WILLS, Department of Psychology, Kent State University, Kent, OH 44242-0001

PREFACE

Relative to many of the people who have contributed to this volume, I am a newcomer to the sexual aggression field. Richard Hirschman and I invited people we consider to be the leading experts in the field to the fourth Kent Psychology Forum "think tank" meeting, which took place April 7–10, 1992 at the Inn at Honey Run in Ohio's Amish country. This volume is the result of that meeting. Over the past decade I have had the good fortune of getting to know many of the people who have contributed to this volume and in this preface I would like to briefly review my experiences in the field.

My original goal was to devote my career as a clinical psychologist to the study of ethnic minority issues, particularly Asian-American issues. I went to graduate school in Southern California for this purpose, fully intending to settle there. However, because of relatively limited career opportunities in working with Asians, I sought to broaden my interests and expertise during my internship at my alma mater, the University of Washington.

My introduction to the sexual aggression field was in 1981, during my internship, when I had a child molester case in therapy. This man wanted to avoid discussing his child molesting. Rather than confront him about his behavior, my supervisor suggested that I "work around" his resistance and deal with his depression. Needless to say, therapy was not productive and I was not very encouraged about working with sex offenders.

My next experiences in the field of sexual aggression were several intriguing forensic evaluations of sex offenders, which occurred during my postdoctoral year with Roland Maiuro at the University of Washington Department of Psychiatry and Behavioral Sciences. My interest in work with sex offenders was solidified after hearing a very charismatic presentation by Nicholas Groth on his theory of rape. I bought and read Groth's book, *Men Who Rape,* but soon discovered that there was very limited empirical research to support Groth's theory.

Undaunted by my discouragement about Groth's work, I took a job as a psychologist at Western State Hospital in the Sex Offender Program. I was aware that there was much political turmoil and infighting about the direction of the program following a highly publicized reoffense of a former patient from the Sex Offender Program. However, Bill Proctor, who later became Chief of Psychology, believed that I could have a positive impact. In preparation for this job, I ravenously devoured any published literature that I could find on sexual aggression. Joe Becker, who was one of my supervisors during my internship, advised that I conduct research at Western State Hospital if I had any aspirations of returning to academia. Thus, I negotiated that 10% of my time at Western State Hospital be devoted to research.

Just before I began working at Western State Hospital, I attended the meeting of the International Society for Research on Aggression in Victoria, British Columbia. I heard Neil Malamuth give a talk on sexual aggression and was very impressed with his command of conceptual and empirical issues in research. I was also impressed with how young he was. I eagerly approached him after his talk to offer the possibility of gathering data on sex offenders at my new job at Western State Hospital. As it turned out, it would be several years before we would get to work together.

Heeding Joe Becker's sage advice, I sought out research opportunities in my new job at Western State Hospital in 1983. When I inquired about whose permission I needed to conduct research, I was informed that there was no internal review board and that I should contact someone at the state level. The state official I contacted saw no problem with my conducting archival research and granted me permission to do so. I discovered hundreds of MMPI sex offender profiles and undertook a mammoth study, which took two years to complete, in search of the alleged "MMPI sex offender profile." I also began a prospective study to assess and treat anger problems in the Western State sex offender population. This prospective research was permissible, since it was part of the treatment program and not a "pure research" project.

I briefly described the MMPI and anger studies in a May 1984 *APA Monitor* article. Jim Breiling of the National Institute of Mental Health was also quoted in the article as commenting that the Western State Hospital program was "pioneering." I contacted Jim about his comments and he invited me to submit a proposal to participate in a NIMH-sponsored sex offender research conference in St. Louis in 1985. Jim later invited me to present my research on anger problems among sex offenders. I was delighted to accept this invitation, having previously traveled only as far east as Utah, and anticipated an opportunity to meet other colleagues in the field. Many of the major researchers on sex offenders were at the conference, including Howard Barbaree, Judith Becker, and Janice Marques. Despite my lack of credibility and accomplishment at the time, Howard befriended me and took an interest in my work, and has been a supportive influence ever since. I was quite familiar with Howard's research and was astonished at how approachable and helpful he was (and continues to be).

During 1985 I finally completed the MMPI project at Western State Hospital and did not find a model sex offender profile, but multiple profiles. I wrote a manuscript based on this work which I submitted to the *Journal of Consulting and Clinical Psychology* (*JCCP*). I had decided to aim for the best journal, and the rejection of the manuscript that I received from Associate Editor Jim Butcher was not unexpected. Jim suggested that I had overinterpreted statistically significant between-group results that were not necessarily clinically significant. Although I had not expected the manuscript to be accepted, I felt discouraged about continuing research, since I had invested two years in the project.

Another major source of discouragement in 1985 was my new responsibility as Acting Director of the Sex Offender Program at Western State Hospital. As is the case in many institutional settings, the "reward" for good clinical work is administrative responsibilities. I reluctantly accepted the directorship on an acting basis. However, I resigned from my responsibilities as Acting Director in 1986 to return to my regular responsibilities as a psychologist.

In addition to the research that I was conducting, bright spots during my Western State Hospital tenure were clinical work and training. Fortunately, my colleagues Carole Seegert, Lael Zylstra, Beth Bierbaum, Dan DeWaelsche, David Weston, and Joyce Gale steered clear of hospital politics and helped me implement anger management and relapse prevention programs. Our internship program, which gained American Psychological Association (APA) approval, was also rewarding, particularly my work with George Nelson and Darrell Lynch.

My friend and colleague from my postdoctoral fellowship at the University of Washington, Maria Root, offered encouragement during 1985 by suggesting that I call Jim Butcher to see if he would reconsider a revised version of the sex offender MMPI manuscript that was more critical of the discriminative validity of the MMPI. Jim suggested that I resubmit the manuscript to *JCCP,* which was sent to Associate Editor Larry Beutler to review. Not only did Larry decide to accept the article, but, to my surprise, sent me a manuscript to review for *JCCP* and later nominated me to the Editorial Board of *JCCP.* I view the acceptance of this article as a turning point in my research career.

I was invited again in 1986 to the NIMH-sponsored sex offender research conference, which was held in Tampa, where Richard Laws was developing a treatment program for child molesters based on Alan Marlatt's relapse prevention model. I presented a study at the conference in which I had found that the best single predictor of future sex offenses was past sex offenses. In additional analyses that I performed on the data, I found that combinations of past offenses and other actuarial variables (e.g., age, psychometric data) were also superior to clinical judgment about recidivism potential. It was at this conference that I first heard Robert Prentky and Ray Knight present their important taxonomic work, and heard Bill Marshall's enthusiastic and sensitive presentation of his treatment efforts with sex offenders. I got to chat with Bill briefly at the end of the conference. The conference and my consultation there with Howard Barbaree provided renewed impetus for me to continue my research efforts. Because of the emphasis on Laws' relapse prevention at the Tampa conference, I contacted my friend and colleague from internship, Bill George, who had consulted on Richard Laws' relapse prevention program. Bill and his dissertation advisor at the University of Washington, Alan Marlatt, provided training at Western State Hospital and helped me get a relapse prevention component started there.

NIMH stopped sponsoring the sex offender research conference in 1987. The Association for the Behavioral Treatment of Sexual Abusers (ABTSA) sponsored the conference in the spring of 1987 in Newport, Oregon and invited me to participate. I had the pleasure of having dinner with Howard Barbaree and Bill Marshall at Gleneden Beach. I also heard Bill Pithers present his important work on relapse prevention, and got to meet him. As always, Howard was very encouraging when I told him of my uncertain situation at Western State, and said that most people doing sexual aggression research had ups and downs during their careers but eventually landed on their feet. I presented a paper in Oregon that was critical of plethysmograph assessment of child molesters.

During 1987, the state of Washington was in the process of moving sex offender treatment from the state hospital to the prison system. If I wanted to continue research and clinical work with sex offenders, I would need either to move to the prison system or consider a new career setting. Inspired by the Oregon ABTSA conference, I decided to consider the possibility of an academic career. Although I had been able to get my research published, I was skeptical of my chances for an academic job because I had been out of academia for four years, since my postdoctoral training. Sexual aggression is also not a mainstream topic studied in most psychology departments. I made an appointment with Alan Marlatt to discuss the feasibility of my getting an academic job. Alan was encouraging and even offered, unsolicited, to write a letter of reference. He also suggested that his area of addictive behaviors was not considered mainstream at one time. I decided to apply to positions primarily on the West and East coasts, but I also applied to Kent State University because I was familiar with Jack Graham and his work with the MMPI.

While I was applying for academic jobs, Irv Dreiblatt, a prominent Seattle clinical psychologist who is a pioneer in work with sex offenders, approached me about private practice. He suggested that he was considering retiring within the next few years and wanted someone to continue his work with sex offenders. Although I was flattered by this offer, which would have allowed me to stay in Seattle, I was intent on an academic job.

When I was invited by Jack Graham for my job interview at Kent State University, I was uncertain of where Kent State was located. However, after my interview there, I was convinced that Kent State would be the best place for me to pursue my interests in sexual aggression. I enthusiastically accepted the job at Kent State and have received much professional and personal support from my colleagues here. I have had the pleasure of collaborating with Richard Hirschman and several graduate students who have contributed to this volume. My colleagues in the Ohio clinical community, who also contributed to this volume, have made it possible for me to continue my research on sexual offenders.

This volume was inspired by a symposium on Theories of Sexual Aggression that I organized for the 1990 APA Convention in Boston. Howard Barbaree, Robert Prentky, and Neil Malamuth participated in the symposium. Larry Beutler, now Editor of *JCCP*, recognized the importance of this topic and published a Special Series in *JCCP* based on the APA symposium that also included Lee Ellis' biosocial approach. The purpose of the current volume is to facilitate the development of such theories of sexual aggression and their application to research and clinical practice.

I would like to express my deepest gratitude to the people who have contributed to this volume and have offered encouragement to me at various junctures in my career both through their scholarly work and personal support. I also would like to thank Stevan Hobfoll and the Applied Psychology Center for organizing the Forum and this Taylor & Francis series on Law and Psychology, and particularly Judy Jerkich who tirelessly helped organize this volume to make it a reality. The work on this volume was also supported by National Institute of Mental Health Grant RO1 MH45700 awarded to Gordon Nagayama Hall and Richard Hirschman. Most of all, I would like to thank Jeanne Nagayama Hall for her constant support and adaptability.

Gordon C. Nagayama Hall
Kent, Ohio
September, 1992

CONCEPTUALIZING SEXUAL AGGRESSION: PROGRESS AND FUTURE NEEDS

Gordon C. Nagayama Hall
Richard Hirschman
Kent State University

Sexually aggressive behavior is a biopsychosocial phenomenon that primarily is engaged in by males. The multidetermined nature of sexual aggression is reflected in the wide range of different forms of sexually aggressive behavior that are addressed in this volume. Although much recent scholarly work on sexual aggression has addressed victim issues (e.g., Coyne & Downey, 1991; Hanson, 1990; Koss & Burkhart, 1989; Mandoki & Burkhart, 1991; Wyatt, Notgrass, & Newcomb, 1990), this volume focuses on the perpetrators of sexual aggression who ultimately are responsible for the act (Gilbert, Heesacker, & Gannon, 1991). Although the empowerment of victims and potential victims of sexual aggression is critically important (Harney & Muehlenhard, 1991; Levine-MacCombie & Koss, 1986; Prentky, Burgess, & Carter, 1986), there is no other type of aggressive act (e.g., murder, burglary, assault) in which the victim is so routinely blamed (White & Sorenson, 1992). Thus, we hope that our focus on perpetrators serves to shift the emphasis away from victim responsibility and assist in the understanding, treatment, and prevention of sexually aggressive behavior.

Sexually aggressive behavior certainly is not restricted to adults. At one end of the age continuum are sexually aggressive adolescents and pre-adolescents, as discussed in Becker, Harris, and Sales' chapter (chapter 12) on juveniles who commit sexual offenses. Although adolescent sexual behavior is often considered exploratory or not deviant, adolescent sexual aggression against victims ages 12 or over appears common (Fagan & Wexler, 1986). Moreover, many men who are sexually aggressive as adults began their "careers" during adolescence.

The behavior of college students might be considered the next stage on the age continuum. Barbaree and Serin (chapter 6) review studies in which college men's sexual arousal in response to rape stimuli has been disinhibited by variables such as anger and cognitive distortions about a woman. Hall and Hirschman (chapter 7) attempt to identify an observable act of sexual imposition in the laboratory. Their paradigm, in which men present unwanted erotic stimuli to a female confederate, might be considered analogous to a mild form of in vivo sexual aggression.

The work of Malamuth, Heavey, and Linz (chapter 5) involves college men's self- and partner-reported acts of sexually aggressive behavior. Although some of these college men admitted to rape of women, most admitted to lesser acts of coercive sexual behavior, such as touching a woman against her will. At the extreme end of the continuum are the adult clinical populations described by Prentky and Knight (chapter 4), Marshall (chapter 9), Pithers (chapter 10), and Marques, Day, Nelson, and West (chapter 11). These populations differ from the others in terms of high levels of coercion and physical force.

The heterogeneity of sexually aggressive behavior is also reflected in the range of different variables that have been proposed as motivating it. The broadest approaches are those of Malamuth, Heavey, and Linz (chapter 5) and Ellis (chapter 3), who view sexually aggressive behavior from ecological perspectives that include family, cultural, and evolutionary influences, albeit with different emphases for these influences. The developmental context of sexually aggressive behavior is addressed by Becker, Harris, and Sales in the chapter on juvenile sexual offenders (chapter 12) and by Prentky and Knight's chapter on adult sexual offenders (chapter 4). Individual motivational factors are central to the work of Barbaree and Serin (chapter 6) and of Hall and Hirschman (chapter 7). Barbaree and Serin discuss the role of sexual arousal in motivating sexually aggressive behavior. In addition to physiological sexual arousal, Hall and Hirschman identify cognitions, affect, and developmentally related personality problems as motivational precursors of sexually aggressive behavior.

The treatment approaches presented by Becker et al., Marshall, Marques et al., and Pithers target many of the individual psychological factors associated with sexually aggressive behavior in the above theoretical models. The treatment approaches for rapists described in this volume have evolved from treatment programs for child molesters. The relative emphasis in treatment that is placed on particular psychological factors differs between rapists and child molesters. Treating anger dyscontrol receives a greater emphasis among violent rapists than it would among less violent child molesters, and deviant sexual arousal is typically less of a primary motivational factor for rapists than it is for child molesters. Similarly, the cognitive distortions of rapists focus on women rather than on children.

Because most sexual aggressors eventually will be returned to the community, treatment is warranted from a cost–benefit perspective. Victim- and offender-related treatment and incarceration costs per each reoffense of child molesters totaled approximately $180,000 in a recent study (Prentky & Burgess, 1990). These costs to society underscore the importance of understanding, treating, and preventing sexually aggressive behavior.

When treatment programs have been implemented via social policy, the policy seldom has included a mandate for program evaluation. Treatment programs typically are evaluated only when there is a perceived failure, such as a highly publicized reoffense. Programs with an evaluation mandate, such as Marques' California sex offender treatment program, are exceptional. However, the equivocal effectiveness of treatment programs for sexual aggressors against adults warrants evaluation of all treatment methods with this population (Becker et al, chapter 12; Hall, Shondrick, & Hirschman, in press).

The purpose of this volume is to present state-of-the-science theory and research on sexual aggression. We believe that the major approaches to sexual aggression are represented in this volume. We hope that this volume stimulates future research and clinical advances in understanding, treating, and preventing sexually aggressive behavior.

REFERENCES

Coyne, J. C., & Downey, G. (1991). Social factors and psychopathology: Stress, social support, and coping processes. *Annual Review of Psychology, 42,* 401–425.

Fagan, J., & Wexler, S. (1986). Explanations of sexual assault among violent delinquents. *Journal of Adolescent Research, 3,* 363–385.

Gilbert, B. J., Heesacker, M., & Gannon, L. J. (1991). Changing the sexual aggression-supportive attitudes of men: A psychoeducational intervention. *Journal of Counseling Psychology, 38,* 197–203.

Hall, G. C. N. (1988). Criminal behavior as a function of clinical and actuarial variables in a sexual offender population. *Journal of Consulting and Clinical Psychology, 56,* 773–775.

Hall, G. C. N., Shondrick, D. D., & Hirschman, R. (in press). Conceptually-derived treatments for sexual aggressors. *Professional psychology: Research and practice.*

Hanson, R. (1990). The psychological impact of sexual assault on women and children: A review. *Annals of Sex Research, 3,* 187–232.

Harney, P. A., & Muehlenhard, C. L. (1991). Factors that increase the likelihood of victimization. In A. Parrot & L. Bechhofer (Eds.), *Acquaintance rape: The hidden crime* (pp. 159–175). New York: Wiley.

Koss, M. P., & Burkhart, B. R. (1989). A conceptual analysis of rape victimization: Long-term effects and implications for treatment. *Psychology of Women Quarterly, 13,* 27–40.

Levine-MacCombie, J., & Koss, M. P. (1986). Acquaintance rape: Effective avoidance strategies. *Psychology of Women Quarterly, 10,* 311–319.

Mandoki, C. A., & Burkhart, B. R. (1991). Women as victims: Antecedents and consequences of acquaintance rape. In A. Parrot & L. Bechhofer (Eds.), *Acquaintance rape: The hidden crime* (pp. 176–191). New York: Wiley.

Prentky, R., Burgess, A. W., Carter, D. L. (1986). Victim responses by rapist type: an empirical and clinical analysis. *Journal of Interpersonal Violence, 1,* 73–98.

Prentky, R., & Burgess, A. W. (1990). Rehabilitation of child molesters: A cost–benefit analysis. *American Journal of Orthopsychiatry, 60,* 108–117.

White, J. W., & Sorenson, S. B. (1992). A sociocultural view of sexual assault. *Journal of Social Issues, 48,* 187–195.

Wyatt, G. E., Notgrass, C. M., & Newcomb, M. (1990). Internal and external mediators of women's rape experiences. *Psychology of Women Quarterly, 14,* 153–176.

I

ETIOLOGY AND ASSESSMENT

2

INTRODUCTION: ETIOLOGY AND ASSESSMENT

Lori L. Oliver
Karen Chambers
Kent State University

ETIOLOGY

Feminist, evolutionary, and social learning perspectives of sexual aggression could provide organizing contexts for understanding the specific etiological factors of sexual aggression as described in the following chapters. For example, in feminist theory, rape is primarily an economically and politically driven event. Presumably most or all women are affected by the possibility of rape, because this possibility may change women's behavior (Brownmiller, 1975; Donat & D'Emilio, 1992; Griffin, 1971; Riger & Gordon, 1981). Sexual aggression can also be viewed as a consequence of women failing to follow gender-role stereotypes. Female gender-role stereotypes often are negative, particularly relative to male gender-role stereotypes (Sanday, 1981). Masculinity often is associated with power, dominance, and strength, whereas femininity often is associated with submissiveness, passivity, and weakness (Scully & Marolla, 1985). According to this perspective, rape is motivated more by a desire to dominate and be in control than for sexual pleasure (Brownmiller, 1975; Scully & Marolla, 1985). Support for this view is seen by males' hostility toward women and males' sexually aggressive acts. If a man is relatively high in hostility, the woman's suffering during a sexually aggressive act will not inhibit his sexual arousal and may reinforce it (Malamuth, 1981, 1986). Feminists often assert that the prevention of sexual assault lies in the establishment of economic and political equality between the sexes (Brownmiller, 1975; Riger & Gordon, 1981). Educating women to be assertive (Donat & D'Emilio, 1992; Griffin, 1971) as well as educating men not to rape, through attitude and behavioral modification (Donat & D'Emilio, 1992), are also feminist strategies for prevention of sexual assault.

Evolutionary theory is based on the study of the historical adaptation of species to the environment. Biologists study adaptations as long-term products of nonrandom differential reproduction of individuals (Thornhill & Thornhill, 1991). There are both proximate and evolutionary causes for biological characteristics that impact on the success or failure of adaptation. Proximate explanations include immediate causes leading to the expression of a characteristic (e.g., biochemical, developmental, social, and learning causes). Evolutionary explanations focus on causes that exist throughout evolutionary history and lead to the selection of a biological characteristic (Thornhill & Thornhill, 1983). Evolutionary theorists point to many factors of sexual coercion that may have their basis in evolutionary history and different reproductive strategies. One speculative view is that whereas men may attempt to produce many offspring and invest little in each offspring, women are likely to have few offspring and invest a great deal in each offspring (Ellis, 1991). Because women have a greater investment in their offspring, they are likely to be more selective than men about their sexual partners (Buss, 1989; Ellis, chapter 3). In addition, those individuals who lack socially favored characteristics (e.g., status, stability, wealth) are less likely to be selected by the opposite sex to produce offspring (Buss, 1989). Not surprisingly, from this perspective it is the male who has not been chosen by a female who is likely to be sexually coercive toward a desired female in an effort to reproduce his genetic makeup (Ellis, chapter 3). A corollary prediction from this view is that females of reproductive age will be sexually assaulted most frequently, because the primary cause of assaulting is the desire to reproduce (Ellis, chapter 3; Thornhill & Thornhill, 1983, 1991). It also can be predicted that men with high levels of testosterone may be more likely to be sexually aggressive than men with lower levels of testosterone. Presumably, increased testosterone levels result in an increased sex drive and relative insensitivity to the environment (Ellis, chapter 3, 1986). This insensitivity may be manifested in the lack of caring about consequences to oneself as well as the victim, and may increase the likelihood that a sexual assault will occur (Ellis, chapter 3).

Another important organized, explanatory context for the etiological factors of sexual aggression is social learning theory. Specifically, it may be useful to look at the person's culture as a system of units, with the smaller units being influenced by the larger ones. In increasing order, these would be the individual, the family, the peer subculture, and society (Malamuth, Heavey, & Linz, chapter 5). At the smallest unit, the person develops coercive, sexually aggressive techniques. This can occur through family interactions that encourage a manipulative style (Dodge, Bates, & Pettit, 1990; Malamuth et al., chapter 5; Prentky & Knight, chapter 4). The family unit may also influence a particular individual through particularly harsh punishment and poor supervision (Knight,

Prentky, Schneider, & Rosenberg, 1983; Prentky & Knight, chapter 4). A major predictor of sexual aggressiveness is having been sexually victimized as a child (Prentky & Knight, chapter 4). Presumably, the earlier the onset of sexual victimization, the more pathological the abuse; and the longer the period of abuse, the earlier the onset of sexual aggressiveness by the victim (Prentky & Knight, chapter 4). Frequently, those children from a hostile home environment will associate with a delinquent peer group (Patterson, DeBaryshe, & Ramsey, 1989). These peer groups often reinforce the hostile and aggressive tendencies originating in the home (Malamuth et al., chapter 5). Ultimately, this peer subculture is embedded in the general cultural environment.

Similar to the feminist theory, social learning theorists posit that society generally reinforces attitudes that foster the victimization of women (Burt, 1980; Malamuth et al., chapter 5). Pornography most often portrays women as sexual objects who enjoy being raped even if they outwardly resist (Marshall & Barbaree, 1989) and may result in men accepting rape myths and increasing their sexual arousal in further presentations of rape pornography (Malamuth, 1981; Malamuth & Check, 1981). Sexual fantasies serve to entrench the attractiveness of deviant sexual acts (Marshall & Barbaree, 1984). Masturbation paired with such fantasies may reinforce and maintain this deviant sexual arousal (Marshall & Barbaree, 1984, 1989). Malamuth et al. (chapter 5) hypothesize that these experiences affect two trajectory paths that interact to influence aggression toward women. These paths can be thought of as a "hostile masculinity" path and a "sexual promiscuity" path. The hostile masculinity path includes components of dominance motivation and hostility toward women. The sexual promiscuity path includes viewing components of sex as power and delinquency. Malamuth et al. (chapter 5) suggest that it is when these two paths converge that sexual aggression is more likely to be expressed.

It is apparent that, in each of these theories, causes of sexual aggression are viewed from different perspectives. It may be helpful to think of these theories as complementary, rather than trying to determine which theory is unequivocally correct. Sexual aggression may then be viewed as being possibly caused by a cluster of factors (e.g., biological, family, individual) with interdependent variables contributing to each factor.

ASSESSMENT

Regarding the assessment of the potential for a male to commit a sexually aggressive act, there are two well-established methods. One of these methods involves the direct physiological measurement of men's arousal to sexual stimuli via the penile plethysmograph. The other assessment method is self-report. Other direct and indirect laboratory methods designed to measure sexual aggression have been developed (Hall & Hirschman, chapter 7; Malamuth, 1983, 1987, 1988; Malamuth & Check, 1982). Some of these methods are still in the experimental stages (Hall & Hirschman, chapter 7). Unfortunately, no one assessment instrument or method alone has been found to be reliably predictive of sexually aggressive behavior (Malamuth et al., chapter 5). In addition, each method has weaknesses. To appreciate the research on assessment of sexual aggression in the following chapters, it is helpful to look more closely at the specific assessment methods and to understand the strengths and weaknesses associated with each of them.

Self-Report

Much traditional research on sexual aggression has involved post hoc comparisons of sexually aggressive and nonaggressive persons on a variety of variables assessed through self-report (Hall, 1990). The self-report measures used in sexual aggression research have included personality inventories (Eysenck, 1978), sexual activity and interest surveys (Bentler, 1969; Koss & Oros, 1982), and attitudes about women scales (Burt, 1980; Check, 1985; Nelson, 1979). Unfortunately, equivocal relationships generally have been found between such measures and sexually aggressive behavior (Hall, 1990).

One possible explanation for the inconsistent relationship between self-report measures and sexually aggressive behavior is that admitting deviant sexual behavior is socially undesirable. Even the assurance of anonymity in many studies does not necessarily preclude social desirability in self-report (Hall, 1990). Further, there is evidence that the admission of sexually aggressive behavior is socially undesirable even in the presence of corroborating evidence (Hall, 1989; Lanyon & Lutz, 1984; McGovern & Nevid, 1986). Additionally, discrepancies often exist between perpetrator and victim self-reports of sexual aggression. Male perpetrators often have not viewed their behavior as sexually aggressive although female victims have defined it as such (Koss, Gidycz, & Wisniewski, 1987). Thus, social desirability, as well as distorted perceptions of the occurrence of sexual aggression, may limit the validity of information gained from self-report or, at the least, require more evidence of reliability.

Despite these limitations, much valuable information has been learned about perpetrators of sexual aggression, particularly when attempts are made to overcome or limit the influence of these limitations. For instance, Malamuth et al. (chapter 5) uses a wide variety of self-report measures to assess predictors thought to be relevant to sexual aggression. A portion of a self-report instrument development by Nelson (1979) was utilized to measure a dominance motive (e.g., the desire to dominate women) as a predictor for sexual aggression (Malamuth et al., chapter 5). Other such instruments used by Malamuth et al. (chapter 5) included the Hostility Toward Women Scale (Check, 1985), the Acceptance of Interpersonal Violence Against Women Scale (Burt, 1980), the

Psychoticism Scale of the Eysenck Personality Questionnaire (Eysenck, 1978), the Sexual Behavior Inventory (Bentler, 1968), and a measure of sexually aggressive behavior developed by Koss and Oros (1982). Additionally, to corroborate the self-report of male subjects, female partners were questioned regarding aggression and sexual aggression in their relationships with the subjects. The findings of Malamuth et al. (chapter 5) indicated that all of the identified predictors (as assessed by self-report), except psychoticism, were significantly related to naturalistic sexual aggression, as assessed by partner report. In their study, social desirability was not associated with the admission of sexually aggressive behavior. Thus, assessment of sexual aggression through self-report may be more promising than had previously been thought.

Physiological Measurement of Sexual Arousal

Direct physiological measurement of penile erection by using the penile plethysmograph has been demonstrated to be a more reliable index of male sexual arousal than self-report or other physiological measures (Barlow, 1977; Farkas, Sine, & Evans, 1979; Quinsey, Steinman, Bergersen, & Holmes, 1975; Rosen & Keefe, 1978; Zuckerman, 1971). However, the external validity of this assessment instrument has been questioned (Blader & Marshall, 1989; Hall, 1990), because measures of penile erection have not been entirely successful in identifying deviant sexual arousal patterns among sexual offenders (Baxter, Barbaree, & Marshall, 1986; Murphy, Krisak, Stalgaitis, & Anderson, 1984). Arousal to sexually deviant stimuli among sex offenders may simply reflect general arousability, rather than deviant sexual behavior (Hall, 1989). Other researchers (Earls & Proulx, 1986; Quinsey, Chaplin, & Upfold, 1984) have found results supportive of a sexual preference hypothesis, namely, that rapists may show stronger arousal to rape cues than nonoffenders, and stronger arousal to rape cues than to consenting cues. The literature regarding this assessment tool is conflicting; for this reason, Hall, Proctor, & Nelson (1988) advised caution in the interpretation of physiological measures of sexual aggression.

Sexual arousal to rape stimuli, when combined with other predictors, showed a strong relation to actual sexually aggressive behavior (Malamuth et al., chapter 5). Barbaree and Serin (chapter 6) also developed a typology of sexual arousal among rapists that shares some elements with Knight and Prentky's (1987) taxonomy. The typology (Barbaree & Serin, chapter 6) accounts for the heterogeneity in the population of rapists, and supports the idea that sexual arousal and sexual motivation may differ among subtypes of rapists. Although interpretation of sexual arousal may be problematic, it is apparent that the availability of a means of physiologically assessing arousal to sexual stimuli is of crucial importance for the progression of sexual aggression research.

Laboratory Methods for Assessing Sexual Aggression

Given the problems with self-report and the external validity questions associated with the physiological assessment of sexual arousal as predictors of sexual aggression, a more direct behavioral method of assessing sexual aggression would be helpful. Ethical and practical constraints have played a major role in limiting research aimed at developing laboratory analogues of sexual aggression (Hall, Hirschman, & Oliver, 1992). Prior attempts toward this goal have not entirely captured the essence of what is considered to be sexual aggression (Blader, Marshall, & Barbaree, 1988; George & Marlatt, 1986; Lang, Searles, Lauerman, & Adesso, 1980; Pryor, 1987).

Hall et al. (1992) have conceptualized sexual aggression as the imposition of an unwanted sexual experience on a victim. As such, they have developed a laboratory analogue of sexual aggression in which the subject has the opportunity to display sexually imposing behavior within the appropriate ethical and practical constraints (Hall & Hirschman, chapter 7). The method of assessing sexually imposing behavior developed by Hall and Hirschman (chapter 7) is less susceptible to social desirability than self-report, less ambiguous with regard to motives than physiological assessment, and less inferential than other laboratory methods. To the extent that Hall and Hirschman's (chapter 7) procedure is reliable and valid, it may provide a more direct, but analogous, context for examining motivational variables of the perpetrators.

In conclusion, although much is known about sexual aggressors, the assessment tools currently available to assess the potential for sexual aggression have not been entirely satisfactory. More reliable and valid measures must be developed for theory testing. Examples of the state-of-the-science are found in the following chapters.

REFERENCES

Barbaree, H. E., & Serin, R. C. (1992). The role of male sexual arousal during rape in various rapist subtypes. In G. C. N. Hall & R. Hirschman (Eds.), *Sexual aggression: Issues in etiology and assessment, treatment and policy* (pp. 99–114). New York: Hemisphere.

Barlow, D. H. (1977). Assessment of sexual behavior. In A. R. Ciminero, K. S. Calhoun, & H. E. Adams (Eds.), *Handbook of behavioral assessment* (pp. 461–508). New York: Wiley.

Baxter, D. J., Barbaree, H. E., & Marshall, W. L. (1986). Sexual responses to consenting and forced sex in a large sample of rapists and nonrapists. *Behaviour Research and Therapy, 24,* 513–520.

Bentler, P. M. (1969). Heterosexual behavior assessment in males. *Behaviour Research and Therapy, 6,* 21–25.

Blader, J. C., & Marshall, W. L. (1989). Is assessment of sexual arousal in rapists worthwhile? A critique of current methods and the development of a response compatibility approach. *Clinical Psychology Review, 9,* 569–587.

Blader, J. C., Marshall, W. L., & Barbaree, H. E. (1988, June). *The inhibitory effect of coercion on sexual arousal in men and disinhibition by provocation.* Paper presented at the meeting of the Canadian Psychological Association, Montreal.

Brownmiller, S. (1975). *Against our will: Men, women and rape.* New York: Simon & Schuster.

Burt, M. R. (1980). Cultural myths and support for rape. *Journal of Personality and Social Psychology, 38,* 217–230.

Buss, D. M. (1989). Sex differences in human mate preferences: Evolutionary hypotheses tested in 37 cultures. *Behavioral and Brain Sciences, 12,* 1–49.

Check, J. V. P. (1985). *The hostility towards women scale.* Unpublished doctoral dissertation. University of Manitoba, Winnipeg.

Dodge, K. A., Bates, J. E., & Pettit, G. S. (1990). Mechanisms in the cycle of violence. *Science, 250,* 1678–1683.

Donat, P. L. N., & D'Emilio, J. (1992). A feminist redefinition of rape and sexual assault: Historical foundations and change. *Journal of Social Issues, 48,* 9–22.

Earls, C. M., & Proulx, J. (1986). The differentiation of Francophone rapists and nonrapists using penile circumferential measures. *Criminal Justice and Behavior, 13,* 419–429.

Ellis, L. (1986). Evidence of neuroandrogenic etiology of sex roles from a combined analysis of human, nonhuman primate, and nonprimate mammalian studies. *Personality and Individual Differences, 7,* 519–552.

Ellis, L. (1991). A synthesized (biosocial) theory of rape. *Journal of Consulting and Clinical Psychology, 59,* 631–642.

Eysenck, H. J. (1978). *Sex and personality.* London: Open Books.

Farkas, G. M., Sine, R. F., & Evans, I. M. (1979). The effects of distraction, performance demand, stimulus explicitness, and personality on objective and subjective measures of male sexual arousal. *Journal of Consulting and Clinical Psychology, 46,* 25–32.

George, W. H., & Marlatt, G. A. (1986). The effects of alcohol and anger on interest in violence, erotica, and deviance. *Journal of Abnormal Psychology, 95,* 150–158.

Griffin, S. (1971). Rape: The all-American crime. *Ramparts, 10,* 26–35.

Hall, G. C. N. (1989). Self-reported hostility as a function of offense characteristics and response style in a sexual offender population. *Journal of Consulting and Clinical Psychology, 57,* 306–308.

Hall, G. C. N. (1990). Prediction of sexual aggression. *Clinical Psychology Review, 10,* 229–245.

Hall, G. C. N., Hirschman, R., & Oliver, L. L. (1992). *Ignoring a woman's protest: sexually impositional behavior in the laboratory.* Manuscript submitted for publication.

Hall, G. C. N., Proctor, W. C., & Nelson, G. M. (1988). Validity of physiological measures of pedophilic sexual arousal in a sexual offender population. *Journal of Consulting and Clinical Psychology, 56*(1), 118–122.

Knight, R. A., & Prentky, R. A. (1987). The developmental antecedents and adult adaptations of rapist subtypes. *Criminal Justice and Behavior, 14,* 403–426.

Knight, R. A., Prentky, R. A., Schneider, & Rosenberg, R. (1983). Linear causal modeling of adaptation and criminal history in sexual offenders. In D. Van Dusen & S. Mednick (Eds.), *New directions in psychological research* (pp. 43–62). Toronto: Van Nostrand.

Koss, M. P., Gidycz, C. A., & Wisniewski, N. (1987). The scope of rape: Incidence and prevalence of sexual aggression and victimization in a national sample of higher education students. *Journal of Consulting and Clinical Psychology, 55,* 162–170.

Koss, M. P., & Oros, C. (1982). Sexual experiences survey: A research instrument investigating sexual aggression and victimization. *Journal of Consulting and Clinical Psychology, 50,* 455–457.

Lang, A. R., Searles, J., Lauerman, R., & Adesso, V. (1980). Expectancy, alcohol, and sex guilt as determinants of interest in and reaction to sexual stimuli. *Journal of Abnormal Psychology, 89,* 644–653.

Lanyon, R. I., & Lutz, R. W. (1984). MMPI discrimination of defensive and nondefensive felony sex offenders. *Journal of Consulting and Clinical Psychology, 52,* 841–843.

Malamuth, N. M. (1981). Rape fantasies as a function of exposure to violent sexual stimuli. *Archives of Sexual Behavior, 10,* 33–48.

Malamuth, N. M. (1983). Factors associated with rape as predictors of laboratory aggression against women. *Journal of Personality and Social Psychology, 45,* 432–442.

Malamuth, N. M. (1986). Predictors of naturalistic sexual aggression. *Journal of Personality and Social Psychology, 50,* 953–962.

Malamuth, N. M. (1987, August). *Sexual aggression and domineeringness in conversations with male vs. female targets.* Paper presented at the Annual Meeting of the American Psychological Association, New York.

Malamuth, N. M. (1988). Predicting laboratory aggression against male and female targets: Implications for sexual aggression. *Journal of Research in Personality, 22,* 474–495.

Malamuth, N. M., & Check, J. V. P. (1981). The effects of mass media exposure on acceptance of violence against women: A field experiment. *Journal of Research in Personality, 15,* 436–446.

Malamuth, N. M., & Check, J. V. P. (1982, June). *Factors related to aggres-*

sion against women. Paper presented at the Annual Meeting of the Canadian Psychological Association, Montreal, Canada.

Malamuth, N. M., Heavey, C. L., & Linz, D. (1992). Predicting men's aggression against women: Research contributing to the development of the confluence model of sexual aggression. In G. C. N. Hall & R. Hirschman (Eds.), *Sexual aggression: Issues in etiology and assessment, treatment and policy* (pp. 63–97). New York: Hemisphere.

Marshall, W. L., & Barbaree, H. E. (1984). A behavioral view of rape. *International Journal of Law and Psychiatry, 7,* 51–77.

Marshall, W. L., & Barbaree, H. E. (1989). Sexual violence. In Howells & Hollin (Eds.), *Clinical approaches to violence* (pp. 205–246). New York: Wiley.

McGovern, F. J., & Nevid, J. S. (1986). Evaluation apprehension on psychological inventories in a prison-based setting. *Journal of Consulting and Clinical Psychology, 54,* 576–578.

Murphy, W. D., Krisak, J., Stalgaitis, S., & Anderson, K. (1984). The use of penile tumescence measures with incarcerated rapists: Further validity issues. *Archives of Sexual Behavior, 13,* 545–554.

Nelson, P. A. (1979). *Personality, sexual functions, and sexual behavior: An experiment in methodology.* Unpublished doctoral dissertation, University of Florida.

Patterson, G. R., DeBaryshe, B. D., & Ramsey, E. (1989). A developmental perspective on antisocial behavior. *American Psychologist, 44,* 329–335.

Pryor, J. B. (1987). Sexual harassment proclivities in men. *Sex Roles, 17,* 269–290.

Quinsey, V. L., Chaplin, T. C., & Upfold, D. (1984). Sexual arousal to nonsexual violence and sadomasochistic themes among rapists and non-sexoffenders. *Journal of Consulting and Clinical Psychology, 52,* 651–657.

Quinsey, V. L., Steinman, C. M., Bergersen, S. G., & Holmes, T. F. (1975). Penile circumference, skin conductance, and ranking responses of child molesters and "normals" to sexual and nonsexual visual stimuli. *Behavior Therapy, 6,* 213–219.

Riger, S., & Gordon, M. T. (1981). The fear of rape: A study in social control. *Journal of Social Issues, 37,* 1–27.

Rosen, R. C., & Keefe, F. J. (1978). The measurement of human penile tumescence. *Psychophysiology, 15,* 366–376.

Sanday, P. R. (1981). The socio-cultural context of rape. *Journal of Social Issues, 37,* 1–27.

Scully, D., & Marolla, J. (1985). Riding the bull at Gilley's: Convicted rapists describe the rewards of rape. *Social Problems, 32,* 251–263.

Thornhill, R., & Thornhill, N. W. (1983). Human rape: An evolutionary analysis. *Ethology and Sociobiology, 4,* 137–173.

Thornhill, R. & Thornhill, N. W. (1991). Coercive sexuality of men: is there psychological adaptation to rape? In E. Graverholz & M. A. Koralewski (Eds.), *Sexual coercion: a source book on its nature, causes, and prevention* (pp. 91–107) Toronto: Lexington Books.

Zuckerman, M. (1971). Physiological measures of sexual arousal in the human. *Psychological Bulletin, 25,* 297–327.

3

RAPE AS A BIOSOCIAL PHENOMENON

Lee Ellis
Minot State University

The overall theme of this chapter is that rape can be best understood as both a biological and a social phenomenon. Within the framework of that theme, certain evolutionary, physiological, and socio-legal processes may be identified as likely to affect the rates at which rape is prevalent in various societies.

The presentation is in three parts: The first gives a brief sketch of prior social science attempts to understand rape. The second outlines a biosocial (or synthesized) theory of rape per se. The third states that rape is linked to an important evolutionary concept, that of *r/K selection*. Also in the third part, evidence is reviewed with respect to how sex, age, and social status may be related to rape probabilities.

BRIEF HISTORY OF SCIENTIFIC ATTEMPTS
TO UNDERSTAND RAPE

Although a few dozen studies on the possible causes of rape were published prior to the mid-1970s, nearly all of them were based on the study of convicted rapists (Amir, 1971; Bonger, 1916; Gebhard, Gagnon, Pomeroy, & Christenson, 1965; Guttmacher, 1951). Given the low rate at which rape offenses are reported to police, and even lower rate at which they result in arrest and conviction (Ellis, 1989a), these early studies did not provide a representative picture of rape offenders or victims.

Beginning in the mid-1970s, social science articles on rape began to be published at an unprecedented rate. By the end of the 1980s, close to a thousand scientific articles had been published bearing on the possible causes of sexual assault. Out of this flurry of scientific research emerged three distinguishable theories of rape: the feminist theory, the social learning theory, and the evolutionary theory (Ellis, 1989a). Each of these theories is described briefly below, followed by an attempt to synthesize them.

The Feminist Theory of Rape

One of the unique features of the feminist theory of rape is that its proponents basically conceive of rape in political and economic terms (Brownmiller, 1975; Dworkin, 1981; Schwendinger & Schwendinger, 1982). Rape is considered one of the outcomes of a long tradition of male domination of most political and economic affairs in numerous societies throughout the world (Brownmiller, 1975).

Male political and economic supremacy is seen from the feminist perspective as fostering and reflecting the exploitation of women at an interpersonal level. Rape as well as prostitution and pornography are considered some of the prime examples of male exploitation (Basow & Companile, 1990; Dworkin, 1981; MacKinnon, 1984). In the case of all these sexual phenomena, women tend to be treated (or portrayed) in subservient and degrading roles, rather than as equal partners in human affairs (Clark & Lewis, 1977; Dworkin, 1981).

As to the causes of the long tradition of male domination and exploitation, most feminist theorists attribute these tendencies to socialization into stereotypic sex roles (Brownmiller, 1975; Quackenbush, 1989). By and large, feminist theorists strenuously resist suggestions that any biological factors are responsible for variations in male tendencies to dominate women, and especially in male tendencies to commit rape (Harding, 1985; Sanday, 1981; Schwendinger & Schwendinger, 1982, 1983).

To proponents of the feminist theory, sexuality has little to do with motivating rape. Instead, the primary objective of rapists, according to the feminist theory, is to dominate and degrade women and ultimately ensure that women are maintained as socially and economically subservient to men. This view is epitomized by pronouncements that rape is, in reality, a "pseudosexual act" (Groth, 1979; Groth & Burgess, 1978; Yourell & McCabe, 1989).

Among the most widely known proponents of the feminist theory of rape are Brownmiller (1975), Clark and Lewis (1977), Dworkin (1981), and Schwendinger and Schwendinger (1983), although there are numerous others. Within a decade of its formulation in the 1970s, the feminist theory had become the dominant social science explanation for rape (Smith & Bennett, 1985).

Because they conceive of rape as having little to do with sexuality, and as being rooted in sex disparities in political and economic power, many proponents of the feminist theory have sought to reduce the risk of rape by eliminating sex disparities in political and economic power (Brownmiller, 1975; Chappell, Geis, Schafer, & Siegel, 1977). Unfortunately, the exact nature of this relationship is not consistently envisioned by all proponents of feminist theory. Whereas some proponents argue that progress in reducing sex disparities in political and economic status will reduce the risk of rape, others have put forth a "frustration version" of the theory. This latter version asserts that as progress is made toward equalizing the sexes in political and economic status, rape rates actually may increase, especially in the short run (Russell, 1975). Such an increase may be the result of many males increasing their use of sexual aggression to re-assert their supremacy and control over women (Ellis, 1989a).

Support for the frustration version of the feminist theory has come from studies that have compared various rape rates in geographical regions, with degrees of disparity between the sexes in social status. For example, in a study of rape rates in 29 U.S. cities (using both official statistics and victimization survey data), Ellis and Beattie (1983) found that cities with the greatest disparity between the sexes in political and economic status, even after controlling for a number of other variables, tended to have lower rape rates than cities with the fewest status disparities between the sexes. Similar findings have been reported by Barron and Straus (1984) in their statewide study of official rape rates in the United States.

The feminist theory also leads to the hypothesis that exposing males to pornography will increase rape rates, primarily because most pornography reflects and reinforces male domination and aggression toward women (Dworkin, 1981; MacKinnon, 1986). The feminist theory shares this hypothesis with the social learning theory, albeit with some subtle differences.

Social Learning Theory of Rape

The social learning theory of rape is rooted most strongly in social psychological research, suggesting that repeated exposure to virtually any type of stimulus fosters positive feelings toward it (Wilson & Nakajo, 1965; Zajonc, 1968). Another theoretical underpinning of the social learning theory of rape has come from Bandura's (1973, 1978) proposal that aggressive behavior can be learned through imitation (or modeling). A third impetus to the social learning theory as it relates to rape has come from proposals by Burt (1980) and others (Wyer, Bodenhausen, & Gorman, 1985; Zillmann & Bryant, 1984), who have contended that many Western cultures (including contemporary American culture) are steeped in beliefs and traditions that tolerate and even encourage rape. Thus, most social learning theorists have asserted that rape is basically a form of male aggression toward women that is gradually learned through the following processes: (a) becoming desensitized to the harm caused by sexual violence, (b) coming to associate violence with sexual pleasure, and (c) becoming persuaded that sexual gratification can be gained via aggression toward women.

Without implying that social learning theorists are all of one mind, major proponents include Malamuth (1981, 1983, 1984),[1] Check and Malamuth (1985), Linz (1985), and Zillmann (1984). They have the following elements in common with feminist theorists: Both give no specific consideration to any biological variables, although social learning theorists seem less antagonistic toward biological variables than feminist theorists. Both groups view rape as reflecting a tradition of female repression by males, and some social learning theorists concur with feminists that sexuality has little to do with rape motivation (Malamuth, 1984; Yourell & McCabe, 1989).

The main difference between the feminist theory and most versions of the social learning theory of rape is that the latter does not emphasize political and economic causes of rape. Instead, most social learning theorists focus on the outcome of exposure to pornography and other aspects of culture that foster male attitudes in which aggression, domination, and sexuality become fused (Check & Malamuth, 1986; Donnerstein, Linz, & Penrod, 1987; Malamuth, 1984). Several social learning theorists have attempted to identify precise features of films that may elicit raping behavior in males and ways to counteract those features (Intons-Peterson, Roskos-Ewoldsen, Thomas, Shirley, & Bult, 1989). Another difference between the two theories is that much of the research by social learning theorists has been experimental, whereas almost none of the research by feminist theorists has been.

Conclusions reached by social learning theorists about the types of filmed stimuli that are most likely to have rape promoting effects have been steeped in controversy. For example, research by Zillmann (1984, 1986) has indicated that prolonged exposure to most forms of hard-core pornography is likely to promote male raping tendencies. On the other hand, studies by Donnerstein, Linz, and Penrod (1987) and Linz (1989) have suggested that R-rated slasher films, in which scenes of gruesome violence are thematically interwoven with pictures of females in sexually provocative attire, may be much more rape promoting than hard-core pornography. Other researchers, such as Check and Malamuth (1986), have reviewed evidence suggesting that only when sexual violence is blended with scenes depicting women in "dehumanizing" (i.e., subservient plus sexually insatiable) roles is pornography likely to foster sexual assault.

Although much of the work of social learning theorists has been experimental, essentially none of the research has used sexual assault per se as a dependent variable (for obvious ethical reasons). Instead, various "proxies" for rape have served as dependent variables, such as males taking the opportunity to shock females, subjective estimates of the seriousness of rape, and paper-and-pencil reports of greater likelihood of committing rape.

---

[1]*In recent years, Malamuth has shifted his theoretical emphasis to one that incorporates some evolutionary concepts as well as social learning (personal correspondence; also see chapter 5 of this volume).*

Evolutionary Theory of Rape

At the heart of the evolutionary (or sociobiological) theory of rape is reproduction. The theory is grounded in evidence that the sexes may optimize their reproductive success differently. Specifically, whereas male reproduction can be optimized by having numerous sex partners, the number of sex partners a female has generally will not increase her reproductive success at all (Daly & Wilson, 1983; Hagen, 1979). The female's reproductive potential depends much more than the male's on being assisted while she gestates and rears the offspring that she bears (Ellis, 1989b). Given such a sex difference in how to leave the greatest number of offspring in the next generation, males would be favored much more than females would be for employing a wider variety of methods (tactics) to gain copulatory access with numerous sex partners. Conceivably, the tendency to resort to physical force, at least when other tactics fail, may have evolved in some species, especially when there is little risk of any successful retaliation (Le Boeuf & Mesnick, 1990).

Proponents of the various versions of the evolutionary theory of rape include Symons (1979), Shields and Shields (1983), Thornhill and Thornhill (1983, 1987), Marshall (1984), and Thiessen (1986). All versions of this theory share the common assumption that genetic factors underlie male tendencies to rape, and that the frequency of these genetic dispositions may vary within a species. However, this assumption does not rule out the involvement of learning, given that both the ability to learn and the tendency to learn certain things often appear to have a genetic foundation (Gould & Marler, 1987).

The evolutionary theory clearly predicts that rape victims should primarily be of reproductive age, and support for this prediction is strong (Ellis, 1989a). Also, according to this theory, there must be significant chances of pregnancy resulting from forced copulation. Although a limited review of the literature brought Harding (1985) to conclude that the likelihood of pregnancy resulting from rape was too low to have been naturally selected, two more extensive reviews have concluded that the probability of pregnancies resulting from rape appear to be almost as high as the probability associated with voluntary copulations (Ellis 1989a; Krueger, 1988).

THE BIOSOCIAL (SYNTHESIZED) THEORY OF RAPE

The theory put forth next has been espoused in somewhat different forms elsewhere (Ellis, 1989a, 1991a). The theory was designed specifically to incorporate what seemed to be the strengths of each of the three theories just outlined. In addition, it incorporates concepts having to do with how sex hormones affect brain functioning, and thereby rape probability. The theory can best be described in terms of four propositions.

Proposition 1. Two unlearned drives motivate rape (as well as essentially all other forms of sexual behavior): one is the sex drive, and the other is the drive to possess and control.

As sexually reproducing animals, humans appear to have a basically unlearned drive to periodically copulate. This is not to suggest that learning is not important to the expression of the sex drive, but simply to assert that the drive itself (like the drive for food and water) is largely unlearned.

A drive to possess and control also appears to be widespread in the animal world, although probably not as universal as the sex drive (Ellis, 1989b, 1991b). Whereas humans often express their drives to possess and control in linguistic forms, nonhuman animals must do so nonlinguistically. These nonlinguistic expressions of the drive to possess and control include: (a) catching, burying, or otherwise hoarding resources (Anderson & Krebs, 1978; Dewsbury, 1978; Roberts, 1979; Smith & Reichmann, 1984); (b) maintaining proximity to resources and guarding them against conspecifics (Kummer, 1973); (c) fighting conspecifics that attempt to usurp their possession and control (Valzelli, 1974); and (d) using a variety of techniques known as *marking* to distinguish the objects over which they claim ownership from other objects (Jolly, 1985; Lumia, Westervelt, & Reider, 1975; Rasmussen & Rasmussen, 1979).

The objects toward which the drive to possess and control are directed primarily include such obvious resources as food, water, shelter, and territory (Dewsbury, 1978; Hinde, 1956; Klopfer, 1969). However, the drive to possess and control is also directed toward other conspecifics, especially in species that tend to form long-term bonding relationships with sex partners (Phillips, Cox, Kakolewski, & Valenstein, 1969; Richard & Schulman, 1982; Sachser & Hendricks, 1982; Wilson & Daly, 1985).

Studies have shown that male rats resisted territorial intrusion by alien males more vigorously if they were allowed to occupy a territory containing a female with whom they had copulated than if they occupied an identical territory containing no female (Albert, Dyson, & Walsh, 1987; Albert, Walsh, Gorzalka, Siemens, & Louie, 1986). Similarly, male mockingbirds who had a female mate more consistently chased off male intruders from their territories than males who had not yet acquired a mate (Lewin, 1987).

In humans, evidence is substantial that males and females are often extremely possessive toward one another as far as mutual control over sexual behavior is concerned (Collins, 1982; Dutton & Painter, 1981; Eibl-Eibesfeldt, 1987; Hirschon, 1984; Paterson, 1979; Spiro, 1977; Stets & Pirog-Good, 1987).

It is certainly reasonable to believe that linguistically mediated learning may shape some of the detailed aspects of this possessiveness toward sex partners in humans. However, given that many animals exhibit a basic drive to possess and control sex partners in the absence of linguistically mediated learning, it is also reasonable to assume that the underlying motivation for such possessive efforts is largely unlearned.

Proposition 2. Natural selection has favored a stronger sex drive in males than in females. As a result, males have a tendency to prefer sex more often than females and to orient their drives to possess and control toward multiple sex partners. On the other hand, natural selection has favored females who are more likely than males to refrain from copulating until assured of their partner's willingness to assist in caring for offspring.

The synthesized theory considers natural selection as playing a major role in producing not only male tendencies to learn forceful copulatory tactics, but also female tendencies to resist these tactics. In general terms, these evolved sex differences can be understood from the standpoint of what each sex can potentially gain in reproductive terms when they learn to perform certain roles.

From the standpoint of a male, there is more to be gained than lost from learning to be pushy when it comes to sex, whereas for females learning to display hesitancy and coyness would generally be favored. Although such behavior is learned, the underlying reasons have to do with the minimum investment of time and energy that each sex must make in any offspring they produce. Specifically, the minimum investment that males must make to sire an offspring is very small relative to the minimum investment by females (in humans, roughly 15 minutes versus 9 months).

From an evolutionary standpoint, the above sex disparity means that natural selection would favor males who learn to use more and pushier copulatory tactics than females. Although this does not mean that forced copulations will necessarily evolve in all species, it does mean that wherever forced copulations are found, they should be predominantly used by males. Such a sex difference has been confirmed in numerous species (Ellis, 1989a; Palmer, 1989; Le Boeuf & Mesnick, 1990).

Another way to understand sex differences in learning copulatory tactics is to think of it as intra-sex competition (Archer, 1986; Daly & Wilson, 1983). In most species, because females must bear much more of the initial burden of the parental investment in each offspring than males, they are favored by natural selection for effectively competing with one another for males who will be stable suppliers of resources useful in rearing offspring. The more time and energy that must be invested in each offspring, the more females should compete with one another in this way.

On the other hand, males should compete with one another for access to sex partners. Males who appear to females to be successful in, or at least capable of, securing and sharing resources, will generally have the least difficulty attracting voluntary sex partners. Males who do not impress females with their resource-procuring potential will attract fewer voluntary sex partners. Although all males may augment their access to voluntary sex partners with forced copulations, especially when the risks of retaliation are high, forced copulations should be primarily used by males with low resource-procuring prospects. More will be said about this issue later in this chapter.

Proposition 3. Although the motivation for sexual assault is essentially unlearned, the behavior surrounding sexual assault is learned, with the major form of learning being experiential (in which probable costs and benefits are roughly weighed), rather than imitative, attitudinal, or instructional.

According to the synthesized theory, no human is simply a "born rapist," although there should be genetic variations in individual dispositions toward readily learning forced copulatory tactics. Whereas both the feminist and the social learning theories of rape hypothesize that imitative learning and/or instructional/attitudinal learning are important in rape etiology, the synthesized theory envisions experiential learning as the most important. Experiential learning is learning based on experiences with varying approximations of a given category of behavior (e.g., using deceptive and pushy tactics in attempting to copulate), and in which the probable costs and likelihood of success are roughly weighed in light of the strength of one's drive to engage in this category of behavior.

The present theory gives little weight to the view that rape is caused by imitating pornographic depictions of sexual aggression or being told that sexual aggression is an effective and acceptable way to gain copulatory access (i.e., acquiring so-called rape myths). Both of these factors may incline males with little sexual experience to at least try mildly aggressive tactics. However, according to the synthesized theory, these individuals would only be likely to persist in their use of sexually aggressive tactics if those tactics proved relatively successful in the past.

According to this third proposition, acts of aggression and domination toward females are not the goals of rapists. Rather, aggressive and dominating behavior are tactics that many males employ in their efforts to copulate. This deduction is supported by evidence that date rapists are more likely than males in general to use other tactics—such as deceptively pledging love and attempting to get his date drunk—to copulate (Kanin, 1967; Koss, Leonard, Beezley, & Oros, 1985).

Proposition 4. Increased exposure of the brain to male sex hormones (androgens) increases an individual's sex drive and reduces sensitivity to the threat of punishment and to the suffering of others, all of which increase the probability of committing rape.

This proposition primarily looks at rape from a biochemical standpoint. Such a perspective is a unique feature of the synthesized theory. It suggests how rape may be neurohormonally motivated. Also, it suggests that rapists tend to be insensitive to the emotional horror and physical pain suffered by their victims. It is contended that two of the important effects of male sex hormones upon behavior are to increase the sex drive and decrease sensitivity to aversive environmental stimuli.

Evidence has shown that sex hormones affect both the structure and functioning of the brain (Diamond, 1988; Durden-Smith & deSimone, 1983; Ellis,

1982; Ellis & Coontz, 1990; Kolata, 1979). Although these effects are complex and still being deciphered, several studies have demonstrated the heuristic value of conceiving of the effects of sex hormones on the brain as occurring in two stages: the organizational stage and the activational stage (Ehrhardt, 1978; Ellis & Ames, 1987).

The organizational stage of brain differentiation takes place during gestation (and, for some species, but not humans, during the first week or two after birth) (Ehrhardt, 1978; Hines & Gorski, 1985). During this organizational stage, male hormone regimes are high and the brain becomes fundamentally masculinized/defeminized instead of remaining feminized/demasculinized (the latter being the "default" course for all mammalian brains) (Jost, Vigior, Prepin, & Perchellet, 1973; MacLusky & Naftolin, 1981; von Berswordt-Wallrobe, 1983).

In other words mammalian brains are basically feminine/demasculine unless genetic instructions located on the Y chromosome trigger a set of diversionary phenotypic patterns to begin falling into place (albeit, always to varying degrees of precision) (Dorus, 1980; Giannandrea, 1985; McLaren, 1990). For humans, within the first 2 months, these genetic instructions located on the Y chromosome cause the fetal gonads to differentiate into testes instead of remaining ovaries. Thereafter, relatively large quantities of testosterone are produced, and, barring any unusual interference caused by chemicals in the mother's blood system, the process of masculinizing/defeminizing the brain will generally proceed in a more or less typically male fashion (Ellis & Ames, 1987).

Attention now is turned to the activational stage of brain differentiation. The activational stage begins with a pubertal surge in the production of sex hormones that normally persists throughout adulthood, with only a slight decline from middle age onward (Ellis & Coontz, 1990). Essentially, the same hormones that were responsible for initiating the process of "sexing" the brain in organizational terms are also responsible for fully activating it in adolescence and adulthood. With this general information about a two-stage process of sexual differentiation as a backdrop, it is possible to focus on how sex hormones influence the sex drive.

Taken together, studies indicate that the human sex drive, like the sex drive of other animals, is primarily controlled by neurohormonal variables (Ellis, 1991a). In particular, exposing the brain to testosterone and other androgens perinatally helps to strengthen the sex drive that will be activated by the pubertal surge in sex hormones following the onset of puberty. Because nearly all males are exposed to much higher levels of testosterone both perinatally and postpubertally than females (Ellis & Coontz, 1990), the male sex drive on average tends to be considerably stronger than that of females (Ellis, 1991a).

The present view is that this stronger male sex drive is one of the reasons that nearly all sexual assaults are perpetrated by males. Furthermore, because males vary in the degree to which their brains have been exposed to testosterone during various prenatal and postpubertal stages, some males will be considerably more prone toward sexual assault than others. Nevertheless, a strong sex drive is not the only cause of sexual assault. Another important factor is the availability of voluntary sex partners. Given the same intensity of their sex drive, males who have little difficulty attracting voluntary sex partners should be less likely to commit rape than males who can attract few sex partners.

Another cause of variation in rape probability has to do with one's sensitivity to the environment, rather than with the sex drive or the drive to possess and control sex partners. According to the biosocial theory, insensitivity to aversive environmental stimuli is directly associated with the probability of sexual assault.

Environmental sensitivity, like the sex drive, appears to be influenced by exposing the brain to testosterone. The evidence comes from three empirical sources. First, 17 studies of humans and 10 studies of other mammals all indicated that, on average, males tolerated pain at a given intensity to a greater degree than females (one study of nonhumans found no significant difference) (Ellis, 1986; see also Feine, Bushnell, Miron, & Duncan, 1991). Second, experiments with laboratory animals have indicated that these sex differences can be eliminated by equalizing the degree to which the brain is exposed to testosterone, especially during crucial periods of neuro-organization (Beatty & Beatty, 1970; Redmond, Baulu, Murphy, Loriaux, & Zeigler, 1976). A third line of evidence comes from studies showing that, with the possible exception of vision (McGuiness, 1980), male mammals are less sensitive to all modes of stimulation than female mammals (Cain, 1981; Doty, Shaman, Applebaum, Giberson, Sikorski, & Rosenberg, 1984; Murphy, 1983; Redmond et al., 1976; Shepherd-Look, 1982).

Studies suggest that more or less adjacent subcortical regions of the brain play crucial roles in controlling the sex drive (Edwards & Einhorn, 1986; Panksepp, 1982; Yahr, 1983) and environmental sensitivity (Joseph, Forrest, Fiducia, Como, & Siegel, 1981; Marx, 1975). Various lines of evidence point to the second trimester as the time when most subcortical regions of the brain are sexually differentiated (Bender & Berch, 1987; Ellis & Ames, 1987). It is unlikely that the critical period for neuro-organization for the strength of the sex drive is exactly the same as that for environmental sensitivity (Grisham, Kerchner, & Ward, 1991). Therefore, although there should be a substantial inverse correlation between the strength of a person's sex drive and his or her environmental sensitivity, anything close to a perfect relationship is unlikely.

If the above reasoning is correct, an important deduction can be made regarding differences in the brains of persons who vary in their probabilities of sexual assault. Persons with high probabilities of sexual assault should have been exposed to higher levels of testosterone at the critical periods (mainly during perinatal development) than persons who are least prone toward such assault. This deduction is represented in Figure 1.

According to this diagram, when the sex drive is more or less fully activated following the onset of puberty, persons with relatively strong sex drives will be less likely than most people to seriously weigh the prospects of adverse consequences to themselves (e.g., arrest, imprisonment) or to their victims (e.g., physical pain, shame, pregnancy). This will substantially increase the prospects of their actually committing the assault under a given set of circumstances.

The above argument could help to explain why rapists seem to be unusually deficient in correctly reading emotional cues from women (Lipton, McDonel, & McFall, 1987), and why they are more likely to be involved in crime generally, especially in all types of violent crime (Virogradov, Dishotsky, Doty, & Tinklenberg, 1988). Resistance to the adverse aspects of one's environment could also help to account for why rapists tend to be as sexually aroused by verbal portrayals of forced intercourse as by verbal portrayals of voluntary sexual intercourse, whereas males in general are less aroused by the latter than by the former (Ellis, 1989a; Murphy, Haynes, Coleman, & Flanagan, 1985).

SOME DEMOGRAPHICS OF SEXUAL ASSAULT AS REFLECTING PART OF A REPRODUCTIVE STRATEGY

This third section elaborates on the biosocial theory of rape by arguing that a basic evolutionary concept may help to explain why certain demographic variables are significantly related to the probability of rape. The concept, *r/K selection,* refers to a theoretical continuum along which all living things are assumed to be positioned (MacArthur, 1962; MacArthur & Wilson, 1967). The concept was devised initially to explain within-species variability in traits (Menge, 1974), although it has been used more recently to account for between-species variability as well (Rushton & Bogaert, 1988).

Before considering how r/K selection and various forms of intra-species victimizing behavior may be linked, it should be emphasized that there is nothing inherently good about an organism's position along the r/K continuum. Currently living species can be found taking up an enormous diversity of positions along this theoretical continuum. If the current conceptualization is correct, it can even be assumed that organisms tend to shift in their position along the r/K continuum with age. Also, it appears to be exceedingly difficult to predict the type of environmental conditions that will favor population shifts along the r/K continuum (Stearns, 1983). Nevertheless, the concept of r/K selection still may help to explain why a variety of traits, both behavioral and physiological, co-vary in fairly specific ways.

Several writers have hypothesized that, in most species including humans, males are more r-selected on average than females (Ellis, 1987; Gould, 1982;

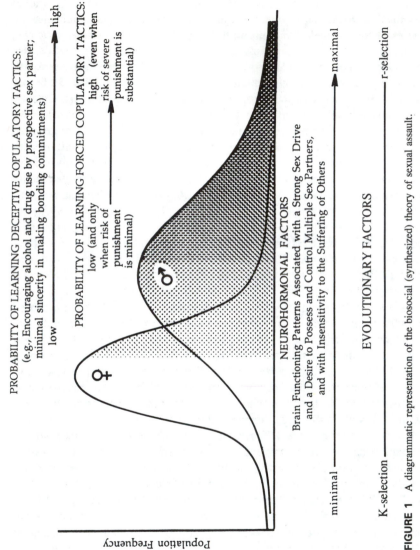

FIGURE 1 A diagrammatic representation of the biosocial (synthesized) theory of sexual assault.

Masters, 1983; Rushton & Bogaert, 1988; Szacka, 1989). This hypothesis was recently tested by reviewing studies across the entire mammalian order (Ellis, 1989/1990). The review showed that nearly all of the traits associated with r-selection (e.g., greater numbers conceived, shorter gestation periods, more rapid development to reproductive functioning, shorter life expectancy) were, as predicted, more characteristic of males than of females. Although there were certain exceptions, this generalization held true for humans as much as for mammals in general.

Elsewhere, the proposal has been made that r-selected organisms should be more inclined than K-selected organisms to victimize conspecifics (Ellis, 1987). The reasoning behind this proposal may be summarized as follows: Basically, the opposite of victimizing behavior is altruistic behavior (Ellis, 1990; Eysenck & Gudjonsson, 1989). Presumably, the first forms of altruism to have been favored by natural selection were those directed toward close relatives (especially offspring). This is because the greater the genetic distance between an altruist and a recipient, the less the altruist's genes stand to gain in reproductive terms from each act of altruism performed (Trivers, 1971).

Because altruism on behalf of offspring would be equivalent to parental investment, it is reasonable to conceive of altruism and K-selection as closely related phenomena. Nevertheless, these concepts should not be thought of as equivalent (Ellis, 1991b, 1991c). Conversely, without equating the concepts, one can deduce that r-selected organisms will victimize conspecifics (even close relatives) to a greater degree than K-selected organisms.

As to why sexually assaultive tactics per se should be more characteristic of r-selected than of K-selected organisms, the argument may be stated as follows: The probability of conception resulting from a sexual assault appears to be roughly similar to the conception probability from voluntary copulations (Ellis, 1989a). Therefore, unless detected and punished severely, males who employ assaultive copulatory tactics are at no reproductive disadvantage relative to other males. In fact, given that these males appear to be more sexually active than males in general (Kanin, 1967, 1983, 1985; Koss et al., 1985), they are likely to leave descendants in subsequent generations at higher rates than other males.

Because females must gestate each offspring conceived (a form of parental investment that females cannot escape), they are prevented from reproductively benefiting from the use of sexual assault nearly to the degree males could benefit (Ellis, 1991a). This unbridgeable gap between the sexes has produced a substantial sex difference in tendencies to commit rape. More fundamentally, females should have been selected to a greater degree than males for K-selected tendencies, which mitigate against victimizing behavior.

Quite apart from any average sex differences, humans as a species are unquestionably very K selected (Daly & Wilson, 1983; Gould, 1982; Jolly, 1985). Therefore, humans are under strong evolutionary pressure to invest heavily in most offspring born (with the exception of offspring who are least reproductively viable). Because this evolutionary pressure for heavy parental investment should weigh heavier on the most K-selected sex (females), females would be favored for choosing mates in ways that help to redress the imbalance between themselves and males in parental investment. As outlined earlier (Proposition 3), females appear to partially redress this imbalance by discriminating in their mate choice against males who appear incapable of, or disinclined to, assist in long-term child care.

The natural selection pressure on females to discriminate against males who appear disinclined to assist in long-term child care has not resulted in anything close to perfect abilities to discriminate. Instead, female tendencies to discriminate against males disinclined to help in child care seem to have caused a spectrum of reproductive strategies to evolve among males. At one end of the spectrum are males who closely accommodate the preferences of females. These males willingly and capably assist the female throughout gestation and afterward by providing her and her offspring with food, shelter, and other environmental conditions conducive to successful child rearing (call this the "good provider" strategy).

At the other end of the spectrum is a male reproductive strategy that relies on any number of deceptive and, ultimately, even forceful copulatory tactics (call this the "cheater" strategy). The deceptive methods used by this type of male might include attempting to get a prospective sex partner drunk or high on drugs to lower her resistance to his copulatory attempts. The "cheater" strategy might also include falsely pretending to have capacities and inclinations to be a good provider, and lying about the degree of commitment he is willing to make to a long-term bonded relationship.

Strictly from a reproductive standpoint, the best male strategy of all might be a "mixed" strategy. A mixed strategy could involve attempting to use a "good provider" strategy with females who were most desired and/or most attainable as permanent sex partners, and resorting to deception and force with other females. Such a strategy might be especially effective in the early years of a male's reproductive career, before major commitments are made toward actually forming an exclusive sexual bond.

As a rule, those males who are most capable of making a sustained parental investment by providing a stable supply of resources to a female and her offspring should gravitate most strongly toward the "good provider" strategy. Males who are least capable in this regard (or are so judged by the females they court) should be most inclined to opt for an exclusive "cheater" strategy. Most males should use a mixed strategy to some extent, especially during their early reproductive years.

The above reasoning leads to a series of hypotheses that may be tested by comparing at least three demographic characteristics of persons with high and low probabilities of rape. If the reasoning just described is correct, one should find rape to be (a) predominantly a male offense, (b) more heavily concentrated in the early than the later reproductive years, and (c) more common in the lower than in the upper social strata. Below is evidence bearing on these three deductions.

Regarding the hypothesis that rape is predominantly a male offense, evidence has been largely supportive. Most studies indicated that somewhere between 1–2% of predatory rapes (or attempted rapes) (Ellis, 1989a, 1991a) and 5–10% of date rapes (Struckman-Johnson, 1991) are perpetrated by females. The only exceptions have been studies in which "sexual assaults" were very liberally defined as including "pressure" to have sex. In these cases, as many as one third of all sexual assaults were committed by females (Anonymous, 1989; Sorenson, Stein, Siegel, Golding, & Burnam, 1987).

Concerning the age at which the perpetration of rape is most likely, the evidence strongly supports the hypothesis that offenses are concentrated in the early reproductive years. Specifically, males are most likely to commit rape between their mid-teens and their late twenties (Amir, 1971; Chappell & Singer, 1977; Goldner, 1972; Henn, Herjanic, & Vanderpearl, 1976; McCaldron, 1967).

With regard to the hypothesis that rape is especially common among males of low social status, the evidence is generally supportive, but in need of further research. Four studies have found a significant inverse correlation between rape probabilities and male social status (Henn et al., 1976; Peterson & Bailey, 1988; Snare, 1984; Weis & Borges, 1973). However, one study failed to find a significant relationship (Alder, 1985).

The biosocial theory implies that the main differences in rape probabilities is between males who are least inclined to help provide for offspring and males who are most inclined. This implies that a rough J-shaped relationship exists between rape probabilities and social status (with the highest rape probabilities in the lower strata, and few if any differences between the middle and upper strata). If so, it is important to include a broad spectrum of males in one's sample, as far as social status is concerned, when testing the hypothesis.

SUMMARY

Following a brief sketch of the three theories of rape that have been proposed since the 1970s, a biosocial (or synthesized) theory of rape was formulated. The theory is based on four propositions, which may be summarized as follows: (a) Two largely unlearned drives (a sex drive and a drive to possess and control) motivate rape, and persons vary in the extent to which these two drives motivate them. (b) On average, males have been naturally selected for being more highly motivated than females to learn both deceptive and forced copulatory tactics, whereas females have been naturally selected for learning how not to succumb to these tactics. (c) At the proximate level of analysis, tendencies to use force in attempts to copulate are largely a function of the strength of the sex drive, plus an individual's estimate of the probability of succeeding minus the probability of being punished divided by sensitivity to aversive stimuli. (d) Genes have evolved mainly on the Y chromosome that increase exposure of the brain to sex hormones (especially testosterone and its metabolite estradiol). These increases in brain exposure to sex hormones in turn affect how the brain functions regarding the strength of the sex drive and sensitivity to aversive stimuli, thereby varying the probability of rape.

In the third section of this chapter, the evolutionary concept of r/K selection was introduced to illustrate how the biosocial theory of rape may be used to predict demographic variations in rape probabilities. In essence, r-selection refers to organisms that emphasize producing relatively larger numbers of offspring, and, in the course of doing so, forego heavily investing time and energy in the nurturing of each offspring. K-selection is the opposite of r-selection.

It was hypothesized that deceptive and assaultive copulatory tactics are part of an r-selected approach to reproduction. Also, it was hypothesized that males are more r-selected than females, especially during their early reproductive years, and that persons of low social status are more r-selected than those of middle and upper status. These hypotheses were tested by reviewing evidence that rape is predominantly a male offense, is most common in the early reproductive years, and is relatively more common in the lower social strata.

In closing, this chapter has argued that rape can best be viewed as both a biological and social phenomenon. It is biological in two important ways. First, from an evolutionary standpoint, rape can serve an offender's reproductive ends essentially as well as voluntary copulations, provided, of course, that victims do not selectively terminate pregnancies resulting from rape, and the punishment of offenders is a fairly minor risk. If supplemented by normal rates of voluntary copulations, raping tendencies could actually result in the genes of rapists becoming increasingly numerous in subsequent generations.

The second sense in which rape is a biological phenomenon has to do with the neurological and hormonal processes, whereby most desires to copulate and control sex partners seem to be motivated. The theory asserts that whereas rape per se is not innately motivated, the two drives that underlie sexual behavior are, and that the strength of these drives varies substantially, both within and between the sexes. The strength of an individual's sex drive or drive to possess and control sex partners (especially the former) is hypothesized to increase the probability of forceful copulatory tactics being learned.

Rape is also seen as a social process in at least two important ways. First, most of the framework within which raping tactics are rewarded and punished involves complex socio-sexual interactions between prospective victims and offenders. Much remains to be learned about the dynamics of these interactions. Second, most of the social factors that offer the greatest hope for reducing rape probably lie at the social institutional level. These factors include both sanctioning and treatment strategies.

Much of the remainder of this book explores issues having to do with various social institutional options for dealing with sexual assault. To the degree that the present theory has merit, the likelihood that these options will succeed will be greatest if they accommodate contributions being made by biological factors.

REFERENCES

Albert, D. J., Dyson, E. M., & Walsh, M. L. (1987). Intermale social aggression: Reinstatement in castrated rats by implants of testosterone propionate in the medial hypothalamus. *Physiology & Behavior, 39,* 555–560.

Albert, D. J., Walsh, M. L., Gorzalka, B. B., Siemens, Y., & Louie, H. (1986). Testosterone removal in rats results in a decrease in social aggression and a loss of social dominance. *Physiology & Behavior, 36,* 401–407.

Alder, C. (1985). An exploration of self-reported sexually aggressive behavior. *Crime and Delinquency, 31,* 306–331.

Amir, M. (1971). *Patterns in forcible rape.* Chicago: University of Chicago Press.

Anderson, M., & Krebs, J. (1978). On the evolution of hoarding behavior. *Animal Behavior, 26,* 707–711.

Anonymous. (1989). Offering resistance: How most people respond to rape. *Psychology Today, 23,* 13.

Archer, J. (1986). Animal sociobiology and comparative psychology: A review. *Current Psychology Research & Review, 5,* 48–61.

Bandura, A. (1973). *Aggression: A social learning process.* Englewood Cliffs, NJ: Prentice-Hall.

Bandura, A. (1978). Social learning theory of aggression. *Journal of Communication, 28,* 12–29.

Baron, R. A., & Strauss, M. (1984). Sexual stratification, pornography, and rape in the United States. In N. M. Malamuth & E. Donnerstein (Eds.), *Pornography and sexual aggression* (pp. 185–209). New York: Academic Press.

Basow, S. A., & Companile, F. (1990). Attitudes toward prostitution as a function of attitudes toward feminism in college students. *Psychology of Women Quarterly, 14,* 135–141.

Beatty, W. W., & Beatty, P. A. (1970). Hormonal determinants of sex differences in avoidance behavior and reactivity to electric shock in rats. *Journal of Comparative and Physiological Psychology, 73,* 446–455.

Bender, B. G., & Berch, D. B. (1987). Sex chromosome abnormalities: Studies of genetic influences on behavior. *Integrated Psychiatry, 5,* 171–178.

Bonger, W. A. (1916). *Criminalite et conditions economiques.* Bloomington: Indiana University Press. (Reprinted in 1935)

Brownmiller, S. (1975). *Against our will: Men, women, and rape*. New York: Simon & Schuster.

Burt, M. R. (1980). Cultural myths and supports for rape. *Journal of Personality and Social Psychology, 38*, 217–230.

Cain, W. S. (1981). Educating your nose. *Psychology Today, 15*, 48–56.

Chappell, D., Geis, G., Schafer, S., & Siegel, L. (1977). A comparative study of forcible rape offenses known to the police in Boston and Los Angeles. In D. Chappell, R. Geis, & G. Geis (Eds.), *Forcible rape: The crime, the victim, and the offender*. New York: Columbia.

Chappell, D., & Singer, S. (1977). Rape in New York: A study of material in the police files and its meaning. In D. Chappell & R. Geis (Eds.), *Forcible rape* (pp. 245–271). New York: Columbia University Press.

Check, J. V. P., & Malamuth, N. M. (1985). An empirical assessment of some feminist hypothesis about rape. *International Journal of Women's Studies, 8*, 414–423.

Check, J. V. P., & Malamuth, N. M. (1986). Pornography and sexual aggression: A social learning theory analysis. *Communication Yearbook, 9*, 181–213.

Clark, L., & Lewis, D. (1977). *Rape: The price of coercive sexuality*. Toronto: Women's Press.

Collins, R. (1982). *Sociological insight*. New York: Oxford University Press.

Daly, M., & Wilson, M. (1983). *Sex, evolution and behavior* (2nd ed.). Belmont, CA: Wadsworth.

Dewsbury, D. A. (1978). *Comparative animal behavior*. New York: McGraw-Hill.

Diamond, M. C. (1988). *Enriching heredity*. New York: Free Press.

Donnerstein, E., Linz, D., & Penrod, S. (1987). *The question of pornography*. New York: Free Press.

Dorus, E. (1980). Variability in the Y chromosome and variability of human behavior. *Archives of General Psychiatry, 37*, 587–594.

Doty, R. L., Shaman, P., Applebaum, S. L., Giberson, R., Sikorski, L., & Rosenberg, L. (1984). Smell identification ability: Changes with age. *Science, 226*, 1441–1443.

Durden-Smith, J., & deSimone, D. (1983). *Sex and the brain*. New York: Warner.

Dutton, D., & Painter, S. L. (1981). Traumatic bonding: The development of emotional attachments in battered women and other relationships of intermittent abuse. *Victimology, 6*, 139–155.

Dworkin, A. (1981). *Pornography: Men possessing women*. New York: Perigee.

Edwards, D. A., & Einhorn, L. C. (1986). Preoptic and midbrain control of sexual motivation. *Physiology and Behavior, 37*, 329–335.

Ehrhardt, A. A. (1978). Behavioral sequelae of prenatal hormonal exposure in animals and man. In M. A. Lipton, A. DiMascio, & K. F. Killam (Eds.), *Psychopharmacology: A generation of progress* (pp. 531–539). New York: Raven Press.

Eibl-Eibesfeldt, I. (1987). Ethological aspects of food sharing and the roots of possession. *South African Journal of Ethology, 10,* 23–28.

Ellis, L. (1982). Developmental androgen fluctuations and the five dimensions of mammalian sex (with emphasis upon the behavioral dimension and the human species). *Ethology and Sociobiology, 3,* 171–197.

Ellis, L. (1986). Evidence of neuroandrogenic etiology of sex roles from a combined analysis of human, nonhuman primate, and nonprimate mammalian studies. *Personality and Individual Differences, 7,* 519–552.

Ellis, L. (1987). Criminal behavior and r/K selection: An extension of gene-based evolutionary theory. *Deviant Behavior, 8,* 149–176.

Ellis, L. (1989a). *Theories of rape.* New York: Hemisphere.

Ellis, L. (1989b). Evolutionary and neurochemical causes of sex differences in victimizing behaviour: Toward a unified theory of criminal behavior and social stratification. *Social Science Information, 28,* 605–636.

Ellis, L. (1989/1990). Sex differences in criminality: An explanation based on the concept of r/K selection. *Mankind Quarterly, 30,* 17–37, 399–417.

Ellis, L. (1990). Conceptualizing criminal and related behavior from a biosocial perspective. In L. Ellis & H. Hoffman (Eds.), *Crime in biological, social and moral contexts* (pp. 18–35). New York: Praeger.

Ellis, L. (1991a). A synthesized (biosocial) theory of rape. *Journal of Consulting and Clinical Psychology, 59,* 631–642.

Ellis, L. (1991b). The drive to possess and control as a motivation for sexual behavior: Applications to the study of rape. *Social Science Information, 30,* 663–675.

Ellis, L. (1991c). A biosocial theory of social stratification derived from the concepts of pro/antisociality and r/K selection. *Politics and the Life Sciences, 10,* 5–23.

Ellis, L., & Ames, M. A. (1987). Neurohormonal functioning and sexual orientation: A theory of homosexuality–heterosexuality. *Psychological Bulletin, 101,* 233–258.

Ellis, L., & Beattie, C. (1983). The feminist explanation for rape: An empirical test. *Journal of Sex Research, 19,* 74–93.

Ellis, L., & Coontz, P. D. (1990). Androgens, brain functioning, and criminality: The neurohormonal foundations of antisociality. In L. Ellis & H. Hoffman (Eds.), *Crime in biological, social, and moral contexts* (pp. 162–193). New York: Praeger.

Eysenck, H. J., & Gudjonsson, G. H. (1989). *The causes and cures of criminality.* New York: Plenum.

Feine, J. S., Bushnell, M. C., Miron, D., & Duncan, G. H. (1991). Sex differences in the perception of noxious heat stimuli. *Pain, 44,* 255–262.

Gebhard, P. H., Gagnon, J. H., Pomeroy, W. B., & Christenson, C. V. (1965). *Sex offenders.* New York: Bantam.

Giannandrea, P. F. (1985). The myth of male superiority: Its biopsychosocial importance to male psychological development. *Psychiatric Annals, 15,* 715–724.

Goldner, N. S. (1972). Rape as a heinous but understudied offense. *The Journal of Criminal Law, Criminology and Police Science, 63,* 402–407.

Gould, J. L. (1982). *Ethology: The mechanisms and evolution of behavior.* New York: Norton.

Gould, J. L., & Marler, P. (1987). Learning by instinct. *Scientific American, 256,* 74–85.

Grisham, W., Kerchner, M., & Ward, I. L. (1991). Prenatal stress alters sexual dimorphic nuclei in the spinal cord of mole rats. *Brain Research, 551,* 126–131.

Groth, A. N. (1979). *Men who rape: The psychology of the offender.* New York: Plenum Press.

Groth, A. N., & Burgess, A. W. (1978). Rape: A pseudosexual act. *International Journal for Women's Studies, 1,* 207–210.

Guttmacher, M. (1951). *Sex offences: The problem, causes, and prevention.* New York: Norton.

Hagen, R. (1979). *The bio-sexual factor.* Garden City, NY: Doubleday.

Harding, C. F. (1985). Sociobiological hypotheses about rape: A critical look at the data behind the hypotheses. In S. R. Sunday & E. Tobach (Eds.), *Violence against women: A critique of the sociobiology of rape* (pp. 23–58). New York: Gordian Press.

Henn, F. A., Herjanic, M., & Vanderpearl, R. H. (1976). Forensic psychiatry: Profiles of two types of sex offenders. *American Journal of Sex Offenders, 133,* 694–696.

Hinde, R. A. (1956). The biological significance of territories of birds. *Ibis, 98,* 340–369.

Hines, M., & Gorski, R. A. (1985). Hormonal influences on the development of neural asymmetries. In F. Benson & E. Zaidel (Eds.), *The dual brain* (pp. 75–96). New York: Guilford Press.

Hirschon, R. (1984). *Women and property.* New York: St. Martin's Press.

Intons-Peterson, M. J., Roskos-Ewoldsen, B., Thomas, L., Shirley, M., & Blut, D. (1989). Will educational materials reduce negative effects of exposure to sexual violence? *Journal of Social and Clinical Psychology, 8,* 256–275.

Jolly, A. (1985). *The evolution of primate behavior* (2nd ed.). New York: MacMillan.

Joseph, R., Forrest, N. M., Fiducia, D., Como, P., & Siegel, J. (1981). Electrophysiological and behavioral correlates of arousal. *Physiological Psychology, 9,* 90–95.

Jost, A., Vigior, B., Prepin, J., & Perchellet, J. P. (1973). Studies on sex differentiation in mammals. *Recent Progress in Hormone Research, 29,* 1–41.

Kanin, E. J. (1967). An examination of sexual aggression as a response to sexual frustration. *Journal of Marriage and the Family, 3,* 428–433.

Kanin, E. J. (1983). Rape as a function of relative sexual frustration. *Psychological Reports, 52,* 133–134.

Kanin, E. J. (1985). Date rapists: Differential sexual socialization and relative deprivation. *Archives of Sexual Behavior, 14,* 219–231.

Klopfer, P. H. (1969). *Habitats and territories.* New York: Basic Books.

Kolata, G. B. (1979). Sex hormones and brain development. *Science, 205,* 985–987.

Koss, M. P., Leonard, K. E., Beezley, D. A., & Oros, C. J. (1985). Nonstranger sexual aggression: A discriminant analysis of the psychological characteristics of undetected offenders. *Sex Roles, 12,* 981–992.

Krueger, M. M. (1988). Pregnancy as a result of rape. *Journal of Sex Education and Therapy, 14,* 23–27.

Kummer, H. (1973). Dominance versus possession, an experiment on Hamadryas baboons. In E. W. Menzel (Ed.), *Precultural primate behavior* (pp. 226–231). (Symposia of the 4th International Congress of Primatology, Vol. 1). Basel: Karger.

Le Boeuf, B. J. & Mesnick, S. (1990). Sexual behaviour of male northern elephant seals: I. Lethal injuries to adult females. *Behaviour, 116,* 143–162.

Lewin, R. (1987). Mockingbird song aimed at mates, not rivals. *Science, 236,* 1521–1522.

Linz, D. G. (1985). *Sexual violence in the media: Effects on male viewers and implications for society.* Unpublished doctoral dissertation, University of Wisconsin–Madison.

Linz, D. G. (1989). Exposure to sexually explicit materials and attitudes toward rape: A comparison of study results. *Journal of Sex Research, 26,* 50–84.

Lipton, D. N., McDonel, E. C., & McFall, R. M. (1987). Heterosocial perception in rapists. *Journal of Consulting and Clinical Psychology, 55,* 17–21.

Lumia, A. R., Westervelt, M. O., & Rieder, C. A. (1975). Effects of olfactory bulb ablation and androgen on marking and agonistic behavior in male mongolian gerbils. *Journal of Comparative and Physiological Psychology, 89,* 1091–1099.

MacArthur, H. H. (1962). Some generalized theorems of natural selection. *Proceedings of the National Academy of Science, 48,* 1893–1897.

MacArthur, R. H., & Wilson, E. O. (1967). *The theory of island biogeography.* Princeton, NJ: Princeton University Press.

MacKinnon, C. (1984). Not a moral issue. *Yale Law and Policy Review, 2,* 321–345.

MacKinnon, C. (1986). *Feminism unmodified.* Cambridge, MA: Harvard University Press.

MacLusky, N. J., & Naftolin, F. (1981). Sexual differentiation of the central nervous system. *Science, 211,* 1294–1302.

Malamuth, N. M. (1981). Rape proclivity among males. *Journal of Social Issues, 37,* 138–157.

Malamuth, N. M. (1983). Factors associated with rape as predictors of laboratory aggression against women. *Journal of Personality and Social Psychology, 45,* 432–442.

Malamuth, N. M. (1984). Aggression against women: Cultural and individual causes. In N. M. Malamuth & E. Donnerstein (Eds.), *Pornography and sexual aggression* (pp. 19–52). New York: Academic Press.

Marx, J. L. (1975). Opiate receptors: Implications and applications. *Science, 189,* 708–710.

Masters, R. D. (1983). Explaining "male chauvinism" and "feminism": Cultural differences in male and female reproductive strategies. In M. Watts (Ed.), *Biopolitics and gender* (pp. 165–210). New York: Haworth Press.

McCaldron, R. J. (1967). Rape. *Canadian Journal of Corrections, 9,* 37–59.

McGuiness, D. (1980). Strategies, demands and lateralized sex differences. *The Behavioral and Brain Sciences, 3,* 244.

McLaren, A. (1990). What makes a man a man? *Nature, 346,* 216–217.

Menge, B. A. (1974). Effect of wave action and competition on brooding and reproductive effort in the seastar, lept asterias hexactis. *Ecology, 55,* 84–93.

Murphy, C. (1983, October). Men and women: How different are they? *Saturday Evening Post,* vol. 255, 41–48, 101.

Murphy, W. D., Haynes, M. R., Coleman, E. M., & Flanagan, B. (1985). Sexual responding of nonrapists to aggressive sexual themes: Normative data. *Journal of Psychopathology and Behavioral Assessment, 7,* 37–47.

Palmer, C. (1989). Rape in nonhuman animal species: Definitions, evidence, and implications. *Journal of Sex Research, 26,* 355–374.

Panksepp, J. (1982). Toward a general psychobiological theory of emotions. *Behavioral and Brain Sciences, 5,* 407–467.

Paterson, E. J. (1979). How the legal system responds to battered women. In D. M. Moore (Ed.), *Battered women* (pp. 79–99). Beverly Hills: Sage.

Peterson, R. D., & Bailey, W. C. (1988). Forcible rape, poverty, and economic inequality in U.S. metropolitan communities. *Journal of Quantitative Criminology, 4,* 99–119.

Phillips, A. G., Cox, V. C., Kakolewski, J. W., & Valenstein, E. S. (1969). Object-carrying by rats: An approach to the behavior produced by brain stimulation. *Science, 166,* 903–905.

Quackenbush, R. L. (1989). A comparison of androgynous, masculine sex-typed and undifferentiated males on dimensions of attitudes toward rape. *Journal of Research in Personality, 23,* 318–342.

Rasmussen, D. R. & Rasmussen, K. L. (1979). Social ecology of adult males in a confined troop of Japanese macaques. *Animal Behavior, 27,* 434–445.

Redmond, D. E., Baulu, J., Murphy, D. L., Loriaux, D. L, & Zeigler, M. G. (1976). The effects of testosterone on plasma and platelet monoamine oxidase in rhesus monkeys. *Psychosomatic Medicine, 37,* 80.

Richard, A. F., & Schulman, S. R. (1982). Sociobiology: Primate field studies. *Annual Review in Anthropology, 11,* 231–255.

Roberts, R. C. (1979). The evolution of avian food-storing behavior. *American Naturalist, 114,* 418–438.

Rushton, J. P., & Bogaert, A. F. (1988). Race versus social class difference in sexual behavior: A follow-up test of the r/K dimension. *Journal of Research in Personality, 22,* 259–272.

Russell, D. (1975). *The politics of rape.* New York: Stein & Day.

Sachser, N., & Hendricks, H. (1982). *A longitudinal study on the social structure and its dynamics in a group of guinea pigs.* Munchen: BLV Verlagsgesellschaft mbH.

Sanday, P. R. (1981). The socio-cultural context of rape: A cross-cultural study. *Journal of Social Issues, 37,* 5–27.

Schwendinger, J. H., & Schwendinger, H. (1982). Rape, the law, and private property. *Crime & Delinquency, 15,* 270–291.

Schwendinger, J. H., & Schwendinger, H. (1983). *Rape and inequality.* Beverly Hills: Sage.

Shepherd-Look, D. L. (1982). Sex differentiation and the development of sex roles. In B. B. Walman (Ed.), *Handbook of developmental psychology* (pp. 403–433). Englewood Cliffs, NJ: Prentice-Hall.

Shields, W. M., & Shields, L. M. (1983). Forcible rape: An evolutionary perspective. *Ethology and Sociobiology, 4,* 115–136.

Smith, C. C., & Reichmann, O. J. (1984). The evolution of food caching by birds and mammals. *Annual Review of Ecological Systems, 15,* 329–351.

Smith, M. D., & Bennett, N. (1985). Poverty, inequality, and theories of forcible rape. *Crime and Delinquency, 31,* 295–305.

Snare, A. (1984). Sexual violence against women: A Scandinavian perspective. *Victimology: An International Journal, 9,* 195–210.

Sorenson, S. B., Stein, J. A., Siegel, J. M., Golding, J. M., & Burnam, M. A. (1987). The prevalence of adult sexual assault: The Los Angeles Epidemiologic Catchment Area Project. *American Journal of Epidemiology, 126,* 1154–1164.

Spiro, M. E. (1977). *Kinship and marriage in Burma.* Berkeley: University of California Press.

Stearns, S. (1983). The genetic basis of differences in life-history traits among six populations of mosquitofish (Gambusia Affinis) that shared ancestors in 1905. *Evolution, 37,* 610–627.

Stets, J. E., & Pirog-Good, M. A. (1987). Violence in dating relationships. *Social Psychology Quarterly, 50,* 237–246.

Struckman-Johnson, C. (1991). Male victims of acquaintance rape. In A. Parron & L. Bechhogen (Eds.), *Acquaintance rape: The hidden crime* (pp. 192–213). New York: Wiley.

Symons, D. (1979, October). Sex and the sociobiologist. *Psychology Today, 13,* 125–130.

Szacka, B. (1989). Biology and bureaucracy or what the school textbooks teach. *Social Science Information, 28,* 599–604.

Thiessen, D. D. (1986). The unseen roots of rape: The theoretical untouchable. *Revue Europeenne des Sciences Sociales, 24,* 9–40.

Thornhill, R., & Thornhill, N. W. (1983). Human rape: An evolutionary analysis. *Ethology and Sociobiology, 4,* 137–173.

Thornhill, R., & Thornhill, N. W. (1987). Human rape: The strengths of the evolutionary perspective. In C. Crawford, M. Smith, & D. Krebs (Eds.), *Sociobiology and psychology: Ideas, issues, and applications* (pp. 269–292). Hillsdale, NJ: Lawrence Erlbaum.

Trivers, R. L. (1971). The evolution of reciprocal altruism. *Quarterly Review of Biology, 46,* 35–57.

Valzelli, L. (1974). 5-hydroxytryptamine in aggressiveness. *Advances in Biochemical Psychopharmacology, 11,* 255–263.

Virogradov, S., Dishotsky, N. I., Doty, A. K., & Tinklenberg, J. R. (1988). Patterns of behavior in adolescent rape. *American Journal of Orthopsychiatry, 58,* 179–187.

von Berswordt-Wallrobe, R. (1983). Antiandrogenic actions of progestins. In C. Wayne (Ed.), *Progesterone and progestins* (pp. 109–119). New York: Raven Press.

Weis, K., & Borges, S. S. (1973). Victimology and rape: The case of the legitimate victim. *Issues in Criminology, 8,* 71–115.

Wilson, M. I., & Daly, M. (1985). Competitiveness, risk taking, and violence: The young male syndrome. *Ethology and Sociobiology, 6,* 59–73.

Wilson, W., & Nakajo, H. (1965). Preference for photographs as a function of frequency of presentation. *Psychonomic Science, 3,* 577–578.

Wyer, R. S., Jr., Bodenhausen, G. V., & Gorman, T. F. (1985). Cognitive mediators of reactions to rape. *Journal of Personality and Social Psychology, 48,* 324–338.

Yahr, P. (1983). Hormone influences on territorial marking behavior. In B. B. Svare (Ed.), *Hormones and aggressive behavior* (pp. 145–175). New York: Plenum.

Yourell, A. M., & McCabe, M. P. (1989). The motivations underlying male rape of women. *Australian Journal of Sex, Marriage, and Family, 9*, 215–224.

Zajonc, R. B. (1968). Attitudinal effects of mere exposure. *Journal of Personality and Social Psychology Monograph Supplement, 9*, 1–27.

Zillmann, D. (1984). *Connections between sex and aggression.* Hillsdale, NJ: Lawrence Erlbaum.

Zillmann, D. (1986). Effects of prolonged consumption of pornography. In E. P. Mulvey & J. L. Haugaard (preparers). *Report of the Surgeon General's Workshop on Pornography and Public Health.* Washington, DC: U.S. Public Health Service.

Zillmann, D., & Bryant, J. (1984). Effects of massive exposure to pornography. In N. M. Malamuth & E. Donnerstein (Eds.), *Pornography and sexual aggression* (pp. 115–138). Orlando, FL: Academic Press.

4

AGE OF ONSET OF SEXUAL ASSAULT: CRIMINAL AND LIFE HISTORY CORRELATES

Robert A. Prentky
Massachusetts Treatment Center

Raymond A. Knight
Brandeis University and Massachusetts Treatment Center

The course of criminal conduct generally follows a rather well-established, age-related pattern. Criminal behavior emerges in early adolescence, peaks in late adolescence, and declines thereafter, with the sharpest decline occurring between late adolescence and the mid-twenties (Hirschi & Gottfredson, 1983). The exception appears to be psychopaths, whose decline may be as late as the mid-forties (Hare, McPherson, & Forth, 1988). This pattern is operationalized in terms of contact with the criminal justice system (e.g., age at first arrest). However, it is reasonable to speculate that disruptive conduct is manifest prior to first arrest. Indeed, Hirschi and Gottfredson (1988) hypothesized that signs of criminality are observable by ages 8–10.

The stability of early aggression, and the importance of its contribution to subsequent adolescent and adult aggression and violence, has been well established (Farrington, 1989; Huesmann, Eron, Lefkowitz, & Walder, 1984; Loeber, 1982; Magnusson, Stattin, & Duner, 1983; McCord, McCord, & Zola, 1962; Moskowitz, Ledingham, & Schwartzman, 1985; Olweus, 1979; Robins, 1966; Stattin & Magnusson, 1989). Age of onset of criminal behavior predicts subsequent criminality. Boys who begin offending in childhood or early adolescence are more likely to become chronic offenders than those who begin in late adolescence or adulthood (Farrington, 1983; Hanson, Henggeler, Haefele, & Rodick, 1984; Loeber, 1982). One study also documented an association between onset age and the degree of violence. Guttridge, Gabrielli, Mednick, and Van Dusen (1983) found that as the age of first arrest increased, the probability of subsequent violence decreased.

Although there is substantial empirical support for the predictive validity of the age of onset of criminal behavior, the causes and consequences of early aggressive behavior still require further clarification (Tremblay et al., 1992), and its etiological significance has been the subject of considerable debate (Blumstein, Cohen, & Farrington, 1988; Farrington, 1986; Farrington, Ohlin, & Wilson, 1986; Hirschi & Gottfredson, 1983, 1986). This debate has focused on the role of onset age in predicting an offender's peak age of acceleration in criminal activity, the career or cumulative incidence of his crimes, and the defining criminal offense characteristics of his career. The relevance of the type of onset crime to subsequent criminal behavior has also been discussed.

Despite the interest in criminal onset age in the general criminal literature, this has been a relatively neglected topic in studies of sexual aggression. To our knowledge, only one study has examined the role of onset age in sexually aggressive behavior (Abel & Rouleau, 1990). In their sample of 561 male offenders, Abel and Rouleau (1990) found that slightly over half reported at least one deviant sexual interest prior to the age of 18. The authors noted that "ample evidence . . . confirms that sex offenders with chronic careers do develop that interest at a very early age" (p. 14).

No longitudinal studies of sexually coercive children or adolescents have been undertaken, and most of the empirical studies of juvenile sexual offenders have simply tallied the frequencies of offender and offense descriptive characteristics, such as the offenders' ages, the history of their previous sexual and nonsexual offenses, the types of sexual crimes they have committed, and the ages and sexes of their victims (Davis & Leitenberg, 1987). Indeed, only a handful of studies has actually compared juvenile sexual offenders to normal or delinquent controls. Consequently, we must infer distinguishing characteristics of these offenders from poorly controlled cross-sectional studies, and little is known about either the covariation of early sexual aggression with other variables or the consequences of different onset ages for such behavior.

There is reason to believe that age of onset of disruptive behavior may be especially important for sexual offenders. Many writers (Finkelhor et al., 1986; Kempe & Kempe, 1984; Lanyon, 1986; Rogers & Terry, 1984) have speculated that sexually coercive behavior may be due, in part, to the offender's recapitulation of his own sexual victimization. If this notion has any validity, one domain in which juvenile sexual offenders should be differentiated from nonsexual juvenile offenders is their early sexual histories and adjustment. Moreover, it is consistent with this notion that the earlier and the more serious or protracted the sexual abuse, the more likely the recapitulation will occur early. It is also possible that this recapitulation will be moderated by other variables, such as the level of impulse control of the abused child. The high incidence of sexual victimization reported in samples of juvenile sexual offenders (Becker, Kaplan, Cunningham-Rathner, & Kavoussi, 1986; Fehrenbach, Smith, Monastersky, & Deisher, 1986; Friedrich & Luecke, 1988; Longo, 1982) and the high frequency of sexual experience these offenders report (Abel & Rouleau, 1990;

Becker et al., 1986; Longo, 1982; McCord et al., 1962) are consistent with this recapitulation hypothesis. Prentky and Burgess (1991) hypothesized further that the content of the sexual fantasies of repetitive sexual offenders derive from "protracted sexually deviant and pathological experiences first sustained at a young age" (p. 241). It is consistent with their "traumagenic model" that the earlier the age of onset of sexual abuse, the longer the abuse was sustained, and the more violent and intrusive the abuse was, the earlier the onset of sexually coercive, fantasy driven behavior will be.

Despite their methodological inadequacies, studies of other behavioral domains suggest that juvenile sexual offenders share with nonsexual juvenile offenders a high incidence of physical abuse in their families, poor social competence, histories of other criminal activity and behavioral problems, poor school achievement, and, among the most violent offenders, a high incidence of neurological and cognitive deficits (see Knight & Prentky, in press, for a review). These similarities indicate that, in addition to the special significance of onset age in sexually coercive offenders, onset age might also play a similar role among these offenders as it does in general criminal populations.

The present study sought to examine the importance of the onset age of sexually coercive behavior in a sample of sexual offenders. Sexual offenders were administered a computerized interview in which they were guaranteed complete confidentiality. On the basis of the age at which they reported they engaged in their first sexually coercive behavior, we divided the sample into three groups—first sexually coercive behavior before age 15, first sexually coercive behavior between ages 15 and 18, and first sexually coercive behavior after age 19. To explore the role that onset age might play in sexual aggression, these three groups were compared on their early sexual victimization and subsequent sexual pathology. The groups were also compared on the domains we have just cited, in which juvenile sexual offenders were found to be similar to other juvenile delinquents. If the recapitulation and sexual fantasy speculations are valid, the younger onset groups should be higher than the adult offenders in their sexual victimization as children and adolescents, and they should be higher on measures of sexual fantasy and deviance. If the factors that characterize juvenile delinquents and juvenile sexual offenders are related to onset age, the younger groups should be higher on measures of these domains than adult offenders.

METHOD

Subjects

The subjects in this study were 131 male rapists and child molesters who had been observed at the Massachusetts Treatment Center for Sexually Dangerous Persons in Bridgewater, Massachusetts. The Center was established in 1959 under special legislation for the purpose of evaluating and treating individuals convicted of repetitive and/or aggressive sexual offenses. The legislation provided for a civil, day-to-life commitment for those deemed to be "sexually dangerous." In the present study, the term *rapist* refers to an adult male whose sexual offenses were committed against adult women (i.e., age ≥ 16). The term *child molester* refers to an adult male whose sexual offenses were committed against victims under the age of 16. A *sexual offense* was defined as any sexually motivated assault involving physical contact with the victim.

Embedded in a 541-item, confidential, computerized developmental interview was the question, "Regardless of whether anyone ever knew or if you were caught, how old were you when you committed your first sexual offense?" On the basis of offenders' responses to this question, three groups were created: (a) those who reported that their first sexual offense was prior to the age of 15 (referred to in the text as "Pre-JOs"), (b) those who reported that their first sexual offense was between the ages of 15 and 18 (referred to in the text as "JOs"), and (c) those who reported that their first sexual offense was after the age of 18 (referred to in the text as "AOs"). For rapists, the number of offenders falling into each of these three groups was 13, 25, and 40, respectively. For child molesters, the number of offenders falling into each of these three groups was 17, 16, and 20, respectively.

All six groups, rapists and child molesters, were of average intelligence (ranging from 95 to 102). The three groups of child molesters were almost exclusively Caucasian (approximately 95% for each group). The rapists were slightly more diverse, with 77% of the Pre-JOs, 88% of the JOs, and 85% of the AOs being Caucasian. The comparable groups of rapists and child molesters were almost identical with respect to marital status. Among the Pre-JOs, 77% of the rapists and 76.5% of the child molesters were *never* married. Among the JOs, 68% of the rapists and 69% of the child molesters were *never* married. Among the AOs, 52.5% of the rapists and 40% of the child molesters were *never* married. Finally, education level was differentiated among the three groups of rapists, but not the child molesters. Among child molesters, the last grade completed averaged 10 for Pre-JOs and AOs, and 9.2 for the JOs. Among rapists, the last grade completed was 8.54, 9.20, and 10.50 for the Pre-JOs, JOs, and AOs, respectively (Table 1).

Procedure

File Coding

The primary data source for subtyping subjects and for coding variables was an offender's extensive clinical file, which included all information gathered during the man's evaluation and commitment periods at the Treatment Center. Information collected during the man's observation period included, in addition

TABLE 1 Social, Academic, and Vocational Competence Among Rapists

	Age at First Sexual Assault (X/SD)			
Variable	≤ 14	15–18	> 18	F
Education				
(last grade completed)	$8.54^a/1.66$	$9.20^a/1.78$	$10.50^b/2.03$	6.84**
Adult relationship[1]				
(highest level achieved)	$3.62^a/2.40$	4.28/2.44	$5.20^b/2.24$	2.70[+]
Achieved skill level[2]	1.17/1.64	1.33/1.24	1.88/1.36	1.85
Independence[3]	1.46/1.61	1.42/1.64	2.28/1.57	2.68[+]
No. years employable	5.68/4.35	$2.90^a/2.35$	$6.33^b/4.74$	5.61**
Overall life management skills[4]	$-0.28^a/0.53$	$-0.15/0.55$	$0.09^b/0.50$	3.19*

Note. When two means do not share a common alpha superscript, they are significantly different (at least $p < .05$, Duncan Multiple Range Test).

[+] $p < .10$.

* $p < .05$.

** $p < .005$.

[1] 9-point Guttman scale reflecting the highest achieved level of heterosexual pair bonding: 0 = never involved in any male/female dating relationship; 8 = subject married with children and never divorced or separated.

[2] 7-point Guttman scale: 0 = unskilled; 6 = high-level professional.

[3] 5-point Guttman scale: 0 = subject has never maintained himself in the community; 4 = subject maintained himself independently for ≥ 2 years.

[4] Scale consisting of five Guttman-scaled items: achieved skill level and consistency of skill level in employment; degree of independent living in the community; and two assessments of degree of involvement in peer-age relationships.

to reports of diagnostic and psychometric assessments and clinical interviews conducted as part of the evaluation, data from multiple sources external to the Treatment Center, such as records from past institutionalizations, school and employment reports, police reports, court testimony, parole summaries, probation records, and social service notes. These reports not only originated from different agencies, but were also written at different points in the subject's life to describe events as they were occurring at that time. In almost all cases (90% or higher), social service and school reports were available that predated the subject's first arrest for a sexual offense. Access to these original reports helped to counteract the retrospective biases inherent in file research based largely on summary reports of a subject's life written after events of particular importance have already taken place (in the case of this study, after the onset of criminal activity). Postcommitment information routinely available included such Treatment Center records as treatment reports, behavioral observation reports, work reports, and summaries of program participation.

Two trained research assistants independently coded and rated each institutional file according to a detailed questionnaire. They then met and reached a consensus agreement on their ratings. This double coding, although very time consuming, was done to increase the accuracy of coded information. The reliability estimates are the Spearman-Brown transformations of the Pearson correlations of the preconsensus ratings, reflecting the increased consistency provided by the consensus judgments (Roff, 1981). The reliability for the Delinquency and Antisocial Behavior scale and the Juvenile Unsocialized Behavior scale, reported in Tables 2 and 3, was .90 and .88, respectively. The reliability for the Adult Unsocialized Behavior scale, reported in Tables 4 and 5, was .88. The reliability for the Life Management Skills scale, reported in Tables 1 and 6, was .72. The reliabilities of all other archival variables ranged from .80 to .97 (mean = .896).

Developmental Interview

The developmental interview, compiled by the authors, consisted of 541 questions and statements regarding the subject's family, developmental experiences, school experiences, peer relations through childhood, and numerous events that may or may not have occurred (e.g., serious illness, death of a family member, divorce or separation, institutionalization). There was also a lengthy section containing self-descriptive statements. Items were selected on a rational basis after reviewing several interview schedules that explored developmental histo-

TABLE 2 Delinquency and Lifestyle Impulsivity Among Rapists

Variable	Age at First Sexual Assault (X/SD)			
	≤ 14	15–18	>18	F
Number of juvenile sexual assaults[1]	$1.23^a/1.24$	$0.56^a/1.04$	$0.10^b/0.38$	9.82***
Delinquency and antisocial behavior[2]	$0.53^a/0.70$	$0.43^a/0.63$	$0.04^b/0.48$	5.35*
Disruptiveness in school: verbal or physical assault on peers[3]	$0.90^a/0.32$	$0.71^a/0.46$	$0.38^b/0.49$	6.10**
Disruptiveness in school: verbal or physical assault on teachers[3]	0.56/0.53	0.57/0.51	0.31/0.47	2.08+
Fighting[3]	$1.00^a/0.00$	0.70/0.47	$0.50^b/0.51$	5.13*
Juvenile unsocialized behavior[4]	$0.79^a/0.33$	0.66/0.34	$0.36^b/0.37$	9.63***

Note. When two means do not share a common alpha superscript, they are significantly different (at least $p < .05$, Duncan Multiple Range Test).
+$p < .10$.
*$p < .01$.
**$p < .005$.
***$p < .001$.
[1]Reflect number of criminal charges for victim-involved offenses.
[2]Scale consisted of 18 dichotomously scored items, including stealing, truancy, rebelliousness, physical aggression, impulsivity, running away, temper tantrums, destructiveness, and homicide.
[3]Dichotomous variables: 0 = absent; 1 = present (coded prior to age 16).
[4]Mean of six dichotomously scored items on MTC:R3 Juvenile Unsocialized Aggression scale.

TABLE 3 Delinquency and Lifestyle Impulsivity Among Child Molesters

Variable	Age at First Sexual Assault (X/SD)			
	≤ 14	15–18	> 18	F
Number of juvenile sexual assaults[1]	0.94^a/1.34	0.75^a/1.13	0.05^b/0.22	4.21*
Delinquency and antisocial behavior[2]	0.04/0.64	0.06/0.65	−0.36/0.47	2.84+
Disruptiveness in school: verbal or physical assault on peers[3]	0.57/0.51	0.73^a/0.46	0.26^b/0.45	4.38*
Disruptiveness in school: verbal or physical assault on teachers[3]	0.46^a/0.52	0.45^a/0.52	0.06^b/0.24	4.37*
Fighting[3]	0.44/0.51	0.60^a/0.51	0.24^b/0.44	2.27+
Juvenile unsocialized behavior[4]	0.51^a/0.42	0.53^a/0.35	0.25^b/0.35	3.14*

Note. When two means do not share a common alpha superscript, they are significantly different (at least $p < .05$, Duncan Multiple Range Test).
+$p < .10$.
*$p < .05$.
[1]Reflect number of criminal charges for victim-involved offenses.
[2]Scale consisted of 18 dichotomously scored items, including stealing, truancy, rebelliousness, physical aggression, impulsivity, running away, temper tantrums, destructiveness, and homicide.
[3]Dichotomous variables: 0 = absent; 1 = present (coded prior to age 16).
[4]Mean of six dichotomously scored items on MTC:R3 Juvenile Unsocialized Aggression scale.

TABLE 4 Aggressive and Antisocial Behavior in Adulthood Among Rapists

Variable	Age at First Sexual Assault (X/SD)			
	≤ 14	15–18	> 18	F
Age at first adult incarceration	19.33^a/3.05	18.46^a/2.04	22.49^b/4.32	10.35**
Adult unsocialized behavior[1]	0.61/0.27	0.63^a/0.24	0.47^b/0.30	3.07*
Aggressive response to frustration[2]	0.78/0.44	0.73/0.46	0.61/0.50	0.61
Degree of nonsexual aggression[3]	3.19/1.65	3.00/1.29	2.30/1.35	2.95+
Degree of sexual aggression[4]	2.67/0.70	2.41/0.87	2.30/0.96	0.16

Note. When two means do not share a common alpha superscript, they are significantly different (at least $p < .05$, Duncan Multiple Range Test).
+$p < .10$.
*$p < .05$.
**$p < .001$.
[1]Mean of eight dichotomously scored items on MTC:R3 Adult Unsocialized Behavior scale.
[2]Dichotomously scored variable: 0 = absent; 1 = present.
[3]7-point Guttman scale, ranging from 0 (no aggression) to 6 (extreme aggression); excludes sex-related aggression.
[4]5-point Guttman scale, ranging from 0 (no sexual aggression) to 4 (extreme sexual aggression).

TABLE 5 Aggressive and Antisocial Behavior in Adulthood Among Child Molesters

Variable	Age at First Sexual Assault (X/SD)			
	≤ 14	15–18	> 18	F
Age at first adult incarceration	23.53/7.34	23.08/6.51	27.94/6.63	2.43[+]
Adult unsocialized behavior[1]	0.31/0.32	0.40/0.30	0.25/0.23	1.31
Aggressive response to frustration[2]	0.62/0.51	0.85[a]/0.38	0.35[b]/0.49	4.19*
Degree of nonsexual aggression[3]	2.03/1.62	3.00[a]/1.40	1.43[b]/1.39	4.91**
Degree of sexual aggression[4]	1.20/1.16	1.28/0.77	1.40/1.12	0.16

Note. When two means do not share a common alpha superscript, they are significantly different (at least $p < .05$, Duncan Multiple Range Test).
[+]$p < .10$.
*$p < .05$.
**$p < .01$.
[1]Mean of eight dichotomously scored items on MTC:R3 Adult Unsocialized Behavior scale.
[2]Dichotomously scored variable: 0 = absent; 1 = present.
[3]7-point Guttman scale, ranging from 0 (no aggression) to 6 (extreme aggression); excludes sex-related aggression.
[4]5-point Guttman scale, ranging from 0 (no sexual aggression) to 4 (extreme sexual aggression).

ries, most notably the Minnesota-Briggs History Record (Briggs, 1955), the developmental interviews used in Project Competence at the University of Minnesota (Garmezy, available on request from the author), and the interview schedule designed by Finkelhor (1979) for his study on childhood sexual victimization. In addition to covering areas of conventional developmental psychopathology, items were also selected for their hypothetical relevance in defining the various dimensions found by others to antecede aggressive and/or antisocial behavior. Although most of the items had a multiple-choice response format, a small proportion of the items required a simple dichotomous (i.e., yes/no) response.

The interview was programmed for computer administration using AVID, a software package from Advanced Interactive Systems, Inc. AVID permitted considerable flexibility in the presentation of the interview. In addition, AVID provided for the hierarchical tree structuring of questions as well as follow-up questions that were contingent on the responses to previous questions. Depending on a subject's responses, the interview went into subroutines gathering more information in a given area or going on to another area. For example, if a subject indicated that he had no siblings, those sections dealing with siblings were skipped.

The interview was administered by a DEC PRO350–D System Unit. Instructions regarding the use of the computer terminal were given individually. The keyboard was masked so that only the keys required for responding were available to the subject. Although each subject had privacy during the interview, a research assistant was available to answer questions. Prior to the administration of the interview, a very brief life history was taken by the research assistant to determine those individuals who had played a significant role during the subject's formative years. For the most part, these individuals included grandparents, stepparents, foster parents, and aunts and uncles. Additional questions pertaining to these individuals were included only if the subject or the research assistant felt that the individual had impacted significantly on the subject's life. In such cases, "secondary caregiver" sections that duplicated the questions in the mother or father sections were administered. The headings and references in these secondary caregiver sections were changed to the name of the designated caregiver.

Each interview lasted between 2–3 hours, depending on the number of subroutines necessary for a given individual. When the subject expressed fatigue or was observed to be fatigued or anxious, the interview was terminated and one or two additional, shorter sessions were scheduled.

TABLE 6 Social, Academic, and Vocational Competence Among Child Molesters

Variable	Age at First Sexual Assault (X/SD)			
	≤ 14	15–18	> 18	F
Education				
(last grade completed)	10.00/3.03	9.21/1.67	10.00/2.49	0.50
Adult relationship[1]				
(highest level achieved)	$3.18^a/2.56$	3.88/2.70	$5.00^b/2.51$	2.35^+
Achieved skill level[2]	1.41/1.62	$0.88^a/0.96$	$2.20^b/1.61$	3.82^*
Independence[3]	$2.00^a/1.69$	$2.00^a/1.63$	$3.40^b/1.27$	5.16^{**}
No. years employable	$8.21^a/6.84$	$7.07^a/5.58$	$15.47^b/4.86$	11.55^{****}
Overall life management skills[4]	$-0.23^a/0.54$	$-0.11^a/0.49$	$0.34^b/0.55$	6.07^{***}

Note. When two means do not share a common alpha superscript, they are significantly different (at least $p < .05$, Duncan Multiple Range Test).
$^+p < .10$.
$^*p < .05$.
$^{**}p < .01$.
$^{***}p < .005$.
$^{****}p < .001$.
[1]9-point Guttman scale reflecting the highest achieved level of heterosexual pair bonding: 0 = never involved in any male/female dating relationship; 8 = subject married with children and never divorced or separated.
[2]7-point Guttman scale: 0 = unskilled; 6 = high-level professional.
[3]5-point Guttman scale: 0 = subject has never maintained himself in the community; 4 = subject maintained himself independently for ≥ 2 years.
[4]Scale consisting of five Guttman-scaled items: achieved skill level and consistency of skill level in employment; degree of independent living in the community; and two assessments of degree of involvement in peer-age relationships.

Multidimensional Assessment of Sex and Aggression

An inventory was designed to complement our archival data sources by providing information in areas critical for making classification assignments on the third (current) version of our classification system for rapists MTC:R3 (Prentky, Knight & Cerce, in press). The items in the inventory were generated by a five-step process. First, we surveyed all extant, appropriate self-report inventories (Chambless & Lifshitz, 1984; Eysenck, 1973; Langevin, Handy, Paitich & Russon, 1985; Mosher & Anderson, 1986; Nichols & Molinder, 1984; Singer & Antrobus, 1972; Thorne, 1966), including an 80-item protocol that we had created for examples of items that appeared relevant to all domains of MTC:R3.

Second, four clinicians who were very familiar with MTC:R3 scales and rating criteria judged the appropriateness of each item in the preliminary pool for assessing each of the a priori specified constructs. Third, a subset of items was selected when three or four of the raters agreed. In a few instances in which there were too few items in a particular domain, additional items on which two of the four raters agreed were added. Fourth, we adapted the final item sets both in content and format to fit the assessment requirements of MTC:R3. Fifth, we evaluated the final item sets and created new items to cover critical areas for which no items had been identified. Finally, the items were grouped according to major thematic content and randomized within these content blocks.

The interview consists of five separate sections and can be administered in two sessions, each lasting 1–1.5 hours. The five sections assess the major components of MTC:R3—social competence, juvenile and adult unsocialized behavior, pervasive anger, expressive aggression, sexualization, sadism, and offense planning.

We administered this inventory to 127 of the sexual offenders, and repeated administration after a 6-month interval to a subsample of 35 of these offenders. The test–retest reliabilities were reasonably good, with 84% of the variables equaling or exceeding .70 and 58.3% of the scales equaling or exceeding .80. It is noteworthy that 91.7% of the scales equaled or exceeded the test–retest reliability of the MMPI K scale, which is a widely used scale in criminal populations (Gearing, 1979). In addition, the a priori composed Likert scales proved to have high internal consistency. The alphas of all scales exceeded .60, and 94% of the scales achieved alphas greater than .70.

RESULTS

The three groups of rapists did not differ in the incidence of physical or sexual abuse that they experienced during childhood (Table 7). The one area of victimization that did discriminate among the groups was emotional neglect. All of

TABLE 7 Childhood Abuse and Victimization Among Rapists

Variable	Age at First Sexual Assault (X/SD)			
	≤ 14	15–18	> 18	F
Physical abuse[1]	0.82/0.40	0.65/0.49	0.55/0.51	1.22
Emotional neglect[1]	$1.00^1/0.00$	$0.44^b/0.51$	$0.28^b/0.46$	6.61*
Age of onset of sexual abuse[2]	0.92/0.86	1.12/1.01	0.70/0.91	1.57
Nature of sexual abuse[3]	1.84/2.03	2.44/2.06	1.60/2.07	1.28

Note. When two means do not share a common alpha superscript, they are significantly different (at least $p < .05$, Duncan Multiple Range Test).

*$p < .005$.

[1]Dichotomous variables: 0 = absent; 1 = present (archivally derived).

[2]4-point scale: 0 = no sexual abuse; 1 = 12.9–9.0; 2 = 8.9–6.0; 3 = <6.

[3]6-point scale: 0 = no sexual abuse; 1 = touching; 2 = kissing; 3 = oral sex; 4 = attempted penetration; 5 = completed penetration (last two variables come from the interview).

those who reported committing their first sexual offense at 14 years of age or younger were neglected as children, compared with less than half of those who reported offending for the first time between the ages of 15 and 18 and about one quarter of those who reported committing their offense after the age of 18.

Although the three groups of child molesters did not differ in the incidence of physical abuse or emotional neglect experienced in childhood or adolescence, they did differ on both sexual abuse measures. The Pre-JOs were sexually abused at a significantly earlier age than the AOs. In addition, the Pre-JOs were subjected to significantly more invasive abuse than the AOs. On the average, the Pre-JOs were abused between the ages of 6 and 9, and experienced oral

TABLE 8 Childhood Abuse and Victimization Among Child Molesters

Variable	Age at First Sexual Assault (X/SD)			
	≤ 14	15–18	> 18	F
Physical abuse[1]	0.67/0.49	0.77/0.44	0.41/0.51	2.20
Emotional neglect[1]	0.36/0.50	0.69/0.48	0.47/0.52	1.38
Age of onset of sexual abuse[2]	$1.82^a/0.88$	1.31/0.87	$0.95^b/1.00$	4.10*
Nature of sexual abuse[3]	$3.41^a/1.62$	3.19/2.04	$1.90^b/2.07$	3.34*

Note. When two means do not share a common alpha superscript, they are significantly different (at least $p < .05$, Duncan Multiple Range Test).

*$p < .05$.

[1]Dichotomous variables: 0 = absent; 1 = present.

[2]4-point scale: 0 = no sexual abuse; 1 = 12.9–9.0; 2 = 8.9–6.0; 3 = <6.

[3]6-point scale: 0 = no sexual abuse; 1 = touching; 2 = kissing; 3 = oral sex; 4 = attempted penetration; 5 = completed penetration.

sex and/or attempted penetration. The AOs were abused between the ages of 9 and 13, and experienced touching and/or kissing.

For rapists, the variables associated with delinquency and impulsive, antisocial behavior are reported in Table 2. AO rapists evidenced less delinquent and antisocial behavior, less aggressiveness against peers in school, and fewer juvenile sexual assaults. In addition, AO rapists were lower on the Juvenile Unsocialized Behavior scale than the Pre-JO and JO rapists. Pre-JO and JO rapists did not differ from each other on these variables. The AOs also evidenced less fighting than the Pre-JOs. Although the JOs occasionally fell between the Pre-JOs and AOs (e.g., number of juvenile sexual assaults and fighting), the JOs typically were much closer to the Pre-JOs than to the AOs (e.g., delinquency and antisocial behavior, disruptiveness in school, and juvenile unsocialized behavior).

Although the magnitude of group differences for child molesters was lower than for rapists, the pattern was the same. Pre-JOs and JOs were similar, and both differed from the AOs (Table 3). The AO child molesters evidenced less aggressiveness against teachers, fewer juvenile sexual assaults, and less juvenile unsocialized behavior than the Pre-JO and JO child molesters. In addition, the AO child molesters engaged in less fighting and were less assaultive against peers in school than the JO child molesters. Overall, the amount of delinquent and antisocial behavior among the child molesters was less than it was for the rapists.

The amount of aggressive and antisocial behavior manifest in adulthood for rapists is presented in Table 4. The AOs were older when first incarcerated than the Pre-JOs and JOs. The AOs also evidenced less adult unsocialized behavior than the JOs. Although the groups did not differ in their degree of nonsexual aggression, the Pre-JOs and JOs tended to be higher than the AOs. It is noteworthy that the three groups were very similar in their degree of sexual aggression (i.e., the group means were 2.67, 2.41, and 2.30 for the Pre-JOs, JOs, and AOs, respectively).

Adulthood aggressive and antisocial behavior for the child molesters is presented in Table 5. Although the groups did not differ in the age at which they were first incarcerated, the AOs tended to be older ($M = 28$) than the Pre-JOs and JOs ($M = 23$). The groups did not differ in adult unsocialized behavior. However, the AOs were significantly lower than the JOs in degree of nonsexual aggression and aggressive response to frustration. As in the case of the rapists, the three child molester groups were very similar in their degree of sexual aggression (i.e., the group means were 1.20, 1.28, and 1.40 for the Pre-JOs, JOs, and AOs, respectively).

The self-reported incidence of sexual preoccupation, compulsivity, and related sexual problems among the rapists is presented in Table 9. There were no significant group differences in any variable examined except for pornography use. The JOs were significantly higher than the AOs in reported use of pornography. The JOs also were higher, albeit nonsignificantly, in offense planning. In

TABLE 9 Sexual Fantasy and Behavior Among Rapists

Variable[1]	Age at First Sexual Assault (X/SD)			
	≤ 14	15–18	> 18	F
Sexual preoccupation	− .13/.52	.26/.79	.08/.64	0.61
Sexual compulsivity	− .24/.53	.20/.68	.08/.70	0.76
Masculine sexual identity conflict	− .22/.75	− .15/.47	− .17/.56	0.03
Sexual inadequacy	− .29/.28	− .05/.46	− .23/.38	0.97
Sexual guilt	− .43/.34	.10/.58	.07/.59	1.43
Pornography use	.00/.29	.48[a]/.70	− .05[b]/.47	3.23*
Offense planning	− .18/.97	.52/1.01	.02/.58	1.87

Note. When two means do not share a common alpha superscript, they are significantly different (at least $p < .05$, Duncan Multiple Range Test).
[1]All scales are standardized z-score composites derived from the self-report inventory (MASA).
*$p < .05$.

both instances, the pattern was curvilinear, with the JOs being distinctly higher than the Pre-JOs and the AOs.

The incidence of sexual preoccupation, compulsivity, and related behaviors among the child molesters is reported in Table 10. The three groups were remarkably similar on all of the variables examined, with *F* values below 1.00 in all cases except for pornography use.

The social, interpersonal, and vocational competence of the rapists is presented in Table 1. The AOs achieved a higher level of education than the Pre-JOs and the JOs, and were employable for a greater number of years than the JOs. The AOs possessed superior life management skills and a higher achieved level of heterosexual pair bonding (cf. adult relationship) than the pre-JOs. In

TABLE 10 Sexual Fantasy and Behavior Among Child Molesters

Variable[1]	Age at First Sexual Assault (X/SD)			
	≤ 14	15–18	> 18	F
Sexual preoccupation	− .14/.56	− .13/.51	.04/.29	0.41
Sexual compulsivity	− .15/.61	− .24/.38	.01/.69	0.54
Masculine sexual identity conflict	.08/.65	.15/.64	.29/.64	0.25
Sexual inadequacy	− .01/.54	− .03/.55	.15/.44	0.35
Sexual guilt	.01/.44	.07/.56	.22/.87	0.25
Pornography use	− .17/.76	.26/.55	− .10/.55	1.34
Offense planning	− .16/.78	.01/.84	− .02/.97	0.11

[1]All scales are standardized z-score composites derived from the self-report inventory (MASA).

addition, there was a nonsignificant tendency for the AOs to be higher in independence. Overall, the AOs were more competent than the other two groups.

The same pattern of results was observed for the child molesters (cf. Table 6). The AOs were higher on the Life Management Skills scale, higher on independence, and employable for more years than the Pre-JOs and JOs. Indeed, the AOs were employable for approximately twice as long as the other two groups. The AOs were higher in their achieved level of heterosexual pair bonding (cf. adult relationship) than the Pre-JOs, and higher in their achieved skill level than the JOs. The only competence variable in which the AOs were not higher was achieved level of education. Again, we may conclude that, overall, the AOs were more competent than the other two groups, and that the Pre-JOs and the JOs did not differ.

DISCUSSION

In this investigation of the correlates of onset age of sexually aggressive behavior, we confirmed earlier findings on samples of generic delinquents and samples of juvenile sex offenders in two major areas. First, younger offenders (Pre-JOs and JOs) were much more likely to have a history of impulsive, antisocial acting out than older offenders (AOs). This was the case for both the rapists and the child molesters. Second, those who did not begin offending until late adolescence or adulthood achieved higher levels of competence in most domains that we assessed. Again, this was true for both rapists and child molesters, although the magnitude of the group differences was larger for the child molesters.

Interestingly, the average achieved level of heterosexual pair bonding (adult relationship) for each group was very similar for rapists and child molesters (M = 3.62 and 3.18, 4.28 and 3.88, 5.20 and 5.00 for the Pre-JOs, JOs, and AOs, respectively; cf. Tables 1 and 6). The only noteworthy difference involved the number of years employable. Because the child molesters were first incarcerated at a later age (4.2, 4.6, and 5.45 years later, respectively; cf. Tables 4 and 5), they were consistently higher in number of years employable. However, this did not translate into any difference in achieved skill level. The AO child molesters, for instance, were on the street for an average of 15.47 years prior to incarceration and had an average achieved skill level of 2.20. The AO rapists were on the street for an average of 6.33 years prior to incarceration and had an average achieved skill level of 1.88.

The positive relation between onset age and competence (i.e., earlier onset delinquent behavior being associated with lower competence) is consistent not only with our previous work (Knight & Prentky, in press), but with the general literature on delinquency. An early onset of antisocial and aggressive behavior often triggers a chain of events that includes school failure, peer rejection, disciplinary actions that exacerbate the perceived failure to achieve, and increased association with (and reliance on) delinquent peers (Patterson, DeBary-she, & Ramsey, 1989). These adaptational failures inevitably undermine aca-demic success and vocational achievement, and thwart the normal process of developing social and interpersonal skills.

Group differences in aggressive and antisocial behavior in adulthood were, not surprisingly, less impressive. Overall, the AOs tended to be lower than the Pre-JOs and the JOs. Among rapists, the AOs were significantly lower in unso-cialized behavior, an eight-variable scale that captures a broad range of antiso-cial behavior, and were nonsignificantly lower ($p < .10$) in degree of nonsexual aggression. Among child molesters, the opposite was the case. The AOs were significantly lower in degree of nonsexual aggression, but were only marginally lower in unsocialized behavior.

Overall, these findings are congruent with the literature on the develop-ment of antisocial and criminal behavior among generic offenders. The earlier onset offenders (Pre-JOs and JOs) were higher than later onset offenders (AOs) on a wide range of variables capturing lifestyle impulsivity, delinquent and antisocial behavior, behavior management problems in school, assaultiveness, and fighting. Previous reports have yielded comparable results, namely the earlier onset "careers" tend to be more chronic and perhaps more violent (Farrington, 1983; Guttridge et al., 1983; Hanson et al., 1984; Loeber, 1988). In fact, Hanson et al. (1984) found that the adolescent's age at first arrest was the second most powerful predictor of serious and repeated arrests. There was evidence from the present study that the AOs not only were less "active," but they were also less violent. On a measure of nonsexual violence (degree of nonsexual aggression), the AO child molesters were significantly lower than the JO child molesters. Among rapists, the AOs were nonsignificantly ($p < .10$) lower than the other two groups.

One of the most noteworthy findings was the remarkable comparability among groups, for rapists as well as child molesters, in degree of sexual ag-gression. Indeed, the F values of 0.16 for both rapists and child molesters must be considered overdetermined. Although we did not posit a priori predictions regarding sexual aggression, it certainly would have been plausible to have hypothesized that earlier onset sexual aggression would be more insidious, and, arguably, more prone to an escalation of violence. However, we found that onset age was unrelated entirely to the amount of violence committed in sexual offense.

No comparisons on any components of "sexualization" (sexual fantasy as reflected in "preoccupation," pornography use, and detailed offense planning; sexually compulsive behavior; and sexual problems, such as inadequacy con-cerns, guilt feelings, and masculine self-image problems) yielded significant group differences. These results represent a major disconfirmation of the hy-pothesis that earlier onset of sexual offending would be associated with greater sexual pathology. Among child molesters, there was only one F value above

1.00. Among rapists, there were three F values above 1.00, only one of which, pornography use, was significant.

Our results regarding paraphilic and nonparaphilic fantasies and behaviors do, however, support those of Abel, Becker, Cunningham-Rathner, Mittelman, and Rouleau (1988), who found extensive self-reported paraphilic activity in their subjects. In our study, all three groups reported comparably high levels of paraphilic fantasies and behaviors. Thus, the lack of support for our a priori hypothesis that earlier onset offenders would evidence more sexual pathology was due to the uniformly high report of such pathology for all groups.

A commonly reported clinical and theoretical explanation for the origin of sexually aggressive behavior, particularly behavior with an early onset, is recapitulation (Finkelhor et al., 1986; Kempe & Kempe, 1984; Lanyon, 1986; Rogers & Terry, 1984). Although the cycle of violence is neither inevitable nor inexorable (Garland & Dougher, 1990; Kaufman & Zigler, 1987; Widom, 1989), there is ample speculation and some empirical evidence that sexual violence may, at the very least, increase the risk for subsequent sexual violence (Becker et al., 1986; Condy, Templer, Brown, & Veaco, 1987; Fehrenbach et al., 1986; Friedrich & Luecke, 1988; Gebhard, Gagnon, Pomeroy, & Christianson, 1965; Longo, 1982; Prentky & Burgess, 1991; Prentky, Knight, Sims-Knight, Straus, Rokous, & Cerce, 1989; Seghorn, Prentky, & Boucher, 1987; Tingle, Barnard, Robbins, Newman, & Hutchinson, 1986). As noted, Prentky and Burgess (1991) hypothesized that protracted sexual abuse of an intrusive nature that was first sustained at an early age would be importantly related to the development of sexually deviant and aggressive fantasies.

The present study provided no evidence that either sexual abuse or sexual fantasies were disproportionately observed among Pre-JO or JO rapists. However, we did find that Pre-JO child molesters, when compared to AO offenders, were sexually abused at an earlier age and were subjected to more invasive or severe abuse. Thus, the recapitulation hypothesis received some support for the child molesters, but not for the rapists.

The lack of any substantive difference between those who reported offending between the ages of 15 and 18 and those who reported offending at 14 or younger was perhaps the most surprising finding in this study. Our juvenile offenders looked like our pre-juvenile offenders, and both were differentiable from our adult offenders. Although our age cut at 14 may have been suboptimal, it was dictated by how our sample was distributed. That is, we had too few offenders acknowledging an onset age of 10 years or below to permit formation of a pure child offender group. In addition to the small sample size of the earliest onset offenders, it may well be, of course, that we did not examine the critical variables necessary for differentiating between child and juvenile onset offenders.

Given the obvious limitations of the sample size, we were unable to (a) examine, as a group, child offenders, (b) examine possible taxonomic differences between the groups, and (c) employ multivariate strategies for examining the interrelations among variables. Nevertheless, the results did corroborate two important hypotheses concerning social/vocational competence and juvenile antisocial behavior, as well as a partial confirmation of the apparent association between sexual abuse and early onset offending for child molesters. Clearly, this is a fertile and crucial area for continued inquiry into the etiology of sexual aggression.

REFERENCES

Abel, G. G., Becker, J. V., Cunningham-Rathner, J., Mittelman, M., & Rouleau, J.-L. (1988). Multiple paraphilic diagnoses among sex offenders. *Bulletin of the American Academy of Psychiatry and the Law, 16,* 153–168.

Abel, G. G., & Rouleau, J.-L.. (1990). The nature and extent of sexual assault. In W. L. Marshall, D. R. Laws, & H. E. Barbaree (Eds.), *Handbook of sexual assault: Issues, theories, and treatment of the offender* (pp. 9–21). New York: Plenum Press.

Becker, J. V., Kaplan, M. S., Cunningham-Rathner, J., & Kavoussi, R. (1986). Characteristics of adolescent incest sexual perpetrators: Preliminary findings. *Journal of Family Violence, 1,* 85–97.

Blumstein, A., Cohen, J., & Farrington, D. P. (1988). Criminal career research: Its value for criminology. *Criminology, 26,* 1–35.

Briggs, P. F. (1955). *Preliminary validation of a standard personal history for psychiatric diagnosis.* Unpublished doctoral dissertation, University of Minnesota, Minneapolis.

Chambless, D., & Lifshitz, J. L. (1984). Self-reported sexual anxiety and arousal: The expanded Sexual Arousability Inventory. *The Journal of Sex Research, 20,* 241–254.

Condy, S. R., Templer, D. I., Brown, R., & Veaco, L. (1987). Parameters of sexual contact of boys with women. *Archives of Sexual Behavior, 16,* 379–394.

Davis, G. E., & Leitenberg, H. (1987). Adolescent sex offenders. *Psychological Bulletin, 101,* 417–427.

Eysenck, H. J. (1973). Personality and attitudes to sex in criminals. *The Journal of Sex Research, 9,* 295–306.

Farrington, D. P. (1983). Offending from 10 to 25 years of age. In K. T. Van Dusen & S. A. Mednick (Eds.), *Prospective studies of crime and delinquency* (pp. 17–37). Boston: Kluwer-Nijhoff.

Farrington, D. P. (1986). Age and crime. In M. Tonry & N. Morris (Eds.), *Crime and justice* (vol. 7). Chicago: University of Chicago Press.

Farrington, D. P. (1989). Early predictors of adolescent aggression and adult violence. *Violence and Victims, 4,* 79–100.

Farrington, D. P., Ohlin, L. E., & Wilson, J. Q. (1986). *Understanding and controlling crime.* New York: Springer-Verlag.

Fehrenbach, P. A., Smith, W., Monastersky, C., & Deisher, R. W. (1986). Adolescent sexual offenders: Offender and offense characteristics. *American Journal of Orthopsychiatry, 56,* 225–233.

Finkelhor, D. (1979). *Sexually victimized children.* New York: Free Press.

Finkelhor, D., Araji, S., Baron, L., Browne, A., Peters, S. D., & Wyatt, G. E. (1986). *A sourcebook on child sexual abuse.* Beverly Hills, CA: Sage.

Friedrich, W., & Luecke, W. (1988). Young school age sexually aggressive children. *Professional Psychology: Research and Practice, 19,* 155–164.

Garland, R. J., & Dougher, M. J. (1990). The abused/abuser hypothesis of child sexual abuse: A critical review of theory and research. In J. R. Feierman (Ed.), *Pedophilia biosocial dimensions* (pp. 488–509). New York: Springer-Verlag.

Gearing, M. L. (1979). MMPI as a primary differentiator and predictor of behavior in prison: A methodological critique and review of the recent literature. *Psychological Bulletin, 86,* 929–963.

Gebhard, P. H., Gagnon, J. H., Pomeroy, W. B., & Christianson, C. V. (1965). *Sex offenders: An analysis of types.* New York: Harper & Row.

Guttridge, P., Gabrielli, W. F., Mednick, S. A., & Van Dusen, K. T. (1983). Criminal violence in a birth cohort. In K. T. Van Dusen & S. A. Mednick (Eds.), *Prospective studies of crime and delinquency* (pp. 211–224). Boston: Kluwer-Nijhoff.

Hanson, C. L., Henggeler, S. W., Haefele, W. F., & Rodick, J. D. (1984). Demographic, individual, and family relationship correlates of serious and repeated crime among adolescents and their siblings. *Journal of Consulting and Clinical Psychology, 52,* 528–538.

Hare, R. D., McPherson, L. M., & Forth, A. E. (1988). Male psychopaths and their criminal careers. *Journal of Consulting and Clinical Psychology, 56,* 710–714.

Hirschi, T., & Gottfredson, M. (1983). Age and the explanation of crime. *American Journal of Sociology, 89,* 552–584.

Hirschi, T., & Gottfredson, M. (1986). The distinction between crime and criminality. In T. F. Hartnagel & R. A. Silverman (Eds.), *Critique and explanation: Essays in honor of Gwynne Nettler.* New Brunswick, NJ: Transaction Books.

Hirschi, T., & Gottfredson, M. (1988). Towards a general theory of crime. In W. Buikhuisen & S. A. Mednick (Eds.), *Explaining criminal behaviour* (pp. 8–26). Leiden: E. J. Brill.

Huesmann, L. R., Eron, L. D., Lefkowitz, M. M., & Walder, L. O. (1984). Stability of aggression over time and generations. *Developmental Psychology, 20,* 1120–1134.

Kaufman, J., & Zigler, E. (1987). Do abused children become abusive parents? *American Journal of Orthopsychiatry, 57,* 186–192.

Kempe, R. S., & Kempe, C. H. (1984). *The common secret: Sexual abuse of children and adolescents.* New York: W. H. Freeman.

Knight, R. A., & Prentky, R. A. (in press). Exploring characteristics for classifying juvenile sexual offenders. In H. E. Barbaree, W. L. Marshall, & D. R. Laws (Eds.), *The juvenile sexual offender.* New York: Guilford.

Langevin, R., Handy, L., Paitich, D., & Russon, A. (1985). A new version of the Clarke Sex History Questionnaire for males. In R. Langevin (Ed.), *Erotic preference, gender identity, and aggression in men: New research studies* (pp. 287–305). Hillsdale, NJ: Lawrence Erlbaum.

Lanyon, R. I. (1986). Theory and treatment in child molestation. *Journal of Consulting and Clinical Psychology, 54,* 176–182.

Loeber, R. (1982). The stability of antisocial and delinquent child behavior: A review. *Child Development, 53,* 1431–1446.

Loeber, R. (1988). Behavioral precursors and accelerators of delinquency. In W. Buikhuisen & S. A. Mednick (Eds.), *Explaining criminal behaviour* (pp. 51–67). Leiden: E. J. Brill.

Longo, R. F. (1982). Sexual learning and experience among adolescent sexual offenders. *International Journal of Offender Therapy and Comparative Criminology, 26,* 235–241.

Magnusson, D., Stattin, H., & Duner, A. (1983). Aggression and criminality in a longitudinal perspective. In K. T. Van Dusen & S. A. Mednick (Eds.), *Prospective studies of crime and delinquency* (pp. 277–301). Boston: Kluwer-Nijhoff.

McCord, W., McCord, J., & Zola, I. K. (1962). *Origins of crime.* New York: Columbia University Press.

Mosher, D. L., & Anderson, R. D. (1986). Macho personality, sexual aggression, and reactions to guided imagery of realistic rape. *Journal of Research in Personality, 20,* 77–94.

Moskowitz, D. S., Ledingham, J. E., & Schwartzman, A. E. (1985). Stability and change in aggression and withdrawal in middle childhood and early adolescence. *Journal of Abnormal Psychology, 94,* 30–41.

Nichols, H. R., & Molinder, I. (1984). *Multiphasic Sex Inventory Manual: A test to assess the psychosexual characteristics of the sexual offender* (Research Edition Form A). Tacoma, WA: Nichols & Molinder.

Olweus, D. (1979). Stability of aggressive reaction patterns in males: A review. *Psychological Bulletin, 86,* 852–875.

Patterson, G. R., DeBaryshe, B. D., & Ramsey, E. (1989). A developmental perspective on antisocial behavior. *American Psychologist, 44,* 329–335.

Prentky, R. A., & Burgess, A. W. (1991). Hypothetical biological substrates of a fantasy-based drive mechanism for repetitive sexual aggression. In A. W.

Burgess (Ed.), *Rape and sexual assault III* (pp. 235–256). New York: Garland.

Prentky, R. A., Knight, R. A., & Cerce, D. (1993). Development, reliability and validity of an inventory for the multidimensional assessment of sex and aggression. In press.

Prentky, R. A., Knight, R. A., Sims-Knight, J. E., Straus, H., Rokous, F., & Cerce, D. (1989). Developmental antecedents of sexual aggression. *Development and Psychopathology, 1,* 153–169.

Robins, L. N. (1966). *Deviant children grown up.* Baltimore: Williams & Wilkins.

Roff, J. D. (1981). Reminder: Reliability of global judgments. *Perceptual and Motor Skills, 52,* 315–318.

Rogers, C. M., & Terry, T. (1984). Clinical interventions with boy victims of sexual abuse. In I. Stuart & J. Greer (Eds.), *Victims of sexual aggression* (pp. 91–104). New York: Van Nostrand Reinhold.

Seghorn, T. K., Prentky, R. A., & Boucher, R. J. (1987). Childhood sexual abuse in the lives of sexually aggressive offenders. *Journal of the American Academy of Child and Adolescent Psychiatry, 26,* 262–267.

Singer, J. L., & Antrobus, J. S. (1972). Daydreaming, imaginal processes, and personality: A normative study. In P. Sheehan (Ed.), *The function and nature of imagery* (pp. 175–202). New York: Academic Press.

Stattin, H., & Magnusson, D. (1989). The role of early aggressive behavior in the frequency, seriousness, and types of later crime. *Journal of Consulting and Clinical Psychology, 57,* 710–718.

Thorne, F. C. (1966). The Sex Inventory. *Journal of Clinical Psychology, 22,* 367–374.

Tingle, D., Barnard, G. W., Robbins, L., Newman, G., & Hutchinson, D. (1986). Childhood and adolescent characteristics of pedophiles and rapists. *International Journal of Law and Psychiatry, 9,* 103–116.

Tremblay, R. E., Masse, B., Perron, D., Leblanc, M., Schwartzman, A. E., & Ledingham, J. E. (1992). Early disruptive behavior, poor school achievement, delinquent behavior, and delinquent personality: Longitudinal analyses. *Journal of Consulting and Clinical Psychology, 60,* 64–72.

Widom, C. S. (1989). The intergenerational transmission of violence. In N. A. Weiner & M. E. Wolfgang (Eds.), *Pathways to criminal violence* (pp. 137–201). Newbury Park, CA: Sage.

5

PREDICTING MEN'S ANTISOCIAL BEHAVIOR AGAINST WOMEN: THE INTERACTION MODEL OF SEXUAL AGGRESSION

Neil M. Malamuth
University of Michigan

Christopher L. Heavey
University of Nevada

Daniel Linz
University of California at Santa Barbara

OVERVIEW

In this chapter, we describe an interactive or confluence model of sexual aggression and relevant research. This model is an integration and elaboration of our earlier work, particularly the research reported by Malamuth (1986) and Malamuth, Sockloskie, Koss, and Tanaka (1991). The model proposes that men who are sexually aggressive are characterized by relatively high scores on several risk variables, which can be conceptualized as motivational and/or disinhibitory and which interact with opportunity factors to affect the likelihood that sexual coercion occurs. We further propose that such characteristics may be meaningfully organized into two primary paths—the hostile masculinity and the sexual promiscuity paths. We hypothesize and provide supporting data that most sexual aggressors in the general population have relatively high scores on characteristics comprising both of these two paths.

Our work focuses on men from the general population rather than those in criminal samples, although we recognize that there may be important differences as well as similarities between these groups (Prentky & Knight, 1986).

The authors express their appreciation to David Buss, Bruce Ellis, and Todd Koop for very helpful comments on an earlier draft of this chapter. The writing of this chapter and some of the research presented here were supported by NIMH Grant MH31618 to Neil M. Malamuth and Daniel Linz.

We have also examined the ability of some of the characteristics associated with sexual aggressors to predict other antisocial behaviors against women.

THE CAUSES AND CONSEQUENCES
OF AGGRESSION AGAINST WOMEN

The causes and consequences of men's aggression and discrimination against women are topics of concern throughout the world. Researchers have documented high rates of sexual coercion[1] (e.g., rape) and nonsexual violence (e.g., wife battering when sexuality is not the source of conflict) in many countries, including the United States (Hotaling & Sugarman, 1986; Russell, 1984). Numerous women are also confronted regularly with more subtle forms of antisocial behavior, both from male acquaintances and strangers, including sexual harassment, discrimination in the workplace, and putdowns at home and elsewhere (Russell, 1984).

Sexually coercive behaviors are much more likely to be perpetrated by males against females than vice versa. Although it is true that males in most societies are more likely than females to commit most other forms of aggressive and antisocial behaviors, there is an even more dramatic difference between men and women in the commission of sexually aggressive acts. Research has also documented serious long-term consequences of such acts in victims of both stranger and acquaintance rape (Koss, Dinero, Seibel, & Cox, 1988).

In the area of nonsexual aggression between intimates, there may be less disparity between males and females (Straus & Gelles, 1990), although there may be significant differences between men and women in their motivations for aggression (e.g., defensive vs. offensive) and in the damage resulting from the acts (Dobash, Dobash, Wilson, & Daly, 1992). Physical abuse among cohabitants has serious effects not only for the participants and their children, but appears to be a factor in the transmission of violence from one generation to the next (Straus, 1987; Straus & Gelles, 1990). Instability and distress in relationships, sexism, and discrimination against women may not be as easily observable and quantifiable as physical violence, but they also have long-term negative consequences (Sampson & Laub, 1990).

THE INTERACTION MODEL
OF SEXUAL AGGRESSION

In this section, we describe some of the key aspects of the proposed interactive model. These include emphasis on the convergence of factors, domain specificity, manifestations in behaviors other than overt sexual aggression, and the

---

[1]*Terms such as* coercive sex *and* sexual aggression *are used synonymously in this chapter to refer to sexual acts that are not mutually consenting.*

importance of the environment. As we describe these characteristics, we also note where we believe our model differs from some others proposed to account for sexual aggression.

Convergence of Factors

Our model has four central components. The first suggests that for an individual to commit an act of sexual aggression, several factors must converge for the behavior to occur (Malamuth, 1986). Our approach is analogous to other psychological theorizing in such areas as creativity (cf. Sternberg & Lubart, 1991). These theorists have noted the utility of a multivariate approach that includes intellectual processes, knowledge, intellectual style, personality, motivation, and environmental context in predicting creative performance. Creative performance results from a confluence of these elements. Similarly, we maintain that sexual aggression is the result of the confluence or interactive combination of the motivation, disinhibition, and opportunity predictor variables, and that a relatively high level needs to be reached at all of these levels for sexual aggression to occur. We also suggest that the motivation and disinhibition factors form constellations that may be meaningfully organized into two major paths. Sexual aggression may be best understood as the interaction between relatively high promiscuous sex, and hostile, controlling characteristics. These enable the individual to both overcome inhibitions that could prevent the use of coercive tactics, and enhance the gratification derived by a man using sex to assert his power and vent his anger.

This approach differs from others such as the quadripartite model of Hall and Hirschman (1991), which suggests that sexually aggressive men are primarily motivated by a particular characteristic (e.g., sexual arousal to aggression, cognitions that justify sexual aggression, etc.). Instead, our model suggests that it is the confluence of several factors that characterizes sexual aggressors. Relatively elevated scores on several critical dimensions are most predictive or serve as the best marker for men who will commit rape and other related behaviors.

Our approach suggests a move away from a reliance on a typological approach characterized by one particular characteristic to a focus on a prototypical approach (Broughton, 1990; Rosch, 1978), which emphasizes various combinations or blends of critical variables or paths that are predictive of sexual aggression. As indicated, our model suggests a prototype of the sexual aggressor in the general population as a person who is relatively high in hostile masculinity and sexual promiscuity. We maintain that a greater amount of variance in the prediction of sexual violence is not accounted for because hostility and promiscuity are alternative paths that lead to sexual aggression (an explanation that is most consistent with typologies by Hall & Hirschman's [1991] Quadripartite Model), but because these paths interact to produce aggression.

Domain Specificity

A second aspect of our model is that there is considerable domain specificity in the causes of aggression against women. We therefore expected that the factors predicting male sexual aggression toward females and related behaviors will not be equally successful in predicting male aggression or related behaviors directed toward other men. This is not to deny that there is some overlap in the factors contributing to various types of aggression and that individuals who may be aggressive generally may also aggress toward women. However, this approach differs considerably from that of investigators (Ageton, 1983) who suggest that sexual aggression is simply another manifestation of the causes leading to any other antisocial behavior. We consider the fact that men's behavior is directed toward females an important factor to take into account in understanding the causes of such acts, particularly when there are sexual elements directly or indirectly involved. We discuss a potential explanation for the importance of this factor below.

Behaviors Other than Sexual Aggression

A third aspect of our model is the prediction that the factors contributing to sexual aggression may be expressed in behaviors that are not overtly aggressive. In our work, sexually aggressive behavior has not been considered an isolated response, but an expression of a general way of dealing with social relationships and conflicts with women. We have predicted that many of the same factors that contribute to self-reports of sexual aggression and aggression in the laboratory would also contribute to responses such as men's domineeringness in conversations with women (Malamuth & Briere, 1986).

The Importance of the Environment

As discussed below, we believe that it is important to develop vertically integrated theoretical models that incorporate knowledge derived from evolutionary psychology and from the study of genetic and hormonal factors. However, the fourth characteristic of our model is its emphasis on the role of the social environment in increasing or decreasing the likelihood that a male would sexually coerce a female. This model differs from others (Ellis, 1991) that emphasize individual differences in genetic or hormonal factors. We believe our focus is actually more consistent with the basic tenets of evolutionary psychology. It contends that the basic psychological mechanisms that guide complex human behaviors are similar in all humans, although some of these may differ as a function of gender and age (Tooby & Cosmides, 1990). Differences in the activation of these mechanisms best account for individual differences in behavior, and such activations are largely due to environmental factors (Tooby & Cosmides, 1990).

In keeping with Bronfenbrenner (1979), we find it useful to distinguish among several types of environmental factors: (a) individual childhood developmental factors such as certain family experiences, (b) social units such as peer groups, (c) broader cultural values and belief systems, and (d) stimuli in the immediate setting.

THE POTENTIAL CONTRIBUTION OF EVOLUTIONARY PSYCHOLOGY

Although much of our model's development has been based on feminist and social learning theories (Check & Malamuth, 1986; Malamuth, 1981, 1986, 1989; see also Malamuth, Feshbach, & Jaffe, 1977, for a brief discussion of the contribution of evolutionary processes), we believe that evolutionary psychology can also provide important theoretical guidance for our work, and that it is a useful framework to explain some of the key elements of our model. This approach (Buss, 1991; Symons, 1987; Tooby & Cosmides, 1990) contends that to fully understand current behaviors, it is essential to understand the natural selective processes in our ancestral environments that contributed to the development of species-typical mechanisms that underlie these behaviors. It emphasizes that current behavior is not a product of "nature vs. nurture," but of "nature interacting with nurture." Although some view feminism and evolutionary approaches as inconsistent with each other, in fact they have much in common and may be used to strengthen each other (Gowaty, 1992; Smuts, 1992).

Evolutionary Psychology and Domain Specificity

Evolutionary psychology provides a useful theoretical framework to help explain why male sexual coercion directed at females is so much more frequent than vice versa and for understanding the issue of domain specificity. This approach contends that the evolution of the human mind is similar to the evolution of the body. Just as the anatomy of the human body evolved by the processes of natural selection to solve many specialized physiological problems (e.g., sweat glands to solve the problem of thermoregulation, the heart to solve the problem of blood circulation, etc.), the human mind (with underlying physiological apparatuses in the brain, of course) evolved in ancestral periods to solve many specialized psychological problems (e.g., acquisition of food, competition for status, access to mates, etc.). Therefore, to understand the workings of the human mind, it is necessary to study the many specialized psychological mechanisms (i.e., information processing mechanisms or decision rules that govern the transformation of "inputs" from the environment into "outputs" such as behavior) that evolved to solve specific problems in the environments of our ancestors (Buss, 1991; Symons, 1987; Tooby & Cosmides, 1990).

An aspect of this approach that is particularly relevant here is that the human brain is sexually dimorphic in those areas where in evolutionary history males and females faced different recurrent problems (Buss & Schmitt, in press). One such area is sexuality (Symons, 1979), where the different reproductive opportunities and constraints encountered by females and males led natural selection to design brain/mind differences that led to somewhat different information processing mechanisms affecting various sexuality related responses, particularly their degree of sexual choosiness. Males could have potentially benefited reproductively from mating with any fertile female (close kin excepted), because the minimal investment for males to produce offspring is only to have intercourse with a female. In contrast, females did not similarly benefit from mating with any available male, because there is a much greater minimal investment required for her to reproduce (e.g., 9 months of gestation, the risks of parturition, etc.) (Trivers, 1972; Williams, 1975). This may have created an evolutionary based proclivity for males to be less choosy sexually and to be more inclined than females to seek impersonal sex. It would also be likely to result in situations of sexual conflict of interest when some males would want to have sex with females who would not have reciprocal desires. This would create a motive for males to seek to control female sexuality (Hammerstein & Parker, 1987). Coercion may be one of several tactics that some males use to exert control over female sexual choices to get females to mate with them (Shields & Shields, 1983). Smuts (1992) concluded in her review that such behavior is common in other primates: "Male use of aggression toward females, particularly in a sexual context, is common in primates, which suggests that male aggression against women may often represent species-specific manifestations of wide-spread male reproductive strategies aimed at control of female sexuality" (p. 2). Although she noted the importance of studying each species individually, she suggested that there is considerable support for the idea that control of female sexuality played an important role in the evolution of human male sexuality, generally, and sexual coerciveness, specifically (see also Ellis, 1991; Malamuth et al., 1977). This analysis provides a clear rationale for why sexual coercion by males is expected to be much more frequent than sexual coercion by females.

Moreover, it seems to follow that if one exerts control and dominance over women in nonsexual spheres as well (e.g., their mobility, associates, etc.), it is likely that control of a female's sexuality will be more effectively achieved. Consequently, we also anticipated that some of the factors predicting sexual aggression against women will also predict other related behaviors directed against women (e.g., domineeringness, laboratory aggression), but not necessarily be equally successful in predicting similar behaviors directed toward males.

Ultimate and Proximate Causes of Aggression Against Women

To place the interactive model of aggression against women within a broader perspective, it is useful to distinguish two interrelated levels of causality suggested by evolutionary psychologists—ultimate and proximate causes. Questions about ultimate causes concern why a particular trait or social behavior has evolved by natural selection (Symons, 1987). For example, we might ask: Does men's greater proclivity to rape, compared to women's proclivity, reflect a natural selective design for a specific function or is it a by-product of other evolved human characteristics (Thornhill & Thornhill, 1992)? In other words, did the environments of our ancestors select men who, under some circumstances, raped or did natural selection favor other, somewhat related behaviors (e.g., impersonal sex, coercion to achieve one's goals, control of female sexuality) that included rape as a by-product or an extension?

A related but different level of analysis concerns proximate causes or how a characteristic or behavior developed. In other words, this level concerns the processes in a person's own lifetime by which a trait or behavior came to exist (Symons, 1987). Such research could include analyzing people's genetic endowments, the brain, and the types of environments encountered during development (e.g., prenatal, early childhood, cultural, etc.). It could also include study of the various psychological or information processing mechanisms comprising the mind (i.e., mental structure). These psychological mechanisms affect responses (cognitive, emotional, etc.) that mediate between various circumstances or situational stimuli and overt behavior.

PREDICTOR FACTORS USED IN OUR INTERACTIVE MODEL: MOTIVATION, DISINHIBITION, AND OPPORTUNITY VARIABLES

As Symons (1987) and others have suggested, it is important to consider both ultimate and proximal causes of human behaviors. The focus in the present chapter is on environmental (rather than genetic) proximate causes of male sexual aggression against females. To understand the causes of aggression against women, we have considered three interrelated types of proximate causes: (a) the motivation to commit the aggressive act, (b) the reductions in inhibitions that might prevent aggression from being carried out, and (c) the opportunity for aggressive acts to occur. Although it is useful to think of these as distinct categories, in reality they may sometimes not be separable. In our research program, we have primarily used six predictor variables conceived as falling into the motivation, inhibition, and opportunity factors. However, although differentiating these factors into the three categories is theoretically useful (Malamuth, 1986), they may not always fall exclusively into only one category. Some of these variables may have effects at multiple levels. The six predictor variables we frequently used are:

1. *Sexual responsiveness to rape.* The ratio of sexual arousal to rape portrayals compared with arousal to consenting sex portrayals has been suggested as a discriminator between rapists and nonrapists (Abel, Barlow, Blanchard, & Guild, 1977; Barbaree & Marshall, 1991; Quinsey, 1984). Although considerable research has shown that sexual responsiveness to rape alone is not a particularly good indicator of being a rapist (Malamuth & Check, 1981), such responsiveness may reveal some motivation to sexual aggress (Malamuth, Check & Brieve, 1986). We have used a direct genital measures of physiological arousal to depictions of rape as compared with arousal to mutually consenting sex.
2. *Dominance motive.* The view has been widely expressed that the desire to dominate women is an important motive of sexual aggression (Brownmiller, 1975). Studies of convicted rapists have shown the importance of the offender's desire to conquer and sexually dominate his victim (Groth, 1979; Scully & Marolla, 1985). The connection between sexuality and power/coercive elements for some males has been portrayed quite often in Western culture. In the famous opera *Tosca* by Puccini, the police chief Baron Scarpia attempts to blackmail the beautiful diva named Tosca into having intercourse with him. If she submits, he promises to spare the life of her lover, Mario, whom he has condemned to death. Scarpia describes the type of sexual experience he prefers:

> For love of her Mario she will submit to my pleasure.
> The depth of her misery will match the depth of her love.
> A forcible conquest has a keener relish than a willing surrender.
> I find no delight in sighs and sentimental moonlight serenades.
> I cannot strum chords on a guitar, nor tell fortunes from flower-
> petals, nor make sheep's-eyes or coo like a turtle-dove!
> I have strong desire. I pursue what I desire, bloat myself with it
> and discard it, turning to a new diversion. (Puccini, 1980, p. 107)

Our self-report measure used to assess this dominance construct was part of a larger instrument developed by Nelson (1979), who asked respondents the degree to which various feelings and sensations are important to them as motives for sexual behavior. The subscale assessing dominance (eight items) refers to the degree to which feelings of control over one's partner motivate sexuality (e.g., "I enjoy the feeling of having someone in my grasp"; "I enjoy the conquest").

3. *Hostility toward women.* Studies of convicted rapists have also emphasized the role of hostility toward women (Groth, 1979). Such hostility may

motivate the behavior as well as remove inhibitions when the victim shows signs of suffering (Malamuth, 1986). This construct was measured by the Hostility Toward Women scale (30 items) developed by Check (1985). Examples of items are "Women irritate me a great deal more than they are aware of," and "When I look back at what's happened to me, I don't feel at all resentful towards the women in my life."

4. *Attitudes facilitating aggression against women.* Burt (1978, 1980) theorized that certain attitudes play an important role in contributing to sexual aggression by acting as "psychological releasers or neutralizers, allowing potential rapists to turn off social prohibitions against injuring or using others" (1978, p. 282). She developed several scales to measure attitudes that directly and indirectly support aggression against women. The scale developed by Burt that we have used most frequently (because it measures attitudes that directly condone the use of force in sexual relationships) has been the Acceptance of Interpersonal Violence (AIV) against women scale. Five of the six items measure attitudes supporting violence against women, whereas the sixth concerns revenge. An example is "Sometimes the only way a man can get a cold woman turned on is to use force." In some of the studies, we have also used two of Burt's other scales, the Rape Myth Acceptance (RMA) and the Adversarial Sexual Beliefs scales. These scales assess attitudes that are more indirectly supportive of aggression.

5. *Antisocial personality characteristics/psychoticism.* Rapaport and Burkhart (1984) suggested that, although certain factors may provide a context for sexually aggressive behavior, the actual expression of such aggression occurs only if the person also has certain personality "deficits." Studies assessing such deficits (e.g., psychopathy) have generally failed to show correlations between such measures alone and sexual aggression (Koss & Leonard, 1984), although such measures generally relate to antisocial behavior. Moreover, testing of Rapaport and Burkhart's (1984) proposal requires assessment of the interaction between general antisocial personality characteristics and specific factors related to aggression against women. In our research, we have measured such general antisocial personality characteristics with the Psychoticism (P) scale of the Eysenck Personality Questionnaire (Eysenck, 1978).

6. *Sexual experience.* The Sexual Behavior Inventory (Bentler, 1968) was used to assess subjects' conventional heterosexual experiences, including such acts as fondling of breasts, intercourse, and oral sex. In some of the research, we also assessed other aspects of sexual experience, such as age of first intercourse and the number of people with whom the subject had intercourse. In some of our research (Malamuth, 1986), sexual experience was primarily treated as an opportunity variable, reasoning that the degree to which men engaged in dating and sexual behavior may affect the extent to which they had the opportunity to use coercive tactics. In later research

(Malamuth et al., 1991), we placed more emphasis on this variable as an individual difference characteristic of men.

In general, our research to date has been primarily focused on men's traits and has not given much attention to how such characteristics may interact with situational variables, such as the opportunity dimension. As the research progresses further, it will clearly be important to give greater attention to such situational factors.

In addition to these descriptions of the predictors used, we would like to describe briefly the assessment of sexual aggression. It was usually measured by the self-report instrument developed by Koss and Oros (1982), which assesses a continuum of sexual aggression including psychological pressure, physical coercion, attempted rape, and rape. Subjects respond using a true–false format to nine descriptions of different levels of sexual coercion. An example of an item is "I have had sexual intercourse with a woman when she didn't want to because I used some degree of physical force (e.g., twisting her arm, holding her down, etc.)." We have sometimes used sexually aggressive behavior as a predictor (e.g., in longitudinal research). However, most typically it was used as the dependent measure we were interested in predicting.

RESEARCH TESTING PREDICTIONS FROM THE INTERACTIVE MODEL

A Multiplicity of Methods and Measures

In this section, we describe research that tested some of the predictions generated by our model. We believe that our research has been strengthened by a reliance on a multiplicity of methods. We have reasoned that if we are able to detect a consistent pattern of results across a variety of settings, measures, and procedures, our findings can be considered robust. Our research has included the use of both cross-sectional and longitudinal studies of behaviors measured in the laboratory and occurring in naturalistic settings. Behaviors have been assessed by using self-reports, physiological measures, reports by significant others, and direct observation.

Domain Specificity: Distinguishing Aggression Against Men from Aggression Against Women

We now discuss research testing predictions generated from the model described above, beginning with the specific domain prediction. Malamuth (1983) tested whether men's attitudes toward interpersonal violence and their scores on the sexual responsiveness rape index predicted laboratory aggression. About a week after attitudes (on the AIV and RMA scales) and sexual arousal to rape were measured, subjects participated in what they believed was an unrelated extrasensory perception experiment. In that session, they were angered by a female confederate of the experimenter who pretended to be another subject. Later in the session, subjects vented their aggression against her by administering unpleasant noise as punishment for her incorrect responses. They were told that punishment probably would impede rather than aid extrasensory transmission, but they were given the option to try it. Subjects were also asked about their desire to hurt their co-subject with the noise. Men's attitudes supportive of aggression and their level of sexual arousal to rape were both significant "positive" predictors of the men's aggression against the female subject.

Malamuth and Check (1982) successfully replicated these results in a similar experiment that did not consider the subjects' arousal to rape, but did assess attitudes. Later, Malamuth (1988) used a similar paradigm to examine the extent to which there was specificity in the prediction of laboratory aggression against women versus men. As expected, the predictors indicated in Table 1 showed significant relations with aggression against a female confederate, whereas none of these factors were significantly related to aggression against a male confederate. However, sexual aggression was significantly related to laboratory aggression against both female and male confederates. This is not particularly surprising, because, as noted earlier, it would be expected that there would be some overlap between men who are aggressive generally and the likelihood that some would also direct such behavior against women. However, taken together, these three experiments showed that the predictors significantly related to an "objective" assessment of aggression against women and provided additional support for the specificity of the relationships between the predictors and the behavior directed against females.

Predicting Conversational Domineeringness

Malamuth (1987) designed a study to examine whether a subset of the predictor factors reviewed above would have parallel relationships to symbolic aggression against men and women. In this study, 67 males participated in an unstructured conversation with a confederate, following the completion of a "Buss paradigm," in which subjects interacted with a person who pretended to be another participant in the study, but was actually a confederate of the experimenter who was instructed how to behave. About half of the subjects were randomly paired with a female confederate, whereas the other half were paired with a male confederate. These conversations were taped and the level of "domineeringness" expressed by the men was scored by "blind" raters, according to such criteria as bragging, criticizing, derogating, and verbally aggressing against the confederate.

The predictor factors reviewed above, as well as self-reported sexual ag-

TABLE 1 Correlations Between Predictors and Aggression Index

Predictors	Male confederate	Female confederate
Sexual aggression	.34*	.39*
Dominance motive	.06	.41**
Acceptance of interpersonal violence	.09	.33**
Arousal to rape	.03	.25*

Note. For sexual aggression, $n = 40$ for female confederate, $n = 49$ for male confederate. For all other correlations, $n = 60$ for female confederate, $n = 71$ for male confederate. From Malamuth, 1988.
*$p < .05$.
**$p < .01$.

gression, were, on the whole, significantly related to domineeringness for those males who interacted with a female confederate, but not for males who interacted with a male confederate. For example, for those men who interacted with female confederates, the self-reported levels of sexual aggression and dominance as a motive for sex were significantly related to observer ratings of domineeringness (Table 2). Neither of these factors was related to the ratings of domineeringness for those men who interacted with male confederates. However, contrary to expectations, the hostility toward women measure was not significantly related to domineeringness for either the male or the female confederate, although it was in the expected direction in the latter condition (Table 2). Nevertheless, it is apparent that, on the whole, the predictors significantly related to domineeringness toward the female but not toward the male confederate. It is also noteworthy that the Bentler (1968) measure of sexual experience did not significantly correlate with domineeringness toward either the male ($r = .13$, $p =$ ns) or the female ($r = .16$, $p =$ ns) confederates, an observation that we return to later.

A more recent study provided the opportunity to study the usefulness of

TABLE 2 Correlations Between Predictors and Conversational Domineeringness

Predictors	Male confederate ($N = 29$)	Female confederate ($N = 38$)
Sexual aggression	.13	.43***
Dominance motive	−.12	.39**
Attitudes composite	−.24	.27*
Hostility toward women	−.13	.09

Note. From Malamuth, 1987.
*$p < .05$.
**$p < .01$.
***$p < .001$ (one-tailed).

similar ratings of conversation and interactive style more thoroughly, although it did not manipulate whether the interaction was with a female or a male. Malamuth, Heavey, Linz, and Barnes (manuscript in preparation) examined the relationship between independent observers' ratings of men's domineeringness and hostility in interpersonal interactions and these men's own reports and those of their partners regarding the men's behaviors. This study is a 10-year follow-up of men who participated in some of the earlier, cross-sectional studies presented above. In this section, we report on the cross-sectional results within the Time 2 period (i.e., 10 years after the original data collection), although later in this chapter we report some of the longitudinal findings. We collected follow-up data from 176 men and 91 female partners of these men. However, as explained below, the findings reported here used smaller subsamples of these subjects.

We asked those men in our study who were currently involved in a long-term relationship to participate in several videotaped problem-solving discussions with their partners. In a related longitudinal study of violence in intimate relationships, Murphy and O'Leary (1989) concluded that "early in marriage, the general manner of reacting to conflict rather than general dissatisfaction with the relationship is critical in understanding the development of physical aggression" (p. 582). Thus, behavior during conflictual interactions may be both a risk factor for later spousal violence and a marker of an existing proclivity to aggress.

To obtain a sample of each couple's problem-solving behavior, in our research both partners were asked to identify what they believed to be the major problem area in their relationship. The couple was then asked to attempt to reach a resolution to each of these. Each discussion was videotaped and later coded by observers. The "blind" observers were trained to rate the discussions on a variety of dimensions, including the level of anger and hostility the man expressed and the extent to which he behaved in a domineering manner. Domineeringness was defined in a slightly different manner in this study than in the study reviewed earlier. The definition used for this study focused on the extent to which the individual attempted to override the partner's wishes and dominate the discussion through interruption, disagreement, discounting the partner's thoughts and feelings, and not allowing the partner an opportunity to speak or respond. Forty-seven couples participated in the videotaped problem-solving conversations. Composite outcome measures based on self-reports of the men and women were also constructed. These included: (a) the man's self-report of all sexual aggression since 1982 and his partner's reports of his level of sexual coercion directed at her; (b) an aggregate measure of the man's abuse of the woman composed of the Verbal Aggression and the Physical Aggression subscales of the Conflict Tactics Scale (CTS) (Straus, 1979; Straus & Gelles, 1990) and the Spouse Specific Aggression scale (O'Leary & Curley, 1987), as reported by both the man and the woman; and (c) an aggregate measure of relationship distress composed of the Dyadic Adjustment scale (Spanier &

Filsinger, 1983), the Dyadic Trust scale (Larzelere & Huston, 1980), and the Marital Instability scale (Booth & Edwards, 1983), again as reported by both the man and the woman. All measures combined to make aggregate variables were first converted to z scores to ensure equality of scaling. Base 10 log transformations were performed on all measures of sexual and nonsexual violence to normalize the distribution of these naturally non-normally distributed phenomena.

We obtained independent reports from the men and their female long-term partners when available. Overall, these data indicated relatively high levels of agreement between partners on the quality of the relationship and the degree of physical and verbal aggression within the relationship. The men's and women's reports of relationship distress correlated highly ($r = .65, p < .0001$), as did their reports of the extent to which the man engaged in physical and verbal abuse of his partner ($r = .60, p < .0001$). Because we asked the men about their overall level of sexual aggression rather than sexual aggression specifically at their current partners, it was not possible to compute a true agreement correlation for this variable. However, we computed the correlation between men's reports of their overall sexual aggression and their partners' reports of the men's sexual coercion against them, which yielded a significant correlation ($r = .30, p < .01$).

Observer ratings of the man's domineeringness and hostility strongly related to the outcome measures of interest. These correlations are shown in Table 3. For example, observer ratings of the man's hostility correlated with the female's report of the man's use of sexual aggression against her. Moreover, observer ratings of hostility and domineeringness correlated with both the

TABLE 3 Correlations Between Observer Ratings of the Man's Domineeringness and Hostility in Couples' Interactions with Men's and Women's Reports of Sexual Aggression, Partner Abuse and Relationship Distress

Observer ratings	Man's report			Woman's report		
	Sexual aggression	Abuse of partner	Relationship distress	Man's sexual aggression	Man's abuse of her	Relationship distress
Hostility	.09	.64***	.45***	.35*	.56***	.56***
Domineeringness	.05	.58***	.34*	.09	.46***	.28*

Note. From Malamuth, Heavey, Linz, & Barnes, in preparation.
*$p < .05$.
**$p < .01$.
***$p < .001$ (one-tailed).

man's and woman's reports of our composite measures of relationship quality and physical and verbal aggression in the relationship. Thus, with the exception of the man's reports of his sexual aggression, there is considerable correspondence between observers' ratings of the man's behavior while the couples interacted in the research setting and both the man's and the woman's reports of the man's behaviors in naturalistic settings. The correspondence between the objective laboratory assessments and the self-reported data provides support for the validity of both types of measures.

Testing the Interactive Aspect of the Model in a Naturalistic Setting

Using a sample of 155 men, Malamuth (1986) assessed all of the six predictor factors reviewed earlier, including arousal to sexual aggression, dominance as a motive for sex, hostility toward women, attitudes supporting violence, psychoticism, and sexual experience. These predictors were then correlated with self-reports of sexual aggression. Data were available for 95 subjects on all of these predictors and for 155 on all of the measures except penile tumescence (because 60 subjects did not wish to participate in that type of assessment).

This study addressed three interrelated questions. First, would the predictor variables relate significantly to reported sexual aggression? The results revealed that all of the predictors except psychoticism were significantly related to naturalistic sexual aggression, with psychoticism showing a marginally significant relation. Interestingly, when each predictor was examined individually, the predictor that showed the strongest relation to aggression was the penile tumescence index ($r = .43$, $p < .001$). This is somewhat surprising (but encouraging), because this measure did not share method variance (i.e., it was not a self-report assessment) with the dependent variable.

Second, the study examined whether the variables would provide "redundant prediction" or whether a combination of variables would predict sexually aggressive behavior better than each variable alone. It was found that the predictors did not, on the whole, provide "redundant information," in that a combination of them was superior to any individual one for predicting levels of sexual aggressiveness. With all of the six predictors entered into the equation, four made significant unique contributions (arousal to sexual aggression, hostility toward women, attitudes supporting violence, and sexual experience).

Finally, if a combination of factors were superior, would an additive or an interactive combination yield the best prediction? Regression equations containing interactive effects accounted for a significantly greater percentage of the variance (45% for all 155 subjects and 75% for the 95 subjects) than equations containing additive effects only (30% and 45%, respectively) (Table 4).In summary, these data indicated that the predictors were relatively successful in the cross-sectional prediction of self-reported sexual aggression. They suggested a synergistic process, whereby the combined action of several variables yielded considerably higher levels of sexual aggression than would be expected by the additive combination of them. The overall findings have been replicated in another cross-sectional study (Malamuth & Check, 1985).

To illustrate and examine the data further, the following analysis was performed. For each predictor, a relatively high score was defined as above the median of its distribution. Subjects were then divided according to the number of predictors for which they scored either high or low. This approach is analogous to classifying a characteristic as present or not by defining presence as a relatively high score. A person scoring above the median on all the variables would possess all the characteristics. Figure 1 shows the average level of sexual aggression according to this classification scheme.

TABLE 4 Multiple Regression Analyses: Predicting Sexual Aggression ($N = 95$)

	Data from analyses accounting for additive combinations of factors only		Data from analyses including factor interactions	
Predictor	Beta	sr^2	Beta	sr^2
Tumescence arousal to rape (TUMRAPE)	.329	.100***	.206	.026**
Dominance (DOM)	.085	.006	.170	.017*
Hostility toward women (HTW)	.209	.032*	.037	.001
Acceptance of interpersonal violence (AIV)	.207	.035*	.168	.022*
Psychoticism (PSYCH)	.027	.001	.016	.000
Sexual experience (SEXEXP)	.026	.066**	.111	.010
AIV × SEXEXP	—	—	.116	.025**
TUMRAPE × DOM × AIV × PSYCH	—	—	.200	.029
TUMRAPE × DOM × HTW × AIV	—	—	.493	.151****
TUMRAPE × DOM × HTW × AIV × SEXEXP	—	—	.445	.158****
Multiple				
R	.619****		.865****	
R^2	.383		.748	

Note. sr^2 = square semipartial correlation coefficient indicating unique contribution of variable. From Malamuth, 1986.

*$p < .05$.
**$p < .005$.
***$p < .001$.
****$p < .0001$.

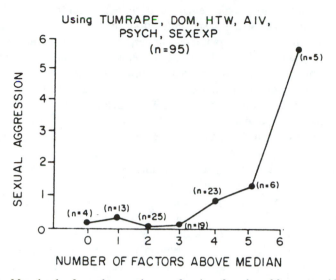

FIGURE 1   Mean levels of sexual aggression as a function of number of factors on which subjects scored above median. TUMRAPE = tumescence arousal to rape index; DOM = dominance motive; HTW = Hostility Toward Women scale; AIV = Acceptance of Interpersonal Violence (against women) scale; PSYCH = psychoticism scale; SEXEXP = sexual experience measure. (From Malamuth, 1986.)

FURTHER EXAMINING THE CAUSES OF AGGRESSION AGAINST WOMEN: THE INTERACTION OF TWO TRAJECTORIES

The Environmental Origins of Coercion Against Women

Up to this point, we have discussed proximate causes of aggression against women in the form of the motivation, disinhibition, and opportunity factors that appear to predispose an individual to sexually aggressive behavior. Malamuth et al. (1991) included the motivation and disinhibition factors in a more broadly conceived model of the environmental factors leading to coercion against women. This model suggests that the ontogeny of coerciveness can often be traced to early home experiences and parent–child interactions. Such interactions within the family milieu lay the foundation for enduring cognitive (Dodge, Baites, & Pettit, 1990), emotional/attachment (Kohut, 1977), and behavioral (Patterson, DeBaryshe, & Ramsey, 1989) responses. Certain home environments, such as those that include violence between parents (O'Leary, 1988) and child abuse, especially sexual abuse (Fagan & Wexler, 1988), may lead to developmental processes that later affect aggression against women. These may include the development of cynical, adversarial, and hostile schema (Huesmann, 1988) concerning male–female and intimate relationships. They may also include feelings of shame (especially about sex) and inadequacy, which are masked by self-protective aggrandizing, anger, and an exaggerated need to control intimates. Additionally, such home environments may not provide the training for the child to develop self-control of emotions and impulsive behaviors.

Children in hostile home environments frequently associate with delinquent peers and engage in a variety of antisocial behaviors (Patterson et al., 1989). Such delinquency experiences may affect various characteristics mediating aggression against women. For example, they may encourage hostile cognitions, including reinforcing those originating in the home environment. They (as well as certain home environments) may also interfere with the mastery of critical developmental skills, such as dealing constructively with frustration, learning to delay gratification, forming a prosocial identity, negotiating disagreements, and other "developmental tasks" (Newcomb & Bentler, 1988). This may result in accelerated adoption of adult roles, including sexual behaviors, but without the necessary growth and development typically needed to ensure success with these roles. Therefore, it may also lead to using domineering and coercive tactics, particularly when dealing with weaker targets, rather than negotiating desired outcomes.

Two Paths Interacting to Lead to Sexual Aggression

Malamuth et al. (1991) were interested in how such delinquent experiences may affect two trajectory "paths" leading, in interaction with each other, to sexual aggression against women.

The Hostile Masculinity Path

Delinquency may affect attitudes, rationalizations, motivations, emotions, and personality characteristics that increase the likelihood of coercive behavior (Patterson et al., 1989). A subculture of delinquent peers may aid in the development of such attitudes and personality characteristics, although the general cultural environment may also foster and/or reinforce attitudes and personality characteristics conducive to violence against women (Burt, 1980). Subcultures and societies that regard qualities such as power, risk taking, toughness, dominance, aggressiveness, honor defending, and competitiveness as masculine may breed individuals hostile to qualities associated with femininity. For these men aggressive courtship and sexual conquest may be a critical component of being good at being a man (Gilmore, 1990). Men who have internalized these characteristics are more likely to be controlling and aggressive toward women in sexual and nonsexual situations.

The path encompassing such characteristics was labeled the "Hostile Masculinity" path by Malamuth et al. (1991). We believe that most of the predictors assessed earlier (Malamuth, 1986) are primarily part of this path. These include sexual arousal in response to aggression, dominance motives, hostility toward women, and attitudes facilitating aggression against women. We believe that these are components of a controlling, adversarial male orientation toward females that is likely to be expressed in diverse ways. As noted later, we believe that other variables commonly used by other investigators in this area of research also probably "load" statistically on this path.

The Sexual Promiscuity Path

The second path, hypothesized to be relevant to sexual aggression, involves delinquent tendencies expressed as sexual acting out (Elliott & Morse, 1989; Newcomb & Bentler, 1988). As noted earlier, the accelerated adoption of adult roles is likely to result in precocious sexual behavior. Boys who develop a high emphasis on sexuality and sexual conquest as a source of peer status and self-esteem may use a variety of means to induce females into sexual acts, including coercion. However, we hasten to add that some boys and men may have the same orientation to sexuality and may engage in similar coercive tactics without necessarily having had a visible delinquent background (Kanin, 1977). Moreover, some males may have a promiscuous sexual orientation without using coercive tactics.

The Interaction of the Two Paths

Malamuth et al. (1991) hypothesized that the degree to which a person possesses characteristics of the hostile path described above will determine whether sexual promiscuity leads to sexual aggression. In other words, the hostility path may moderate (Baron & Kenny, 1986) the relationship between sexual promiscuity and sexual aggression. This would be expressed as a statistical interaction. Because testing for such an interaction effect is problematic when using structural equation modeling with latent variables (Bollen, 1989; Kenny & Judd, 1984), the investigators first tested a simplified model evaluating the sexual promiscuity and hostility path as main effects. Supplementary analyses were then conducted to test the hypothesized interaction effect.

As noted in earlier sections, our model contends that factors that contribute to coercive sexual behavior are likely to be expressed in many ways that have an impact on men's relationships with women (Malamuth & Briere, 1986). In keeping with this expectation, Malamuth et al. (1991) predicted that higher scores on the hostility factor would result in more social isolation from women (i.e., fewer platonic relationships).

A Structural Equation Model Developed and Tested with a National Sample

Using latent-variable structural equation modeling, Malamuth et al. (1991) tested a model based on the theoretical framework described earlier using data from a large nationally representative sample of male college students. This model is represented graphically in Figure 2. According to this model, a hostile home environment (in which child abuse and/or violence between parents occur) is a distal factor leading to aggression against women. The influence of such a home environment on later coercive behavior was postulated to be mediated by several interrelated factors including delinquency, whereby youths become associated with delinquent peers and engage in antisocial behavior.

The two trajectory paths were hypothesized to be influenced by delinquency. First, delinquency may contribute to hostile attitudes and personality characteristics that affect both sexual and nonsexual aggression. To operationalize this hostile masculinity construct, Malamuth et al. (1991) used measures such as the Hostility Toward Women scale described earlier and a Negative Masculinity scale (Spence, Helmreich, & Holahan, 1979), which defines an "unmitigated agentic" style of self-functioning involving controlling, self-absorbed, "one upmanship" personality characteristics. Second, delinquency may also be expressed in a relatively high level of sexual promiscuity. We hypothesized that with increasing levels of hostility, high levels of sexual prom-

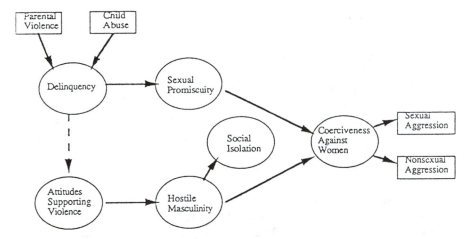

FIGURE 2 Structural model tested and replicated with national college sample. Arrow with broken line designates hypothesized path that was not well supported. (Adapted from Malamuth et al., 1991.)

iscuity would result in more sexual aggression. The model also included a common factor underlying the expression of sexual and nonsexual coerciveness.

Although its development was strongly guided by integrating previous theory and research, the initial model was refined using half of the sample and later cross-validated using the second half. Overall, the model fit the data very well in both sample halves. The only noteworthy exception to the model depicted in the figure, and described earlier, is that although the hostile home variables significantly related to involvement in delinquency, which in turn was strongly related to sexual promiscuity, there was very little relationship between these two factors and the path consisting of hostile attitudes and personality characteristics. This suggests that the hostility and sexual promiscuity paths may be relatively independent trajectories; while the home environmental variables relate to the latter path, they appear not to relate to the former. The development of hostility may be more a function of larger cultural variables than the specific home variables studied here.

As noted earlier, Malamuth et al. (1991) hypothesized that the degree to which a person possesses characteristics of the hostile path will moderate the extent to which sexual promiscuity leads to sexual aggression. To address this hypothesis, the data were submitted to a hierarchical or moderated multiple regression (MMR) analysis (see Bissonnette, Ickes, Bernstein, & Knowles, 1990, for a recent discussion) using component scores on hostile masculinity and sexual promiscuity created for each subject. They found a significant interaction effect between these two dimensions for sexual aggression, but not for nonsexual aggression.

To illustrate this interaction, subjects were divided into three levels for each of the dimensions of hostile masculinity and sexual promiscuity and a 3×3 analysis of variance on the sexual aggression scores was undertaken. This analysis yielded significant effects for hostile masculinity, sexual promiscuity, and the interaction. The form of the interaction is shown in Figure 3.

Follow-up analyses were conducted within each level of sexual promiscuity. Within the low level of sexual promiscuity, no significant effects were found. Within the medium level of sexual promiscuity, a linear trend fitted the curve within statistical error, and all groups were found to differ significantly from each other. Within high level sexual promiscuity, a quadratic term fitted the curve, and the highest level of hostile masculinity differed significantly from the other two levels, which did not differ significantly from each other. It is noteworthy that the group that was relatively high on both sexual promiscuity and hostile masculinity ($M = 5.24$, $n = 88$) was significantly higher in sexual aggression than were all other groups in a manner reminiscent of the synergistic pattern described earlier.

Replicating and Extending the Model:
A Longitudinal Study

We replicated the two-path model of sexual aggression by Malamuth et al. (1991) with the additional sample, described earlier, of men who were followed over a 10-year period (Malamuth et al., in preparation). However, some of the constructs were assessed somewhat differently in this longitudinal study, that is, the early risk factors construct was similar, but not identical, to the assessment by Malamuth et al. (1991) of early abuse experiences and violence in the home.

We also incorporated in this extended model the data for the behaviors assessed at Time 2, about 10 years later (i.e., relationship distress, relationship aggression, and later sexual aggression). In this analysis, we used a path analytical approach without any latent constructs due to the relatively small size of the subsample of our longitudinal study for which Time 1 sexual aggression data are available ($n = 60$).

As shown in Figure 4, we used two paths to predict the early sexual aggression (at an average age of about 20). In the first path, early risk factors predicted delinquent behavior, which in turn predicted sexual acting out (i.e., sexual promiscuity). Early risk factors also directly predicted Time 1 and Time

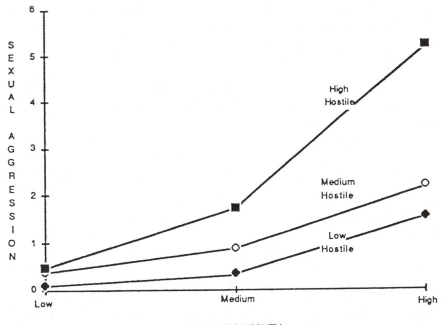

FIGURE 3 Mean sexual aggression as a function of three levels of hostile masculinity and sexual promiscuity. (From Malamuth et al., 1991.)

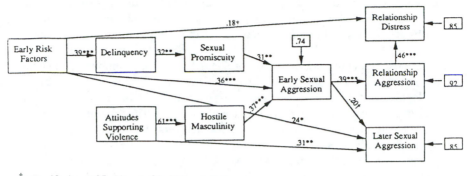

$^{†}p < .10, *p < .05, **p < .01, ***p < .001$
Standardized Regression Coefficients are Shown
NFI = .90
$\chi^2(23) = 14.7, ns$

FIGURE 4 Structural model predicting both early sexual aggression (at about average age of 20 years) and behaviors toward women 10 years later. Data are based on men's self-reports. (From Malamuth, Heavey, Linz, & Barnes, in preparation.)

2 sexual aggression as well as distress in the current relationship. The second path involved attitudes supporting violence predicting hostile masculinity. These two paths converged to predict Time 1 sexual aggression, which in turn predicted Time 2 verbal and physical aggression against the partner as well as sexual aggression ($p < .10$). Relationship aggression had a strong impact on relationship distress.

We are encouraged by the ability of these data to replicate the model based on a national random sample (Malamuth et al., 1991). This model suggests that early sexual aggression is useful for predicting later forms of aggression against women, as well as distress in long-term relationships with women. To our knowledge, this research is the first to attempt to predict antisocial behavior against women in adulthood using data on men's earlier sexual aggression and correlates of such behavior. This may be particularly important, because sexual aggression may often precede the occurrence of later aggression such as marital violence and child abuse. As such, sexual aggression may be an especially useful marker for the occurrence of these later behaviors.

Additional Analyses

Some additional analyses conducted with the longitudinal sample are summarized briefly here. We have addressed the possibility that the predictability we have achieved is due to only a small percentage of the distribution that reports extreme levels of violence. This is often the case in studies of aggression prediction. For example, although research on the longitudinal prediction of aggression has shown that childhood aggression predicts adult aggression, including criminal behavior, the predictive success is based nearly exclusively on 5–10% of the observations at the extreme of the sample distribution (Magnusson & Bergman, 1988). In fact, as Pulkkinen (1988) noted, if the small group of children belonging to the severe multiproblem cluster were removed, the significant statistical relationships " . . . would completely disappear" (p. 195).

To partially examine this issue, we performed a Chi-square analysis in which the predictor measure of sexual aggression at Time 1 (about 10 years ago) was divided into three levels: 0, for subjects who reported no sexual aggression at all ($n = 40$); 1, for those reporting the lowest level of sexual aggression ($n = 13$); and 2, for those indicating any higher level of such aggression ($n = 13$). We examined the ability of such a classification to predict later aggression against women, which was classified simply as "no" versus "yes." For this classification, we used any indication, as reported by either the man or his female partner, of sexual aggression since the earlier assessment and/or physical nonsexual aggression. The results showed a significant Chi-square ($7.9, p < .05$). Based on the three-level classification, the current assessment showed increasing frequencies, with 33%, 46%, and 77% of the men at each of these levels having engaged in aggression against women since the earlier assessment. These data show that the type of aggression we are studying is not restricted to a small percentage of the sample. Similar patterns to those described earlier are found when separating later behavior into types (e.g., sexual aggression only and physical nonsexual aggression only) as well as in separately studying men's and women's reports. Such analyses also demonstrate that the findings are reliable even when using women's reports, which are independent of the men's earlier reports.

The data do not appear to be accounted for solely in terms of social desirability (Crowne & Marlowe, 1980) or method variance biases. For example, the longitudinal findings show strong significant relationships between the men's reports taken 10 years ago and current measures that do not share method variance (e.g., their current female partners' independent reports as well as raters' observations of videotaped interactions). Partialing out shared variance with social desirability scales does not substantially alter these findings.

CONCLUSIONS AND DIRECTIONS
FOR FUTURE RESEARCH

The research described here has provided support for the various components of the interactive model that we described earlier. The findings showed that the factors we studied consistently predicted men's sexual aggression and related antisocial behaviors against women. Further, a combination of factors, particularly using interactive combinations, were better in predicting such behaviors than were individual factors alone. These data support the convergence element of our model. Considerable evidence was also obtained for the domain specificity prediction, so that the factors predictive of overt aggressiveness and similar behaviors (e.g., domineeringness and hostility in conversations) toward women did not equally predict such behaviors when directed against men. The research also showed that such predictive factors could be meaningfully organized in a model comprising two major paths formed by constellations of such factors. These paths also included other environmental proximate influences stemming from a person's early childhood and adolescent experiences.

Future research is needed to better explicate the factors comprising the two major streams or paths we identified. As noted earlier, one of the scales used by Malamuth et al. (1991) as an indicator of the hostile masculinity construct is the Negative Masculinity scale. It is highly correlated with maladaptive components of narcissism (Watson, Biderman, & Boyd, 1989). Buss and Chiodo (1991) recently provided support for the construct of narcissism as a personality syndrome with several constitutive elements that are manifested in behaviors that represent " . . . a dominant and even aggressive display of self-centered impulses with little concern for the negative consequences that such displays might have on others" (p. 213). Findings by Malamuth et al. (1991) suggested that part of the connection between the hostile masculinity path and coercive behaviors toward women may be explained by a general factor that might be described as a reflection of narcissism, particularly the maladaptive components.

However, Malamuth et al. (1991) also found that another part of the connection between hostile masculinity and coercive behaviors appeared to be unique variance specifically linked to hostility toward women. Therefore, the concept of hostile masculinity might be considered to be strongly related to a narcissistic personality, but with hostile elements specifically directed toward women.

The need for incorporation of elements specific to women is supported by other findings presented here, which show some unique connections between the predictor factors and domineering, aggressive behaviors directed toward females. More specifically, as indicated earlier, the research comparing behaviors directed against female as compared to male targets showed that the predictors we studied (e.g., attitudes regarding violence toward women, sexual arousal to aggression against women, etc.) were significantly related to domineeringness and aggression toward females, but not toward males. Furthermore, our longitudinal analyses indicated that factors related to aggression against women did not predict later general antisocial behavior, although they did predict later antisocial behavior against women. These analyses also indicated that assessing hostility toward the specific women with whom the men had a relationship, which was strongly related to their levels of hostility toward women generally, enabled particularly good prediction of their degree of aggression and related behaviors toward them.

It is not clear at this stage whether the specificity in the relationship between the predictors and female targets is due to females' being perceived as
less intimidating or less likely to retaliate in some way, or whether there is a
particular motivation and/or gratification to dominating or controlling females.
We believe that both elements have a contributing role. As suggested by Malamuth (1988), it is important for future research to develop and test theoretical
models that consider the influences of at least three types of factors: (a) those
contributing to any type of coercive behavior (e.g., general hostility); (b) those
more uniquely causing sexism and violence against women (e.g., sexual arousal
to dominance over women); and (c) those promoting antisocial behavior against
targets perceived as "weaker," "outgroups," and so forth (e.g., ego-
defensiveness). Moreover, it is likely that measures that assess hostility toward
the specific woman being victimized (which would be expected to relate
strongly to hostility toward women generally) would be a particularly good
predictor of antisocial behavior against her.

An important component and potential early precursor of the hostile masculinity path that may merit more attention can be described as "rejection-hurt-
anger" feelings and perceptions. Many of the items on the Hostility Toward
Women scale describe such reactions (e.g., "I have been rejected by too many
women in my life" and "I am sure that I get a raw deal from the women in my
life"). Further, Lisak and Roth (1988) compared sexually aggressive and nonaggressive college students with particular focus on the factors underlying anger and power motivations. They concluded that sexually aggressive men were
more likely to perceive themselves as having been hurt by women, including
feelings of being deceived, betrayed, and manipulated. They also found that
variables assessing such hurt were highly intercorrelated with items assessing
anger toward women and a desire to dominate them. It is not clear at this stage
whether such hurt feelings represent some degree of "objective" reality, with
the more aggressive men having experienced more rejection and/or whether
they are hypersensitive to the same type of experiences shared with the nonaggressive men. In any case, these findings suggest that one additional aspect of
the hostile masculinity path consists of adversarial and negative relationships
with women, as well as few close friendships with them.

It is important for research in this area to address more adequately the
question of why some men come to derive particular sexual gratification from
interactions that highlight power and/or coercive elements. It is possible that for
some men the process is related to frustration in attempts to attract desired
sexual partners, resulting in feelings of rejection, anger, and hostility. Some
studies have demonstrated that the temporary priming of hostile feelings results
in greater sexual arousal from coercive sex (Barbaree, 1990; Yates, Barbaree,
& Marshall, 1984). However, once such hostility has been invoked for longer
time periods and sexual arousal has come to be associated with power and/or

coercion, it may not be fully "reversible," even if the man is better able to attract sexual partners.

Certain factors, such as empathy, may statistically "load" inversely on the hostile masculinity path. High scores on such factors are expected to attenuate the relationship between risk factors and later antisocial behavior. With low levels of empathy, the relationships between risk factors and later behavior may be strong, whereas with moderate to high levels of empathy these relationships may not be significant (i.e., the effect of the risk factors on behaviors may be blocked or reduced considerably by counterinfluences, such as empathy). Preliminary analyses of our longitudinal study provided support for these predictions.

The suggestion that having little empathy may be considered part of the hostile masculinity construct is consistent with conceptualizations of the narcissistic personality. One of the components of such a personality is having low empathy, particularly regarding the consequences of one's own behavior on others. However, such a link between empathy and other aspects of this construct has sometimes not been found (Buss & Chiodo, 1991). It is not clear at this point whether it may be more useful to conceptualize variables such as empathy as part of the hostile masculinity path with similar origins or as a dimension that is separate, albeit related, to this path, because the roots of empathic qualities may be quite different from those of the other components of the hostile masculinity path. Theoretical frameworks for understanding this and related issues need to keep in mind the multidimensionality of empathy (Davis, 1980; Davis & Oathout, 1992) and the possible role of both innate and experiential contributing factors (Eisenberg & Lennon, 1983; Hoffman, 1975).

Based on theoretical grounds and some analyses we have conducted, we believe that there are other variables used in research in this area that are also likely to load quite strongly on this hostile masculinity path. Examples include psychopathic deviance, often measured by the MMPI PD Scale 4, a "macho personality" (Mosher & Tomkins, 1988), and possibly the combination of high surgency and high disagreeableness (Buss, 1992), as measured on the five-factor model of personality (McCrae & Costa, 1987).

The second path of particular importance to sexual aggression appears to be related to home environment and to delinquency, when expressed in relatively promiscuous sexuality. This path may also relate quite closely to impulsivity characteristics (Prentky & Knight, 1986, 1991) and to other manifestations of attraction to impersonal sex, such as a relatively high usage of pornography.

The role of this path also needs to be studied more extensively. We suggest that it is not sex drive per se that is critical here, but attraction to impersonal sex and perhaps a relatively strong connection between sex and power. Preliminary analyses of our 10-year longitudinal research are consistent with this view.

They show that being more sexually aggressive earlier in life is predictive of such variables as more frequent reports of sexual arousal by looking at attractive unknown women and of having more extrarelationship affairs in later life. In contrast, it is not predictive of variables such as degree of pleasure derived from sex, frequency of sex with a woman, or number of orgasms per week.

In current American culture, there is considerable evidence to suggest that power motives are often linked with "normal" male sexuality (Nelson, 1979; Winter, 1973; Winter & Stewart, 1978). Whether these are primarily the result of certain cultures encouraging such links or whether there is some evolutionary preparedness for such a link is not clear at this point. In either case, we believe that there are various evolutionary, cultural, and individual converging factors that may affect the extent to which men derive gratification and a sense of self-esteem from using domineering and coercive influence strategies in sexual relations. It would be very helpful to study the extent to which the link between power and sexuality in men varies cross-culturally to help address such issues.

Research should also question whether sexual coercion is "an act of aggression or power" versus "a sexual act" (Brownmiller, 1975; Palmer, 1988). Our findings that the interaction between the sexual promiscuity and hostile masculinity paths best predicts sexual aggression suggest that sexual coercion may be best conceptualized as both an aggressive and a sexual act. This issue may be reframed as a question of what are the ultimate causes of sexual coercion (see earlier discussion of ultimate and proximate causes). We believe that to adequately address such an issue, it is necessary to develop more fully "vertically integrated" multiple-level, complementary explanations of ultimate and proximate causes (Barkow, 1989; Goldsmith, 1991). Our aim is to develop the interactive model described here so that it will be a comprehensive model of this kind. In developing an integrated model of the characteristics of sexual aggressors, it will be important to consider the following: (a) species-wide mechanisms resulting from natural selection that mediate between environmental stimuli and the person's behavior; (b) gender-wide differences in certain psychological mechanisms relating to sexuality and aggressivity; (c) cultural and subcultural differences in ideology, social climate, and so on; and (d) individual variability within males (e.g., genetic, hormonal, experiential, etc.). In a research area focusing on such a critical social problem as rape and related behaviors, it will be particularly important to demonstrate that such an integrated model not only serves heuristic purposes, but that it performs better than current models in such areas as predicting the likelihood that a person will aggress and in generating new hypotheses that otherwise would not have been made.

REFERENCES

Abel, G. G., Barlow, D. H., Blanchard, E., & Guild, D. (1977). The components of rapists' sexual arousal. *Archives of General Psychiatry, 34,* 895–903.

Ageton, S. S. (1983). *Sexual assault among adolescents.* Lexington, MA: Lexington Books.

Barbaree, H. E. (1990). Stimulus control of sexual arousal: Its role in sexual assault. In W. L. Marshall, D. R. Laws, & H. E. Barbaree (Eds.), *Handbook of sexual assault: Issues, theories, and treatment of the sex offender* (pp. 115–142). New York: Plenum.

Barbaree, H. E., & Marshall, W. L. (1991). The role of male sexual arousal in rape: Six models. *Journal of Consulting and Clinical Psychology, 59,* 621–630.

Barkow, J. H. (1989). *Darwin, sex, and status: Biological approaches to mind and culture.* Toronto: University of Toronto Press.

Baron, R. M., & Kenny, D. A. (1986). The moderator-mediator variable distinction in social psychological research: Conceptual, strategic, and statistical considerations. *Journal of Personality and Social Psychology, 51,* 1173–1182.

Bentler, P. M. (1968). Heterosexual behavior assessment 1: Males. *Behaviour Research and Therapy, 6,* 21–25.

Bisonnette, V., Ickes, W., Bernstein, I., & Knowles, E. (1990). Personality moderating variables: A warning about statistical artifact and a comparison of analytic techniques. *Journal of Personality, 58,* 567–587.

Bollen, K. A. (1989). *Structural equations with latent variables.* New York: Wiley.

Booth, A., & Edwards, J. (1983). Measuring marital instability. *Journal of Marriage and the Family, 45,* 387–393.

Bronfenbrenner, U. (1979). *The ecology of human development: Experiments by nature and design.* Cambridge, MA: Harvard University Press.

Broughton, R. (1990). The prototype concept in personality assessment. *Canadian Psychology, 31,* 26–37.

Brownmiller, S. (1975). *Against our will: Men, women, and rape.* New York: Simon & Schuster.

Burt, M. R. (1978). Attitudes supportive of rape in American culture. *House Committee on Science and Technology, Subcommittee on Domestic and International Scientific Planning, Analysis and Cooperation, Research into Violent Behavior: Sexual Assaults* (Hearing, 95th Congress, 2nd session, January 10–12, 1978) (pp. 277–322). Washington, DC: U.S. Government Printing Office.

Burt, M. R. (1980). Cultural myths and supports for rape. *Journal of Personality and Social Psychology, 38,* 217–230.

Buss, D. M. (1991). Conflict in married couples: Personality predictors of anger and upset. *Journal of Personality, 59,* 663–688.

Buss, D. M. (1992). Manipulation in close relationships: Five personality factors in interactional context. *Journal of Personality, 60,* 477–499.

Buss, D. M., & Chiodo, L. M. (1991). Narcissistic acts in everyday life. *Journal of Personality, 59,* 179–215.

Buss, D. M., & Schmitt, D. P. (in press). Sexual strategies theory: A contextual evolutionary analysis of human mating. *Psychological Review.*

Check, J. V. P. (1985). *The hostility towards women scale.* Unpublished doctoral dissertation, University of Manitoba, Winnepeg.

Check, J. V. P., & Malamuth, N. M. (1986). Pornography and sexual aggression: A social learning theory analysis. In M. L. McLaughlin (Ed.), *Communication yearbook* (vol. 9, pp. 181–213). Beverly Hills, CA: Sage.

Crowne, D. P., & Marlowe, D. (1980). *The approval motive: Studies in evaluative dependence.* Westport, CT: Greenwood Press.

Davis, M. H. (1980). A multidimensional approach to individual differences in empathy. *JSAS: Catalog of Selected Documents in Psychology, 10,* 85.

Davis, M. H., & Oathout, H. A. (1992). The effect of dispositional empathy on romantic relationship behaviors: Heterosocial anxiety as a moderating influence. *Personality and Social Psychology Bulletin, 18,* 76–83.

Dobash, R. P., Dobash, R. E., Wilson, M., & Daly, M. (1992). The myth of sexual symmetry in marital violence. *Social Problems, 39,* 71–91.

Dodge, K. A., Bates, J. E., & Pettit, G. S. (1990). Mechanisms in the cycle of violence. *Science, 250,* 1678–1683.

Eisenberg, N., & Lennon, R. (1983). Sex differences in empathy and related capacities. *Psychological Bulletin, 94,* 100–131.

Elliott, D. S., & Morse, B. J. (1989). Delinquency and drug use as risk factors in teenage sexual activity. *Youth and Society, 21,* 32–60.

Ellis, L. (1991). A synthesized (biosocial) theory of rape. *Journal of Consulting and Clinical Psychology, 59,* 631–642.

Eysenck, H. J. (1978). *Sex and personality.* London: Open Books.

Fagan, J., & Wexler, S. (1988). Explanations of sexual assault among violent delinquents. *Journal of Adolescent Research, 3,* 363–385.

Gilmore, D. D. (1990). *Manhood in the making: Cultural concepts of masculinity.* New Haven, CT: Yale University Press.

Goldsmith, T. H. (1991). *The biological roots of human nature.* New York: Oxford University Press.

Gowaty, P. A. (1992). Evolutionary biology and feminism. *Human Nature, 3,* 217–249.

Groth, N. A. (1979). *Men who rape: The psychology of the offender.* New York: Plenum.

Hall, G. C. N., & Hirschman, R. (1991). Toward a theory of sexual aggression: A quadripartite model. *Journal of Consulting and Clinical Psychology, 59,* 662–669.

Hammerstein, P. & Parker, G. A. (1987). Sexual selection: Games between the sexes. In J. W. Bradbury and M. B. Andersson (Eds.). *Sexual selection: Testing the alternatives.* (pp. 119–142). New York: John Wiley & Sons.

Hoffman, M. L. (1975). Developmental synthesis of affect and cognition and its interplay for altruistic motivation. *Developmental Psychology, 11,* 607–622.

Hotaling, G. T., & Sugarman, D. B. (1986). An analysis of risk markers in husband to wife violence: The current state of knowledge. *Violence and Victims, 1,* 101–124.

Huesmann, L. R. (1988). An information processing model for the development of aggression. *Aggressive Behavior, 14,* 13–24.

Kanin, E. J. (1977). Sexual aggression: A second look at the offended female. *Archives of Sexual Behavior, 6,* 67–76.

Kenny, D. A., & Judd, C. M. (1984). Estimating the nonlinear and interactive effects of latent variables. *Psychological Bulletin, 96,* 201–210.

Kohut, H. (1977). *The restoration of the self.* New York: International University Press.

Koss, M. P., Dinero, T., Seibel, C., & Cox, S. (1988). Stranger and acquaintance rape: Are there differences in the victim's experience? *Psychology of Women Quarterly, 12,* 1–24.

Koss, M. P., & Leonard, K. E. (1984). Sexually aggressive men: Empirical findings and theoretical implications. In N. M. Malamuth, & E. Donnerstein (Eds.), *Pornography and sexual aggression* (pp. 213–232). New York: Academic Press.

Koss, M., & Oros, C. (1982). Sexual experiences survey: A research instrument investigating sexual aggression and victimization. *Journal of Consulting and Clinical Psychology, 50,* 455–457.

Larzelere, R., & Huston, T. (1980). The Dyadic Trust scale: Toward understanding interpersonal trust in close relationships. *Journal of Marriage and the Family, 43,* 595–604.

Lisak, D., & Roth, S. (1988). Motivational factors in nonincarcerated sexually aggressive men. *Journal of Personality and Social Psychology, 55,* 795–802.

Magnusson, D., & Bergman, L. R. (1988). Individual and variable-based approaches to longitudinal research on early risk factors. In M. Rutter (Ed.), *Studies of psychosocial risk: The power of longitudinal data* (pp. 45–61). Cambridge: Cambridge University Press.

Malamuth, N. M. (1981). Rape proclivity among males. *Journal of Social Issues, 37,* 138–157.

Malamuth, N. M. (1983). Factors associated with rape as predictors of laboratory aggression against women. *Journal of Personality and Social Psychology, 45,* 432–442.

Malamuth, N. M. (1986). Predictors of naturalistic sexual aggression. *Journal of Personality and Social Psychology, 50,* 953–962.

Malamuth, N. M. (1987, August). *Sexual aggression and domineeringness in conversations with male vs. female targets.* Paper presented at the Annual Meeting of the American Psychological Association, New York.

Malamuth, N. M. (1988). Predicting laboratory aggression against female and male targets: Implications for sexual aggression. *Journal of Research in Personality, 22,* 474–495.

Malamuth, N. M. (1989). Sexually violent media, thought patterns and antisocial behavior. In G. Comstock (Ed.), *Public communication and behavior* (vol. 2, pp. 159–204). New York: Academic Press.

Malamuth, N. M., & Briere, J. (1986). Sexual violence in the media: Indirect effects on aggression against women. *Journal of Social Issues, 42,* 75–92.

Malamuth, N. M., & Check, J. V. P. (1981). The effects of mass media exposure on acceptance of violence against women: A field experiment. *Journal of Research in Personality, 15,* 436–446.

Malamuth, N. M., & Check, J. V. P. (1982, June). *Factors related to aggression against women.* Paper presented at the Annual Meeting of the Canadian Psychological Association, Montreal.

Malamuth, N. M., & Check, J. V. P. (1983). Sexual arousal to rape depictions: Individual differences. *Journal of Abnormal Psychology, 92,* 55–67.

Malamuth, N. M., & Check, J. V. P. (1985). *Predicting naturalistic sexual aggression: A replication.* Unpublished manuscript, University of California, Los Angeles.

Malamuth, N. M., Check, J. V. P., & Briere, J. (1986). Sexual arousal in response to aggression: Ideological, aggressive and sexual correlates. *Journal of Personality and Social Psychology, 50,* 330–340.

Malamuth, N. M., Feshbach, S., & Jaffe, Y. (1977). Sexual arousal and aggression: Recent experiments and theoretical issues. *Journal of Social Issues, 33,* 110–133.

Malamuth, N. M., Heavey, C., Linz, D., & Barnes, G. (in preparation). Longitudinal prediction of sexual and nonsexual aggression against women.

Malamuth, N. M., Sockloskie, R., Koss, M. P., & Tanaka, J. (1991). The characteristics of aggressors against women: Testing a model using a national sample of college students. *Journal of Consulting and Clinical Psychology, 59,* 670–681.

McCrae, R. R., & Costa, P. T., Jr. (1987). Validation of the five-factor model of personality across instruments and observers. *Journal of Personality and Social Psychology, 52,* 81–90.

Mosher, D. L., & Tomkins, S. S. (1988). Scripting the macho man: Hypermasculinization and enculturation. *The Journal of Sex Research, 25,* 60–84.

Murphy, C. M., & O'Leary, K. D. (1989). Psychological aggression predicts physical aggression in early marriage. *Journal of Consulting and Clinical Psychology, 57,* 579–582.

Nelson, P. A. (1979). *Personality, sexual functions, and sexual behavior: An experiment in methodology.* Unpublished doctoral dissertation, University of Florida, Gainesville.

Newcomb, M. D., & Bentler, P. M. (1988). *Consequences of adolescent drug use: Impact on the lives of young adults.* Beverly Hills, CA: Sage.

O'Leary, K. D. (1988). Physical aggression between spouses: A social learning perspective. In V. B. Van Hasselt, R. Morrison, A. Bellack, & M. Hersen (Eds.), *Handbook of family violence* (pp. 31–55). New York: Plenum.

O'Leary, K. D., & Curley, A. D. (1987). *Spouse specific assertion and aggression.* Unpublished manuscript, State University of New York, Stonybrook.

Palmer, C. (1988). Twelve reasons why rape is not sexually motivated: A skeptical examination. *The Journal of Sex Research, 25,* 512–530.

Patterson, G. R., DeBaryshe, B. D., & Ramsey, E. (1989). A developmental perspective on antisocial behavior. *American Psychologist, 44,* 329–335.

Prentky, R. A., & Knight, R. A. (1986). Impulsivity in the lifestyle and criminal behavior of sexual offenders. *Criminal Justice and Behavior, 13,* 141–164.

Prentky, R. A., & Knight, R. (1991). Identifying critical dimensions for discriminating among rapists. *Journal of Consulting and Clinical Psychology, 59,* 643–661.

Puccini, G. (1980). *Tosca.* Hamburg, Germany: Polydor International GMBH.

Pulkkinen, L. (1988). Delinquent development: Theoretical and empirical considerations. In M. Rutter (Ed.), *Studies of psychosocial risk: The power of longitudinal data* (pp. 184–199). Cambridge: Cambridge University Press.

Quinsey, V. L. (1984). Studies of offenders against women. In D. Weisstub (Ed.), *Law and mental health: International perspectives* (vol. 1, pp. 84–121). New York: Pergamon.

Rapaport, K., & Burkhart, B. R. (1984). Personality and attitudinal characteristics of sexually coercive college males. *Journal of Abnormal Psychology, 93,* 216–221.

Rosch, E. (1978). Principles of categorization. In E. Rosch & B. B. Loyd (Eds.), *Cognition and categorization* (pp. 27–71). Hillsdale, NJ: Lawrence Erlbaum.

Russell, D. E. H. (1984). *Sexual exploitation: Rape, child sexual abuse and workplace harassment.* Beverly Hills, CA: Sage.

Sampson, R. J., & Laub, J. H. (1990). Crime and deviance over the life course: The salience of adult social bonds. *American Sociological Review, 55,* 609–627.

Scully, D., & Marolla, J. (1985). Riding the bull at Gilley's: Convicted rapists describe the rewards of rape. *Social Problems, 32,* 251–263.

Shields, W. M., & Shields, L. M. (1983). Forcible rape: An evolutionary perspective. *Ethology and Sociobiology, 4,* 115–136.

Smuts, B. (1992). Male aggression against women: An evolutionary perspective. *Human Nature, 3,* 1–44.

Spanier, G. B., & Filsinger, E. (1983). The Dyadic Adjustment scale. In E. Filsinger (Ed.), *Marriage and family assessment* (pp. 155–168). Beverly Hills, CA: Sage.

Spence, J. T., Helmreich, R. L., & Holahan, C. K. (1979). The negative and positive components of psychological masculinity and femininity and their relationships to self reports of neurotic and acting out behaviors. *Journal of Personality and Social Psychology, 37,* 1673–1682.

Sternberg, R. J., & Lubart, T. I. (1991). An investment theory of creativity and its development. *Human Development, 34,* 1–31.

Straus, M. A. (1979). Measuring intrafamily conflict and violence: The Conflict Tactics (CT) scales. *Journal of Marriage and the Family, 41,* 75–85.

Straus, M. A. (1987, August). *Family patterns and research on primary prevention of family violence.* Paper presented at the American Psychological Association, New York.

Straus, M. A., & Gelles, R. J. (1990). *Physical violence in American families: Risk factors and adaptations to violence in 8,145 Families.* New Brunswick, NJ: Transaction.

Symons, D. (1979). *The evolution of human sexuality.* New York: Oxford University Press.

Symons, D. (1987). An evolutionary approach: Can Darwin's view of life shed light on human sexuality. In J. H. Geer & W. T. O'Donohue (Eds.), *Theories of human sexuality* (pp. 91–125). New York: Plenum.

Thornhill, R., & Thornhill, N. (1992). The evolutionary psychology of men's coercive sexuality. *Behavioral and Brain Sciences, 15,* 363–421.

Tooby, J., & Cosmides, L. (1990). On the universality of human nature and the uniqueness of the individual: The role of genetics and adaptation. *Journal of Personality, 58,* 17–67.

Trivers, R. (1972). Parental investment and sexual selection. In B. Campbell (Ed.), *Sexual selection and the descent of man 1871–1971* (pp. 136–179). Chicago: Aldine.

Watson, P., Biderman, M. & Boyd, C. (1989). Androgyny as synthetic narcissism: Sex role measures and Kohut's psychology of the self. *Sex Roles, 21,* 175–205.

Williams, G. C. (1975). *Sex and evolution.* Princeton, NJ: Princeton University Press.

Winter, D. G. (1973). *The power motive.* New York: Free Press.

Winter, D. G., & Stewart, A. J. (1978). Power motivation. In H. London & J. Exner (Eds.), *Dimensions of personality* (pp. 391–447). New York: Wiley.

Yates, E., Barbaree, H. E., & Marshall, W. L. (1984). Anger and deviant sexual arousal. *Behaviour Therapy, 15,* 287–294.

6

ROLE OF MALE SEXUAL AROUSAL DURING RAPE IN VARIOUS RAPIST SUBTYPES

Howard E. Barbaree
Queen's University

Ralph C. Serin
Joyceville Institution

INTRODUCTION

This chapter is a speculative attempt to integrate two substantive bodies of research in the area of sexual assault. First, a long-standing research effort by Knight and Prentky at the Massachusetts Treatment Center (MTC) has been directed toward the development of a typology of rapists, beginning with clinical attempts and culminating in an empirically based typology. Second, a large number of studies has been conducted comparing rapists and nonoffenders in their erectile responses to descriptions of rape and consenting sexual activities. Based on the sexual arousal literature, Barbaree and Marshall (1991) have described six different models that could account for arousal during rape. These authors suggested that the mechanism of sexual arousal and its role in rape might be different in different rapists, and briefly suggested how different models of rape arousal might apply to different subtypes of rapists. The present chapter is an extension and elaboration of this speculation. It places the MTC subtypes in a two-dimensional table containing two levels of a variable akin to criminal personality, and a second factor comprised of three models of sexual arousal, namely: disinhibition-state, inhibition-trait, and a model of arousal in sadism. These three models, ordered in this way, reflect the manner in which and the degree to which anger or hostility strengthens sexual arousal during rape. Then, various MTC subtypes are allotted, in a rational way, to the six cells in the two-dimensional table. This chapter defines sadism in terms of two possible models of sexual arousal during rape. The speculation presented here makes specific predictions concerning patterns of sexual arousal among various

99

rapist subtypes, and promises to resolve some discrepancies in the literature on sexual arousal among rapists.

Current conceptions of rape can be broadly categorized in two opposing theoretical camps, depending on the perspective of the writer (Malamuth, Check, & Briere, 1986). Feminist writers (Brownmiller, 1975; Burt, 1980; Clark & Lewis, 1977; Darke, 1990; Herman, 1990; Russell, 1975, 1988) have argued that sexual assault is primarily aggressive in nature, and represents a specific instance of a male-centered society's more general hostility toward women and children. In contrast, there is a widely held belief among mental health professionals that rapists are best characterized as sexual deviates. According to a prominent version of the clinical perspective on rape, rapists are motivated by a "sexual preference" for violent or aggressive interactions (Abel, Barlow, Blanchard, & Guild, 1977; Freund & Blanchard, 1981), just as pedophiles show a sexual preference for children. Both perspectives recognize the basic duality of rape: specifically, they recognize that rape involves both aggressive and sexual elements. However, the perspectives differ in the way they conceive of the interaction between these two components. The feminist perspective minimizes the importance of sexual motivation as an important explanatory concept by describing sexual arousal as a coincidental by-product of the circumstance of rape (Brownmiller, 1975). In contrast, the clinical perspective of rape as a paraphiliac behavior focuses on sexual motivation (Freund, Scher, Racansky, Campbell, & Heasman, 1986) as an explanatory concept, but minimizes the role of aggression toward women as a component in rape. Although both groups can point to empirical support for their views, it is becoming increasingly apparent that no single variable can account for all aspects of rape (Malamuth, 1986).

This chapter takes the position that rape is best defined as an integration of both sexual and aggressive components, and that our understanding of rape will be best advanced by an investigation of the psychological processes in which these two elements of rape interact.

Both approaches to rape have postulated and identified dispositional factors that are apparently responsible for the aggressive acts of rapists. Craig (1990) argued convincingly that men with particular dispositions toward sexual aggression are at increased risk for committing rape. These dispositional factors include: (a) acceptance of interpersonal aggression as a viable form of interpersonal expression; (b) more stereotypic views of women and their gender roles; (c) a belief that relationships between men and women are, by definition, adversarial in nature; and (d) membership in a peer group that is supportive of sexual coercion by placing a high value on sexual prowess and loss of virginity. According to Craig (1990), the men with these dispositions will seek out particular women for the perceived sexual possibilities they afford, behave in ways that reduce the woman's likelihood of resistance, and then decrease the responsibility they feel for any coercion that is required by post-hoc distortion of the facts.

Along the same lines, Malamuth (1986) reported that a complex of dispositional factors predict sexually aggressive behavior among men, including: (a) sexual arousal in response to aggression, (b) the identification of dominance as a motive for sexual acts, (c) hostility toward women, and (d) attitudes accepting of violence against women. Similarly, many clinicians have postulated a continuum of individual differences in responses thought to be important in rape in the general population of men (Abel et al., 1977).

According to Craig (1990), however, a more complete analysis of rape will include situational determinants. A significant proportion of rapists report a number of circumstantial factors as being present preceding their rapes, including anger, alcohol intoxication, and sexual arousal (MacDonald & Pithers, 1989; Pithers, Beal, Armstrong, & Petty, 1989).

Recently, it has been suggested that rape is a heterogeneous phenomenon, with different instances of the behavior requiring different explanations. Knight and Prentky (1990) presented a psychological typology of rapists, grounded in empirical investigation, which specified different motives underlying the behavior in different subtypes of rapists. In addition, Malamuth (1986, 1988) presented a predictive model of sexual assault that attributes the behavior to multiple predisposing characteristics. Therefore, current authoritative opinion and empirical data make it increasingly clear that rape is not a unitary phenomenon, but is the result of a complex of interacting dispositional and situational factors.

MODELS OF SEXUAL AROUSAL IN RAPE

Barbaree and Marshall (1991) speculated on the role of sexual arousal in rape. They reviewed a substantial body of research that studied men's sexual arousal to descriptions of rape and mutually consenting sex and compared the responses of rapists with nonrapists. The review indicated that authors in this area hold a variety of theories or models of such arousal, and the review described six separate models. This chapter utilizes four of these models, as described below.

The Sexual Preference Hypothesis

The concept of a sexual preference forms the basis of the modern clinical assessment of sexual deviates. The foremost classificatory systems (see Knight, Rosenberg, & Schneider, 1985, for a review) are based, in part, on the classification of the stimuli that elicit sexual arousal and fantasies in the individual. In the recent revision of the DSM-III (American Psychiatric Association, 1987), the paraphilias are characterized by sexual fantasies and arousal in response to sexual objects or behaviors that are not part of normative arousal-activity patterns. The sexual preference hypothesis states simply that if a man is maximally aroused by a deviant stimulus or act, his eventual gratification will be greater than that resulting from less strong responses to normalized or socially acceptable stimuli or acts.

A sexual preference is thought to be a relatively stable individual trait. When a man is identified as a sexual deviate, it would be usual for the clinician to recommend that he seek and receive treatment to normalize his pattern of sexual arousal. Numerous treatment procedures have been developed over the past 20 years (Quinsey & Marshall, 1983). Following from this model of sexual deviance, the laboratory assessment of sexual preferences has become an important part of a complete clinical assessment of sexual offenders (Earls & Marshall, 1983; Laws & Osborne, 1983). In a laboratory setting, the man's erectile response is monitored, usually by circumferential strain gauge plethysmography, while he is presented with verbal descriptions of consenting sexual activity between adults, and rape in which a male forces intercourse on an adult woman. Sexual arousal to both sexual and nonsexual violence has been interpreted by clinicians as indicating a propensity in an individual man for committing sexual violence (Abel et al., 1977; Malamuth, 1981) and by feminist writers as being indicative of men's inherent potential for violence against women (Russell, 1988). Abel et al. (1977) suggested that rapists are paraphiliacs in the same sense as are pedophiles, except that instead of showing a preference for children as sexual objects, rapists prefer nonconsenting aggressive sexual interactions.

Abel et al. (1977) conducted the first major examination of deviant sexual arousal in rapists by recording the sexual arousal of these offenders and a group of nonrapist sexual deviates during 2-minute verbal descriptions of mutually consenting sex and rape. Abel et al. (1977) found that the rapists were more aroused by descriptions of forced sex than were nonrapists, although the rapists did not show a sexual preference for rape. As a group, the rapists were equally aroused by rape and consenting cues, whereas nonrapists were considerably less aroused by rape than they were by the consenting sexual descriptions.

The findings of Abel et al. (1977) were supported by studies reported soon after (Barbaree, Marshall, & Lanthier, 1979; Quinsey & Chaplin, 1982, 1984). However, later, in strong support of the sexual preference hypothesis, Quinsey, Chaplin, and Upfold (1984) reported that rapists showed stronger arousal to rape cues than did nonoffenders, and stronger arousal to rape cues than to consenting cues (V. L. Quinsey, personal communication, 1988). Earls and Proulx (1986) recently reported similar findings studying a Francophone population of rapists, using translations of Abel, Blanchard, Becker, and Djenderedjian's (1978) verbal descriptions of rape, consenting sex, and assault. However, in contrast to these findings, Baxter, Barbaree, and Marshall (1986) reported results from 60 rapists and 41 nonrapists that indicated that both groups showed significantly less arousal to rape than to mutually consenting cues. Similarly, Murphy, Krisak, Stalgaitis, and Anderson (1984) and Langevin et al. (1985) failed to find significant differences between rapists and nonrapists in their responses to sexual violence.

The findings are confusing in a number of important respects. First, the majority of studies have not found that rapists, on average, have a sexual preference for rape over consenting sexual interactions. Second, among the studies that have not found a sexual preference for rape, some fail to find any substantive differences between rapists and nonrapists, with both groups showing significantly less arousal to rape than to consenting sex. This chapter is, in part, a speculative attempt to account for the discrepancies in this research literature.

Trait Inhibition of Rape Arousal

To account for these discrepant findings, Barbaree et al. (1979) and Marshall and Barbaree (1984) offered an inhibition hypothesis of sexual aggression as an alternative to the sexual preference hypothesis. It was proposed that the descriptions of sexual interactions between the man and woman—the foreplay and intercourse—would be excitatory elements in the compound stimulus presentation and would serve to increase sexual arousal in most men. Similarly, descriptions of the woman, her physical attributes, her sexual arousal, and aspects of her behavior might be excitatory in effect. In contrast, it was hypothesized that nonconsent on the part of the woman and her displays of pain, fear, and discomfort, as well as force on the part of the man, would serve to inhibit the sexual arousal of most men to the interactions. It was argued that the results observed in this study were the product of these two opposing effects. In consenting episodes containing excitatory elements but no inhibitory elements, sexual arousal was greatest. In rape episodes containing inhibitory elements, the sexual arousal that would otherwise be elicited by the excitatory cues was inhibited at least to some degree.

As was pointed out earlier (Barbaree et al., 1979), the mechanism by which inhibitory cues come to reduce arousal is not known. However, we suggest two possible explanations. First, inhibition might come about through the operation of a complex cognitive–psychophysiological response to the violence and pain depicted in the rape episode. The subject may become emotionally aroused by fear or anxiety in response to the descriptions of a violent and criminal act. Similar emotional responses may be evoked as a result of empathy for the victim. These emotional responses may inhibit sexual arousal through activation of the sympathetic nervous system, which is known to decrease the erectile response. Malamuth and Check (1980, 1983) provided indirect support for the competing emotion explanation by showing that when the victim is described as being in greater pain and distress, which might be expected to evoke an even stronger emotional response in the subject, sexual arousal to the rape descriptions was reduced. Second, inhibition might come about through the subject responding to experimenter demands. Subjects recognize that arousal to the rape descriptions would be regarded by most persons, including the experimenter, as inappropriate, and they may wish to appear normal. In addition, they may perceive a purpose to the experiment and want to appear as a cooperative subject. Accordingly, they may consciously and deliberately suppress arousal to the rape descriptions and attempt to enhance arousal to the consenting scenes.

Inhibition of sexual arousal to rape cues can be viewed as a prosocial act. The more concern the subject has for the victim in the description, the more positive his attitudes toward women, and the more sensitive he is to her pain and suffering, the stronger will be his emotional response component which produces the inhibition. Also, the more sensitive the subject is to societal restrictions concerning inappropriate sexual behavior, the more likely he will be to expend the effort required to reduce his arousal to rape in the laboratory.

Barbaree et al. (1979) postulated that, in the general population of men, individuals differ in the strength of their inhibition to rape cues. Other authors have postulated a continuum of individual differences in responses thought to be important in rape in the general population of men. For example, Abel et al. (1977) computed a "rape index" (rape arousal/consenting arousal) and showed that the mean index was higher among rapists than nonrapists, and that this index has been found to be correlated with the rapist's number of previous victims and the likelihood of victim injury (Abel et al., 1978). Presumably, the index quantifies the tendency in the individual to inhibit sexual arousal to cues of nonconsent and force. Similarly, Malamuth and his associates (Malamuth, 1981, 1983, 1986; Malamuth & Check, 1983) suggested that a continuum exists of the "likelihood of raping" among the general male population. Malamuth and Check (1983) reported that when a rape description portrays a woman as abhorring the rape throughout, those men who deny any likelihood of raping show a strong inhibition of arousal to the rape cues, whereas men who admit to some potential for raping if there was no chance of being caught show weaker inhibition. Furthermore, according to Malamuth, sexual arousal to rape cues is only part of an integrated set of behaviors and cognitions that characterize the rapist. Men who admit a potential for raping also have more callous attitudes toward rape and are more likely to believe in rape myths than are men who deny such a potential (Malamuth, 1981; Malamuth & Check, 1983; Malamuth, Haber, & Feshbach, 1980). Additionally, men who respond with relatively strong erectile responses to rape cues, and who also express attitudes accepting of sexual violence toward women, are more likely to aggress against women when given the opportunity in the laboratory (Malamuth, 1983). Finally, Malamuth (1986) reported that a complex of factors predicts sexually aggressive behavior among males in the natural environment, including: sexual arousal in response to aggression, the identification of dominance as a motive for sexual acts, hostility toward women, and attitudes accepting of violence against women.

State Disinhibition of Arousal

When a stimulus loses its inhibitory power abruptly due to some disruptive event, the process is known as disinhibition. This concept has been applied to processes associated with the sexual response (Malamuth, Heim, & Feshbach, 1980; Yates, Barbaree, & Marshall, 1984). Circumstantial variables and events surrounding a sexual assault might influence its occurrence through the disruption of stimulus inhibition. The following review describes laboratory experiments in which the disinhibition of rape arousal has been studied. We describe each in turn.

The manipulations that have served to disinhibit arousal to violent cues have some or all of the following features in common. First, they decrease the subject's motivation to behave in a prosocial way, or to appear to behave in a prosocial way. Second, they create or increase anger or hostility in the subject toward the female victim.

Yates et al. (1984) monitored sexual arousal to verbal descriptions of rape and consenting sex. Subjects were told that the purpose of the study was to examine the effects of physical exercise on sexual arousal. Subjects in the "exercise-only group" were asked to pedal on a bicycle ergometer as fast as they could for 1 minute, after which they were tested in the sexual arousal laboratory. Subjects in the angered condition were also asked to pedal the bicycle ergometer. However, just before they commenced pedaling, a woman dressed in a laboratory coat (actually a confederate of the experimenter) entered the room and asked to borrow a piece of equipment. The experimenter told the woman to wait until she had finished with the subject. At the end of the minute, the subject was told how far he had pedaled. In response to hearing this, the female confederate made a disparaging remark directed toward the subject concerning his performance. This same provocation had been shown in an earlier pilot study to increase aggression in men toward a woman in the laboratory. The subject was then tested immediately in the arousal laboratory. The exercise-only group showed the usual strong inhibition of arousal to the rape cues. However, the angered group showed equally strong response to rape cues as to consenting cues, indicating a complete lack of stimulus inhibition.

Sundberg, Barbaree, and Marshall (1991) examined the role of victim blame in disinhibiting arousal to rape cues in three separate studies. In a pilot study, rape vignettes were rated by 384 university undergraduates, both male and female, on the extent to which the victim was responsible or blameworthy in the assault. The vignettes varied in the clothing worn by the victim and her location when first observed by the rapist. Victims wore revealing or conservative dress and were located in a deserted park or in a library. These two variables were combined factorially to construct four separate vignettes. When the victim wore revealing dress while walking in a deserted park, both male and female raters judged her to be significantly more blameworthy than when the victim wore conservative dress or wore a revealing dress in a library. In a subsequent laboratory experiment, erectile responses were monitored in response to rape vignettes in which victim blame was manipulated by varying the victim's dress and location. For those subjects who listened to the rape of the victim judged earlier to be more blameworthy, the discrimination between rape and consenting cues was reduced markedly, indicating a reduced strength of stimulus inhibition.

Emotional State Augmentation

According to this model, nonsexual emotional states modulate the strength of a sexual response. For example, when a man has strong positive feelings of love or affection for a woman, his emotional state may serve to increase the strength of sexual arousal he experiences in response to sexual interactions with her. Similarly, when a man has strong negative feelings of hate or hostility toward a woman, or women in general, his emotional state may serve to increase the strength of sexual arousal he achieves during a rape or sexually assaultive behavior.

Barbaree (1990) described an experiment conducted on an individual case that illustrates the model. The experiment studied a rapist who, upon earlier plethysmographic assessment, was found to have strong arousal to descriptions of rape and weak arousal to consenting cues. In the experiment, the rapist was monitored for erectile responses and was presented with numerous trials in which he was presented with descriptions of rape. In each trial, he was asked to imagine that the woman in the rape descriptions was a woman he had known previously. Three women from his past were chosen for these imagined rapes, one for whom he held a strong affection, one for whom he held a long-standing animosity, and one for whom his feelings were ambivalent. His pattern of response to the imagined rapes indicated that when he imagined raping a woman toward whom he was hostile, his arousal to the rape cues was the strongest. When he imagined raping the woman for whom he held affection, his rape arousal was attenuated. Therefore, there is a possibility that rape arousal is modulated by the emotional state the subject is in, or by the nature of the emotional response he directs toward the imagined victim of the rape.

Sadism has been described as a synergism between sexual arousal and aggression, or a process in which violence has become eroticized (Knight & Prentky, 1990). The sexual preference model and the emotional state augmentation model of sexual arousal during rape are potential models of sadism, because they both could account for the synergism between sexual and aggressive motivations in rape. According to the sexual preference model, sexual arousal is evoked or elicited, and therefore increased, by violence and cues associated with rape. In the emotional state augmentation model, the sexual arousal is enhanced by the emotional state of anger, which the subject directs toward the victim. At present, there is not sufficient empirical evidence to choose between these models.

THE MTC RAPIST TYPOLOGY

Knight and Prentky and their associates at the Massachusetts Treatment Center (Knight & Prentky, 1990; Prentky, Knight, & Rosenberg, 1988; Prentky, Knight, Rosenberg, & Lee, 1990; Rosenberg, Knight, Prentky, & Lee, 1988) developed a typology of rapists over more than a decade of empirical work. Based initially on clinical typologies, these researchers refined and tested their typology both for its reliability and its validity. It is beyond the scope of this chapter to evaluate the typology or work that led to its development. Suffice it to say here, the MTC typology for rapists is currently the authoritative and most commonly accepted work on rapist subtyping.

This chapter fits the various rapist subtypes into a 2 × 3 factorial grid, which is presented as Table 1. The vertical dimension of the grid is criminal lifestyle and impulsivity. The concept of criminality either as a personality, lifestyle, or behavioral construct has been a central focus of the empirical work leading to the MTC rapist typology (Prentky & Knight, 1986). Measures of criminality abound from self-report measures such as the Socialization Scale (Gough, 1960) and the Psychopathic Deviate scale from the Minnesota Multiphasic Personality Inventory (MMPI) (Dahlstrom & Welsh, 1960) to more stringent definitions of criminal psychopathy using the Psychopathy Checklist-Revised (PCL-R, Hare, 1991). There are several reasons to select the PCL-R beyond those reported by Hare (1985) when comparing all three measures. The PCL-R incorporates lifestyle and behavioral referents as well as personality characteristics (Harpur, Hakstian, & Hare, 1988). It is reliable and valid (Schroeder, Schroeder, & Hare, 1983), with abundant applications in correctional and forensic settings (Hart, Hare, & Harpur, in press). It predicts general (Hart, Kropp, & Hare, 1988; Serin, Peters, & Barbaree, 1990) and violent recidivism (Harris, Rice, & Cormier, in press; Serin, 1991b), but the personality factor appears to be the more important predictor of violent recidivism

TABLE 1 Model of Arousal

Lifestyle and behavior	Disinhibition state	Inhibition trait	Sadism*
Criminal	Opportunistic	Pervasively angry	Overt sadistic
Noncriminal	Nonsadistic sexual	Vindictive	Muted sadistic

*There are two possible models of sexual arousal in sadism. They include the "sexual preference model" and the "emotional state augmentation model."

(Serin, 1991b). Finally, the PCL-R provides incremental predictive validity in sexual offenders (Rice, Harris, & Quinsey, 1990).

Knight and Prentky used the PCL-R to differentiate among subjects in terms of impulsivity and criminality, yet the emerging literature suggests that the PCL-R identifies persistent offenders who are criminally versatile and qualitatively different form nonpsychopaths regarding their use of violence (Serin, 1991a). Considering the recent literature, it may be somewhat misleading to label this dimension as criminal and noncriminal when using the PCL-R for the vertical dimension in offender samples. The dimension reflects both an impulsive and self-centered lifestyle over an extended period of time, however these labels are retained to conform to Knight and Prentky's (1986) MTC rapist typology, as reflected in Table 1.

The horizontal dimension of the grid reflects the way in which aggressive motivation or anger influences sexual arousal. There are three levels of this influence, each reflecting a different model of rape arousal as described earlier (Barbaree & Marshall, 1991). In the first level, the disinhibition state model is in effect. According to this model, rape cues or violence normally inhibit sexual arousal, so such arousal is not usual for the individual, but such arousal may be disinhibited by circumstantial factors such as anger or victim blame. In the second level, the disinhibition trait model is in effect. According to this model, inhibition of arousal by cues of force and violence is not as strong in these individuals, because of a dispositional tendency to anger and hostility. Finally, in the third level, a model of arousal is in effect according to which arousal to rape cues or violence is enhanced by aggression, often referred to as sadism. There are two possible models here, and currently available empirical data do not allow us to make an informed choice between them. In one model, the sexual preference model, men are sexually aroused by the force and violence. In the emotional state augmentation model, anger enhances the level of arousal to cues of violence and force.

Fitting the MTC subtypes into the grid, we begin with the two subtypes in the left-most cells. These subtypes normally show inhibition of arousal, but circumstantial factors disinhibit their rape arousal. First, for the criminal subtype called the opportunistic subtype, the rape seems to be an impulsive, unplanned, and predatory act controlled more by circumstantial or immediately antecedent factors than by any obvious planning or protracted use of sexual fantasy. The rape seems to be only one among many examples of the individual's poor impulse control, and these men tend to have an extensive history of criminal behavior of various kinds (Knight & Prentky, 1990). These men seem not to have a great deal of empathy for their victims (Knight & Prentky, 1990) and their use of violence tends to be more instrumental. Second, for the noncriminal subtype called the nonsadistic sexual type, the individual's sexually aggressive behavior is thought to involve a combination of sexual arousal, distorted male cognitions about women and sex, and feelings of inadequacy about their sexuality and masculine self-image. The fantasies that may accompany their rapes do not include the synergistic relation of sex and aggression that is true for the sadistic types (Knight & Prentky, 1990). For these men, there is less nonsexual aggression in their history than in any other subtype (Knight & Prentky, 1990).

Moving to the right in the grid, we now deal with the two subtypes that operate according to the trait disinhibition model of rape arousal. In these men, inhibition to rape cues, or descriptions of force and violence, will be less strong because their anger and hostility will not produce the same level of prosocial feelings and action required to inhibit arousal. Therefore, in tests of sexual arousal, these men show greater arousal to rape cues than other men, and a level of arousal to rape that more closely equates to their level of arousal to consenting sexual interactions. First, the criminal subtype called the pervasively angry subtype shows generalized anger toward many different targets, including women, but this anger is not restricted to women. These subtypes engage in gratuitous violence in their rapes, even without any apparent victim resistance, although victim resistance may make their violence worse (Knight & Prentky, 1990). These men frequently cause serious physical harm to their victims up to and including death (Knight & Prentky, 1990). Their anger is not sexualized, and these men do not report any antecedent sexual fantasies motivating their rapes (Knight & Prentky, 1990). As with the opportunistic subtype, the sexual assaults of the pervasively angry subtype are only one instance of their generally criminal or impulsive behaviors (Knight & Prentky, 1990). Second, for the noncriminal vindictive subtype rapists, their anger is directed specifically toward women, and their assaults are characterized by a range of aggressive behavior including verbal threats and abuse to brutal physical assaults, and often include elements of degradation and humiliation. The harm done to victims by these subtypes includes physical injury, but may extend to victim death. Unlike the pervasively angry subtype, the vindictive subtypes do not show generalized anger, and, unlike the sadistic subtypes, these men show no evidence that their anger is eroticized (Knight & Prentky, 1990).

Finally, in the far right column of Table 1 are the subtypes in which the anger or aggression has been eroticized, or in which there is seen a synergism between aggression and sexual arousal. In these subtypes, it is not clear which of two models of sexual arousal in rape is appropriate to describe here. There is simply not sufficient empirical data to make a choice between the two models. The two possibilities are the sexual preference model and the emotional state augmentation model. Whichever of these are finally used to understand the synergism between aggression and sexual arousal in sadism, these two subtypes are characterized by the eroticization of anger and aggression or the mutual facilitation of anger and sexual arousal. For the sadistic subtypes, there is poor differentiation between sexual and aggressive motivations. They often have erotic and destructive thoughts and fantasies. For the overt sadistic type, the

rape involves physically damaging behavior. Like the pervasively angry subtypes, these men appear to be angry, belligerent rapists, but, unlike the pervasively angry subtypes, these men often plan their rapes and their rapes are often
driven by sexual fantasies involving violence (Knight & Prentky, 1990). The
noncriminal muted sadistic subtypes show very similar characteristics to the
overt sadistic rapists, except their physical assaults are less severe and they
inflict less victim damage (Knight & Prentky, 1990).

CONCLUSION

The MTC typology, a division of rapists into categories, is reliable and has been
validated at least to some extent. The typology accounts for the heterogeneity in
the population of rapists in a clinically meaningful way. In the typology, the
various subtypes are differentiated according to their motivation for their assaults and the nature of their assaultive behavior. The role of sexual arousal and
sexual motivation differs among the subtypes.

The research literature comparing rapists and nonrapists in their sexual
arousal to rape and consenting sexual stimuli indicates inconsistent findings
among the studies. The inconsistency may indicate a heterogeneity of responding in the rapist group, with some rapists showing a preference for rape, some
rapists showing a preference for consenting activity, and the remainder showing
an equality of response between the stimulus categories.

It is possible that the various MTC subtypes show different patterns of
sexual arousal. This chapter offers a speculative account of the way in which
sexual arousal processes and patterns might differ among the various subtypes.
Empirical investigation of the arousal differences between subtypes should be
straightforward. It would be predicted that the opportunistic and nonsadistic
sexual subtypes would show preferences for consenting sex. Further, it would
be predicted that the vindictive and pervasively angry subtypes would show
either equal arousal to the two stimulus categories or, at least, somewhat reduced discrimination between categories. Finally, it is predicted that the sadistic
subtypes will show a preference for rape over consenting stimulus categories.

REFERENCES

Abel, G. G., Barlow, D. H., Blanchard, E. B., & Guild, D. (1977). The
    components of rapist's sexual arousal. *Archives of General Psychiatry, 34,*
    895–903.
Abel, G. G., Blanchard, E. B., Becker, J. V., & Djenderedjian, A. (1978).
    Differentiating sexual aggressives with penile measures. *Criminal Justice
    and Behavior, 5,* 315–332.
American Psychiatric Association. (1987). *Diagnostic and statistical manual of
    mental disorders—Revised.* Washington, DC: Author.

Barbaree, H. E. (1990). Stimulus control of sexual arousal: Its role in sexual assault. In W. L. Marshall, D. R. Laws, & H. E. Barbaree (Eds.), *Handbook of sexual assault: Issues, theories, and treatment of the offender* (pp. 115–142). New York: Plenum.

Barbaree, H. E., & Marshall, W. L. (1991). The role of male sexual arousal in rape: Six models. *Journal of Consulting and Clinical Psychology, 59,* 621–630.

Barbaree, H. E., Marshall, W. L., & Lanthier, R. D. (1979). Deviant sexual arousal in rapists. *Behaviour Research and Therapy, 17,* 215–222.

Baxter, D. J., Barbaree, H. E., & Marshall, W. L. (1986). Sexual responses to consenting and forced sex in a large sample of rapists and nonrapists. *Behaviour Research and Therapy, 24,* 513–520.

Brownmiller, S. (1975). *Against our will: Men, women, and rape.* New York: Simon & Schuster.

Burt, M. R. (1980). Cultural myths and supports for rape. *Journal of Personality and Social Psychology, 38,* 217–230.

Clark, L., & Lewis, D. (1977). *Rape: The price of coercive sexuality.* Toronto: The Woman's Press.

Craig, M. E. (1990). Coercive sexuality in dating relationships: A situational model. *Clinical Psychology Review, 10,* 395–423.

Dahlstrom, W. G., & Welsh, G. S. (1960). *An MMPI handbook: A guide to use in clinical practice and research.* Minneapolis: University of Minnesota Press.

Darke, J. L. (1990). Sexual aggression: Achieving power through humiliation. In W. L. Marshall, D. R. Laws, & H. E. Barbaree (Eds.), *Handbook of sexual assault: Issues, theories, and treatment of the offender* (pp. 55–72). New York: Plenum.

Earls, C. M., & Marshall, W. L. (1983). The current state of technology in the laboratory assessment of sexual arousal patterns. In J. G. Greek & I. R. Stuart (Eds.), *The sexual aggressor: Current perspectives on treatment* (pp. 336–362). New York: Van Nostrand Reinhold.

Earls, C. M., & Proulx, J. (1986). The differentiation of Francophone rapists and nonrapists using penile circumferential measures. *Criminal Justice and Behavior, 13,* 419–429.

Freund, K., & Blanchard, R. (1981). Assessment of sexual dysfunction and deviation. In M. Hersen & A. S. Bellack (Eds.), *Behavioral assessment: A practical handbook* (pp. 427–455). New York: Pergamon.

Freund, K., Scher, H., Racansky, I. G., Campbell, K., & Heasman, G. (1986). Males disposed to commit rape. *Archives of Sexual Behavior, 15,* 23–35.

Gough, H. S. (1960). Theory and measurement of socialization. *Journal of Consulting Psychology, 24,* 23–30.

Hare, R. D. (1985). Comparison of procedures for the assessment of psychopathy. *Journal of Consulting and Clinical Psychology, 53,* 7–16.

Hare, R. D. (1991). *The Hare Psychopathy Checklist—Revised (PCL-R)*. Toronto, Ontario: Multi-Health Systems.

Harris, G. T., Rice, M. E., & Cormier, C. A. (1991). Psychopathy and violent recidivism. *Law and Human Behaviour, 15*, 625–637.

Harpur, T. J., Hakstian, A. R., & Hare, R. D. (1988). Factor structure of the Psychopathy checklist. *Journal of Consulting and Clinical Psychology, 56*, 741–747.

Hart, S. D., Hare, R. D., & Harpur (in press). The Psychopathy Checklist—Revised (PCL-R): An overview for researchers and clinicians. In J. Rosen & P. McReynolds (Eds.), *Advances in psychological assessment* (vol. 8, pp. 103–130). New York: Plenum.

Hart, S. D., Kropp, P. R., & Hare, R. D. (1988). Performance of male psychopaths following conditional release from prison. *Journal of Consulting and Clinical Psychology, 56*, 227–232.

Herman, J. L. (1990). Sex offenders: A feminist perspective. In W. L. Marshall, D. R. Laws, & H. E. Barbaree (Eds.), *Handbook of sexual assault: Issues, theories, and treatment of the offender* (pp. 117–193). New York: Plenum.

Knight, R. A., & Prentky, R. A. (1990). Classifying sexual offenders: The development and corroboration of taxonomic models. In W. L. Marshall, D. R. Laws, & H. E. Barbaree (Eds.), *Handbook of sexual assault: Issues, theories, and treatment of the offender* (pp. 23–52). New York: Plenum.

Knight, R. A., Rosenberg, R., & Schneider, B. A. (1985). Classification of sexual offenders: Perspectives, methods, and validation. In A. W. Burgess (Ed.), *Rape and sexual assault* (pp. 222–293). New York: Garland.

Langevin, R., Bain, J., Ben-Aron, M. H., Couthard, R., Day, D., Handy, L. C., Heasman, R., Hucker, S. J., Purins, J. E., Roper, V., Bain, Russon, A. R., Webster, C. D., & Wortzman, G. (1985). Sexual aggression: Constructing a predictive equation: A controlled pilot study. In R. Langevin (Ed.), *Erotic preference, gender identity, and aggression in men: New research studies* (pp. 39–76). Hillsdale, NJ: Lawrence Erlbaum.

Laws, D. R., & Osborne, C. A. (1983). How to build and operate a behavioral laboratory to evaluate and treat sexual deviance. In J. G. Greer & I. R. Stuart (Eds.), *The sexual aggressor: Current perspectives on treatment* (pp. 293–335). New York: Von Nostrand Reinhold.

MacDonald, R. K., & Pithers, W. D. (1989). Self-monitoring to identify high-risk situations. In D. R. Laws (Ed.), *Relapse prevention with sex offenders* (pp. 96–104). New York: Guilford.

Malamuth, N. M. (1981). Rape proclivity among males. *Journal of Social Issues, 37*, 138–156.

Malamuth, N. M. (1983). Factors associated with rape as predictors of laboratory aggression against women. *Journal of Personality and Social Psychology, 45*, 432–442.

Malamuth, N. M. (1986). Predictors of naturalistic sexual aggression. *Journal of Personality and Social Psychology, 50,* 953–962.

Malamuth, N. M. (1988). A multidimensional approach to sexual aggression: Combining measures of past behavior and present likelihood. In R. A. Prentky & V. L. Quinsey (Eds.), *Human sexual aggression: Current perspectives* (pp. 123–132). New York: The New York Academy of Sciences.

Malamuth, N. M. & Check, J. V. P. (1980). Penile tumescence and perceptual responses to rape as a function of victim's perceived reactions. *Journal of Applied Social Psychology, 10,* 528–547.

Malamuth, N. M., & Check, J. V. P. (1983). Sexual arousal to rape depictions: Individual differences. *Journal of Abnormal Psychology, 92,* 55–67.

Malamuth, N. M., Check, J. V. P., & Briere, J. (1986). Sexual arousal in response to aggression: Ideological, aggressive, and sexual correlates. *Journal of Personality and Social Psychology, 50,* 330–340.

Malamuth, N. M., Haber, S., & Feshbach, S. (1980). Testing hypotheses regarding rape: Exposure to sexual violence, sex differences, and the "normality" of rapists. *Journal of Research in Personality, 14,* 121–137.

Malamuth, N. M., Heim, M., & Feshbach, S. (1980). Sexual responsiveness of college students to rape depictions: Inhibitory and disinhibitory effects. *Journal of Personality and Social Psychology, 38,* 399–408.

Marshall, W. L., & Barbaree, H. E. (1984). A behavioral view of rape. Special Issue: Empirical approaches to law and psychiatry. *International Journal of Law and Psychiatry, 7,* 51–77.

Murphy, W. D., Krisak, J., Stalgaitis, S., & Anderson, K. (1984). The use of penile tumescence measures with incarcerated rapists: Further validity issues. *Archives of Sexual Behavior, 13,* 545–554.

Pithers, W. D., Beal, L. S., Armstrong, J., & Petty, J. (1989). Identification of risk factors through clinical interviews and analysis of records. In D. R. Laws (Ed.), *Relapse prevention with sex offenders* (pp. 77–87). New York: Guilford.

Prentky, R. A., & Knight, R. A. (1986). Impulsivity in the lifestyle and criminal behavior of sexual offenders. *Criminal Justice and Behavior, 13,* 141–164.

Prentky, R. A., Knight, R. A., & Rosenberg, R. (1988). Validation analyses on a taxonomic system for rapists: Disconfirmation and reconceptualization. In R. A. Prentky & V. L. Quinsey (Eds.), *Human sexual aggression: Current perspectives* (pp. 21–40). New York: The New York Academy of Sciences.

Prentky, R. A., Knight, R. A., Rosenberg, R., & Lee, A. (1990). A path analytic approach to the validation of a taxonomic system for classifying child molesters. *Journal of Quantitative Criminology, 5,* 231–257.

Quinsey, V. L., & Chaplin, T. C. (1982). Penile responses to nonsexual violence among rapists. *Criminal Justice and Behavior, 9,* 372–381.

Quinsey, V. L., & Chaplin, T. C. (1984). Stimulus control of rapists' and non-sex offenders' sexual arousal. *Behavioral Assessment, 6,* 169–176.

Quinsey, V. L., Chaplin, T. C., & Upfold, D. (1984). Sexual arousal to nonsexual violence and sadomasochistic themes among rapists and non-sex-offenders. *Journal of Consulting and Clinical Psychology, 52,* 651–657.

Quinsey, V. L., & Marshall, W. L. (1983). Procedures for reducing inappropriate sexual arousal: An evaluative review. In J. G. Greer & I. R. Stuart (Eds.), *The sexual aggressor: Current perspectives on treatment* (pp. 267–289). New York: Van Nostrand Reinhold.

Rice, M. E., Harris, G. T., & Quinsey, V. L. (1990). A follow-up of rapists assessed in a maximum security psychiatric facility. *Journal of Interpersonal Violence, 5,* 435–448.

Rosenberg, R., Knight, R. A., Prentky, R. A., & Lee, A. (1988). Validating the components of a taxonomic system for rapists: A path analytic approach. *Bulletin of the American Academy of Psychiatry and the Law, 16,* 169–185.

Russell, D. E. H. (1975). *The politics of rape: The victim's perspective.* New York: Stein and Day.

Russell, D. E. H. (1988). The incidence and prevalence of intrafamilial and extrafamilial sexual abuse of female children. In L. E. A. Walker (Ed.), *Handbook on sexual abuse of children* (pp. 19–36). New York: Springer.

Schroeder, M. L., Schroeder, K. G., & Hare, R. D. (1983). Generalizability of a checklist for the assessment of psychopathy. *Journal of Consulting and Clinical Psychology, 51,* 511–516.

Serin, R. C. (1991a). Psychopathy and violence in criminals. *Journal of Interpersonal Violence, 6,* 423–431.

Serin, R. C. (1991b). Violent recidivism in criminal psychopaths. Manuscript submitted for publication.

Serin, R. C., Peters, R., & Barbaree, H. E. (1990). Predictors of psychopathy and release outcome in a criminal population. *Psychological Assessment: A Journal of Consulting and Clinical Psychology, 2,* 419–422.

Sundberg, S. L., Barbaree, H. E., & Marshall, W. L. (1991). Victim blame and the disinhibition of sexual arousal to rape vignettes. *Violence and Victims, 6,* 103–120.

Yates, E., Barbaree, H. E., & Marshall, W. L. (1984). Anger and deviant sexual arousal. *Behavior Therapy, 15,* 287–294.

7

USE OF A NEW LABORATORY METHODOLOGY TO CONCEPTUALIZE SEXUAL AGGRESSION

Gordon C. Nagayama Hall
Richard Hirschman
Kent State University

Now Dinah, the daughter Leah had borne to Jacob, went out to visit the women of the land. When Shecham son of Hamor the Hivite, the ruler of the area, saw her, he took her and violated her. . . . When Jacob heard that his daughter Dinah had been defiled, his sons were in the fields with his livestock; so he kept quiet about it until they came home. . . . Now Jacob's sons had come in from the fields as soon as they heard what happened. They were filled with grief and fury, because Shechem had done a disgraceful thing in Israel by lying with Jacob's daughter—a thing that should not be done.

—Genesis 34, *New International Version of the Bible*

And though she spoke to Joseph day after day, he refused to go to bed with her or even be with her. One day he went into the house to attend to his duties, and none of the household servants was inside. She caught him by his cloak and said, "Come to bed with me!" But he left his cloak in her hand and ran out of the house. When she saw that he had left his cloak in her hand and had run out of the house, she called her household servants. "Look," she said to them, "this Hebrew has been brought to us to make sport of us! He came in here to sleep with me, but I screamed. When he heard me scream for help, he left his cloak beside me and ran out of the house."

—Genesis 39, *New International Version of the Bible*

So Tamar went to the house of her brother Amnon, who was lying down. She took some dough, kneaded it, made the bread in his sight and baked it. Then she took the pan and served him the bread, but he refused to eat. "Send everyone out of here," Amnon said. . . . And Tamar took the bread she had prepared and brought it to her brother Amnon in his bed room. But when she took it to him to eat, he grabbed her and said, "Come to bed with me, my sister." "Don't, my brother!" she said to him. "Don't force me." But he refused to listen to her, and since he was stronger than she, he raped her. . . . Her brother Absalom said to her, "Has that Amnon, your brother, been with you? Be quiet now, my sister; he is your brother. Don't take this thing to heart." And Tamar lived in her brother Absalom's house, a desolate woman. When King David heard all this, he was furious. Absalom . . . hated Amnon because he had disgraced his sister Tamar.

—2 Samuel 13, *New International Version of the Bible*

"Thomas told me graphically of his own sexual prowess. . . . He spoke about acts he had seen in pornographic films. . . ."

—Professor Anita Hill quoted in *Newsweek,* October 21, 1991.

"I have not said or done the things that Anita Hill has alleged."

—Judge Clarence Thomas quoted in *Newsweek,* October 21, 1991.

"I was yelling, 'No,' and 'Stop,'" she said, "and he slammed me back in the ground and then, and then he pushed my dress up and he raped me. And I thought he was going to kill me."

—William Kennedy Smith's accuser quoted by the *Associated Press,* December 5, 1991.

Her rape claim is "a damnable lie."

—William Kennedy Smith quoted by the *Associated Press,* December 5, 1991.

Smith said he and the woman went to the beach and kissed briefly before the woman removed her underpants, undid his pants, rolled over on top of him and fondled him until he ejaculated. Smith said he then took a short swim. When he got out of the water, Smith said the woman was on the lawn, where they had sex again. He said the woman "sort of snapped" when he called her the name of a former girlfriend.

—*Associated Press,* December 11, 1991.

An 18-year-old Miss Black America contestant said Tyson pinned her on a bed with his forearm, stripped her, raped her, and laughed while she cried in pain and begged him to stop. "I tried to fight. It was like hitting a wall."

—*Associated Press,* February 3, 1992.

"I didn't violate her in any way. She never told me to stop, or I was hurting her, nothing."

—Mike Tyson quoted by the *Associated Press,* February 8, 1992.

Ancient and recent history are replete with allegations and episodes of sexual aggression. In Biblical times, it appears that women's allegations of rape were regarded as truth and alleged perpetrators had no recourse. However, punishments for perpetrators of rape varied. Joseph was imprisoned in Egypt because of the Egyptian official's wife's rape allegation. Although Jacob and his sons, King David, and Absalom were angry about the rapes of their family members and seemed to consider rape a serious crime, nothing was done initially. There is no evidence that Jacob or David took any punitive action against the perpetrators. The status of women as property in Hebrew society may have contributed to this inaction. Absalom tried to minimize the seriousness of the crime, possibly because it was incest. Ultimately, Jacob's sons killed Shechem and his neighbors, after falsely promising to allow Shechem to marry their sister Dinah, but requiring that Shechem and his neighbors first be circumcised. Neither this act nor Absalom's killing of Amnon was sanctioned by the Hebrew men's fathers or by Hebrew society.

In modern society, efforts to prevent Type I errors, or false convictions, have required alleged victims of sexual aggression to substantiate their allegations, and alleged perpetrators of sexual aggression have been provided with opportunities to dispute alleged victims' claims. Anita Hill's testimony in the Clarence Thomas confirmation hearings and the testimony in the William Kennedy Smith and Mike Tyson trials were riveting for a variety of reasons, including the veracity of allegations of sexual harassment, sexual battery, and rape. Hill and Thomas presented such mutually exclusive information on their interactions while they worked together at the Department of Education and the Equal Employment Opportunity Commission that either Hill or Thomas had to be lying or their recollections were tarnished by psychological defensiveness. Many, including some senators on the Senate Judiciary Committee, could not believe that a person of Thomas' stature, or any other "normal" adult male, could engage in such vile behavior. Skeptics of Hill's testimony questioned why she did not file charges of sexual harassment at the time the incidents occurred. Thomas' skeptics argued that Hill's allegations were too detailed to have been fabricated. Moreover, she had nothing to gain by such allegations: if Thomas was confirmed, Hill would implicitly be considered a liar; if he was not confirmed, Hill would be blamed.

Such ambiguity about whom to believe (as well as the "politically correct" position on the issue) is illustrated by Senator Edward Kennedy's apparent alliance with alleged victim Hill in the Thomas hearings, and his alliance with his nephew, who allegedly perpetrated sexual battery. As in the Thomas hearings, Smith's and his accuser's credibility were at issue. Unlike the Thomas hearings, both Smith and his accuser agreed that they had sex. However, they disagreed on whether the sex was coerced. Smith apparently was acquitted because the jury harbored reasonable doubts about the actual occurrence of coercive sexual behavior.

Tyson was charged with rape, confinement, and criminal deviate conduct and was sentenced. Dr. Thomas Richardson, the emergency-room physician who examined Tyson's accuser the day after the alleged rape, found vaginal abrasions consistent with rough or forced intercourse. Dr. Richardson reported that such injuries were uncommon as a result of consensual sex, but occurred in 30% of rape cases. Tyson's defense was "that he was a crude womanizer whose accuser must have known he wanted sex" (*Associated Press,* February 11, 1992). Although Tyson did not admit to raping his accuser, unlike Thomas or Smith he attempted to justify inappropriate sexual behavior.

The earlier cases also illustrate that sexual aggression encompasses a wide range of behavior. Although in all sexually aggressive acts one person imposes an unwanted sexual experience on another, sexually aggressive behavior may be conceptualized as a continuum that varies along a dimension of amount of sexual contact (e.g., harassment, rape) and along dimensions of coercion and physical force (Muehlenhard & Linton, 1987; Shotland, 1992). Thus, sexual harassment (e.g., telling a sexually oriented joke that someone finds offensive or sexually suggestive conversation against another person's wishes) would be considered a relatively mild (but serious) form of sexual aggression, whereas a violent rape would be considered a relatively extreme form of sexual aggression.

Although the purpose of this chapter is not to determine the veracity of alleged victims' and aggressors' statements, the Biblical accounts, the Thomas hearings, and the Smith and Tyson trials underscore the weaknesses of self-report in determining the occurrence of sexually aggressive behavior. Although the alleged perpetrators in the recent cases were under intense pressure not to admit to sexually aggressive behavior, there generally are discrepancies be-tween the self-reports of men and women about sexually aggressive behavior, even when reports of sexual aggression are anonymous. Whereas 25% of men in a nationally representative college sample anonymously admitted to engaging in some degree of sexual aggression, including 7.7% who admitted to rape or attempted rape, 54% of women anonymously claimed to have been sexually victimized, including 27.5% who claimed to have been victims of rape or attempted rape (Koss, Gidycz, & Wisniewski, 1987). Possibly some of the men or the women, or both, were lying. The admission of engaging in sexually aggressive behavior is socially undesirable even in the presence of corroborat-ing information (Hall, 1989; Lanyon & Lutz, 1984; McGovern & Nevid, 1986), and anonymity does not preclude social desirability in self-report (Hall, Hirschman, & Oliver, 1992). Another explanation of discrepancies in reports of sexually aggressive behavior is that men and women have different perceptions of what constitutes sexually aggressive behavior. Indeed, there is evidence that some men do not regard threatening a woman with a weapon and forcing her to have sexual intercourse as rape (Scully & Marolla, 1984). Another possible explanation for the male–female discrepancy in rape rates is that a few men commit multiple rapes.

Given the inadequacies of self-report for understanding descriptively a sex-ually aggressive occurrence and its etiology, there is a need for a direct measure of sexually aggressive behavior. One of the most popular methods of assessing sexual aggressors against adults is to determine their genital response to rape or other aggressive stimuli (Abel, Barlow, Blanchard, & Guild, 1977; Barbaree, Marshall, & Lanthier, 1979; Quinsey, Chaplin, & Upfold, 1984; Quinsey, Chaplin, & Varney, 1981). The popularity of this method is based on its ease of use and purported reliability and face validity as a measure of sexual arousal (Zuckerman, 1971). Penile tumescence data suggest that sexual aggressors against children exhibit sexual arousal to pedophilic stimuli (Abel et al., 1981; Avery-Clark & Laws, 1984; Freund & Blanchard, 1989; Hall, Proctor, & Nelson, 1988; Marshall et al., 1986; Murphy et al., 1986; Quinsey & Chaplin, 1988), but that the majority of sexual aggressors against adults tend not to exhibit patterns of sexual arousal to rape stimuli that differ from those of normal men (Baxter et al., 1984, 1986; Blader & Marshall, 1989; Hall, 1989; Hall, Shondrick, & Hirschman, in press). However, genital response to sexually deviant stimuli is vulnerable to faking, and often may be a function of subjects' general arousability rather than a reflection of a propensity for sexual aggression (Hall, 1990, 1991). Sexually aggressive behavior also may be motivated by variables other than sexual arousal (Barbaree & Marshall, 1991; Blader & Marshall, 1989; Hall & Hirschman, 1991). Most importantly, deviant sexual arousal in the laboratory does not constitute sexually aggressive behavior.

Because it is both impractical and unethical to monitor real-life acts of aggression, clinical research on the antecedents of any form of aggressive behavior requires laboratory analogue models (Hall et al., 1992). Physical aggression has been studied extensively in the laboratory by having subjects deliver shock to another person (Geen & Donnerstein, 1983; Milgram, 1963; Taylor, 1986). Much has been learned about the etiology of aggressive acts using this approach. Typically, a hypothesized causal variable (e.g., anger provocation, alcohol) is introduced and the subject is allowed to aggress against another person (e.g., shocking another subject). Similarly, the delivery of shock by male subjects to female subjects has been investigated as an analogue of sexual aggression (Blader, Marshall, & Barbaree, 1988; Geen & Donnerstein, 1983; Malamuth, 1988). The delivery of shock to a female subject, however, is an analogue of physical aggression, but may not be analogous to sexual aggression.

LABORATORY MODELS OF SEXUAL AGGRESSION

In contrast to the extensive research on laboratory analogues of physical aggression, there has been limited development of laboratory analogues of sexual aggression. This limited progress may be partially a function of ethical and practical constraints (Hall et al., 1992). Pryor (1987) described a laboratory analogue of sexual harassment in which male subjects were instructed to train a female confederate, who was described as novice, how to golf. In a control condition, the subjects were instructed to teach the confederate to play poker.

The dependent measures included the confederate's ratings of how frequent and how sexual the subject's physical contact with her was, as well as a rating of how sexual the subject's comments toward her were. No touching rated as sexual took place in the poker condition. However, the touching of men who were high on a scale measuring the likelihood of sexual harassment was rated as more sexual than that of men low on the scale. Men who were high on the scale were rated as engaging in more sexual touching in the golf versus poker condition, but men who were low on the scale were not rated as engaging in more sexual touching in the golf versus poker condition. The male subjects apparently regarded the training requirements of the golf condition as a legitimate excuse for sexual touching. This procedure may be unacceptable from an ethical perspective, however, in that the confederate is subjected to a situation in which actual sexual contact may occur (Hall et al., 1992). Moreover, the confederate's ratings of how sexual the subject's comments and actions are may be subjective and unreliable.

In another innovative attempt to develop a laboratory analogue of sexual aggression, Blader et al. (1988) exposed college men to a 2-minute erotic videotape and had them administer a neutral (i.e., tone) or aggressive (i.e., shock) stimulus to a female confederate under the guise of attempting to increase the confederate's sexual arousal during a biofeedback task. Male subjects' sexual arousal, as measured by penile erection, decreased while administering the aggressive stimulus, compared with baseline arousal or arousal while subjects administered the neutral stimulus. However, when subjects themselves were shocked seven times prior to the experimental task, ostensibly by the female confederate, subsequent administration of shock to the confederate while viewing the erotic videotape failed to inhibit sexual arousal.

Although the Blader et al. (1988) procedure simulated the conditions of sexual arousal that occur in many forms of sexual aggression, much sexual aggression may not take place in the retaliatory context (i.e., response to being shocked by the female confederate) of the Blader et al. (1988) procedure. As noted earlier, the delivery of shock to a subject is an analogue of physical aggression, but may not be analogous to sexual aggression. Moreover, sexual arousal may not be a precursor to all forms of sexually aggressive behavior (Hall & Hirschman, 1991). Sexually aggressive behavior is not restricted to forced sexual intercourse, but includes imposing other types of unwanted sexual activity (Koss et al., 1987), which may not include sexual arousal as a precursor. Although it could be argued that the subjects in the Blader et al. (1988) study were physically aggressive, the subjects did not impose an unwanted sexual experience on the confederate.

Another approach to assessing sexually aggressive behavior in the laboratory has been the measurement of preferences for sexually aggressive material. Two studies that examined the effects of alcohol on deviant sexual arousal used a subject's preferences for pornographic stimuli (as indicated by ad lib exposure) as a dependent variable (George & Marlatt, 1986; Lang, Searles, Lauerman, & Adesso, 1980). George and Marlatt's (1986) study was of particular relevance to a sexual aggression paradigm, because neutral, erotic, violent, and violent-erotic slides were used. However, subject preferences for sexually aggressive material do not constitute an instrumental act of sexual aggression.

Sexual aggression differs from nonsexual physical aggression in that the victim usually has an unwanted sexual experience (Hall et al., 1992). In a laboratory analogue of sexual aggression, a subject would have to be given an opportunity to be sexually aggressive within appropriate ethical and practical constraints. Extreme forms of sexually aggressive behavior, such as rape, may be difficult, if not impossible, to simulate in a laboratory setting. However, if sexually aggressive behavior is conceptualized as a continuum, it may be possible to simulate mild (but potentially serious) forms of sexual aggression in the laboratory. One approach is to view sexually aggressive behavior as the imposition of an unwanted sexual experience. In this regard, Dermen (1990) developed a procedure in which a male subject shows erotic slides to a female confederate who is described as strongly disliking pornography. Presumably, the instrumental act of showing erotic stimuli to a person who dislikes such stimuli in the laboratory is analogous to an unwanted, sexually impositional act (e.g., offensive sexually oriented jokes, same- or different-gender peer pressure to have heterosexual sex, sexual harassment). Slide showing is an observable behavior that requires the subject to act in the presence of another person (the confederate) and is less of a hypothetical situation than previous methods of assessing sexually aggressive behavior (e.g., what have you done in the past, what would you do if you were not caught). Pilot data suggested that male subjects were willing to show erotic slides to female confederates who indicated that they enjoyed erotic slides, but that male subjects were unwilling to show more than brief exposures of erotic slides to female confederates who expressed a dislike to such slides (Dermen, 1990; Lopez & George, 1992). A disinhibitory condition involving alcohol ingestion was required for males to show erotic slides at length to unwilling female subjects (Dermen, 1990). Erotic slide showing times under the alcohol condition were significantly longer than when the subjects had not ingested alcohol (Dermen, 1990). However, all subjects engaged in sexual imposition to the extent that they showed erotic slides to the unwilling confederate, even for short periods of time. Thus, a procedure is needed that identifies some individuals as sexually imposing and others as not sexually imposing.

A NEW LABORATORY METHODOLOGY

We attempted to develop a laboratory analogue that involves a more deliberate act of sexual imposition than Dermen's (1990) procedure and does not require the subject to ingest alcohol to increase the likelihood of initiating a sexually imposing act (Hall et al., 1992). Although some sexually imposing acts occur under conditions of intoxication, many do not. Moreover, alcohol may function as a disinhibitor rather than as a cause of sexually aggressive behavior. In pilot work, we used Dermen's (1990) procedure under the guise of using erotic slides to distract a female confederate from a bogus memory task, but did not have subjects ingest alcohol. The distraction guise was necessary to reduce the demand characteristic not to show erotic slides to someone depicted as disliking them. In other words, the social undesirability of showing erotic slides to a woman who did not like them was reduced, but the fact remained that she strongly disliked pornography. We found that subjects did not show erotic slides significantly longer than neutral slides. Thus, it appeared that subjects approached the task as one of distraction via slide showing, independent of slide content.

We modified Dermen's (1990) procedure to allow subjects to make a more deliberate choice about which slides they would show to the female confederate (Hall et al., 1992). We grouped the slides into four categories of increasing sexual explicitness and deviance (neutral, erotic, explicit-erotic, and deviant-erotic slides), and required subjects to choose one of these categories of slides to show to the female confederate in an effort to distract her from the bogus memory task. Subjects were not instructed to select the most distracting slide category, but simply to select a slide category that would be distracting. This selection of slides, based on their relative level of deviance, was analogous to subjects' selection of voltage level in the general aggression studies using shock (Geen & Donnerstein, 1983; Taylor, 1986). We found that male subjects who were more supportive of rape myths were more likely to show sexually explicit/ deviant slides to a female confederate than male subjects who were less supportive of rape myths. This occurred despite subjects being informed that the confederate strongly disliked pornography. Thus, some subjects were more willing than others to engage in impositional behavior in the laboratory analogous to a mild form of sexual aggression; their willingness was determined, in part, by their beliefs in rape myths. College men supportive of rape myths have consistently been involved in sexually aggressive activity with women more than have men who are less supportive of rape myths (Lisak & Roth, 1988; Malamuth, 1986; Muehlenhard & Linton, 1987; Rapaport & Burkhart, 1984).

We conducted four other experiments that provide support for the current erotic slide selection/showing method as a laboratory-based example of a sexually imposing behavior (Hall et al., 1992). In the first two experiments that used the erotic and neutral slide categories described earlier, more than 90% of the male subjects (82 of 85 subjects) showed erotic slides to a female confederate who was depicted as strongly disliking pornography. To examine the demand characteristics of the paradigm, in the third experiment an additional set of autopsy slides was added, thus allowing subjects to distract the female confederate without imposing sexual stimuli on her (Hall et al., 1992). The autopsy slides were rated by these subjects to be equally distracting as the erotic slides, but not pornographic. Nevertheless, 73% of 51 subjects chose one of the erotic categories to distract the subject, whereas only 24% of the subjects chose the autopsy slides. Thus, it appeared that most subjects actually were willing to attempt to distract the confederate by being sexually imposing in the laboratory, rather than simply complying with the experimental demand to distract the subject (Hall et al., 1992).

The purpose of these studies was to determine if sexually imposing behavior could be elicited under any conditions using the slide selection procedure, without regard to subjects' intentions to impose. This is not unlike Milgram's (1963) intent to elicit aggressive responses at the request of an authority figure. To the extent that behavior in the laboratory could be an alternative to potentially inaccurate subjective self-reports of sexual aggressiveness, external validity issues are less critical (i.e., the behavior by definition is sexually impositional and self-report may or may not be related to the behavior). Moreover, complying with the demand characteristics of the study could be viewed by a participant as an excuse for being sexually impositional, analogous to excuses for other forms of sexually aggressive behavior (e.g., most women secretly desire to be raped; she was asking for it because she was hitchhiking, drinking, wearing provocative clothing, etc.). Regardless of the reasons for committing a sexually impositional act (e.g., demand characteristics, rationalizations, response to authority), we found that some men were willing to do it in the laboratory.

Defining the subjects' behavior as sexually impositional in our studies was not unlike a similar conclusion from studies in the general aggression field, in which the demand characteristics, such as response to authority (Milgram, 1963) or competition (Taylor, 1986), did not detract from the conclusion that willingness to harm was an operational factor. In our studies, subjects may not have intended to harm the confederate, but simply to distract her. Nevertheless, the subjects' behavior was sexually imposing because of its impact on the confederate, who presumably did not want to see the erotic stimuli. In real-world examples of sexual imposition, the perpetrator often claims an innocent intent or believes his act partially was a function of extrinsic factors (e.g., telling a sexually oriented joke at a party that is not offensive to most people). We believe that sexually imposing behaviors may be intentional or nonintentional, and intentionality is not what defines the behavior as sexually impositional. What makes a given behavior sexually impositional is its negative impact on the victim, regardless of other intrinsic (e.g., psychopathology) or context-sensitive factors.

In contrast, defining sexually impositional behavior by the intent of the perpetrator and not by the impact on the victim might lead to a different conclusion regarding the importance of demand characteristics. From this perspective, it could be argued that the subjects in our studies simply intended to comply with the experimental demand to distract the confederate. To address this possibility, subjects were given a nonerotic, distracting choice in the third and fourth experiments that was rated as distracting as the more explicit erotic slide categories, and subjects were not instructed to select specific stimuli with which to distract the female confederate. Nevertheless, only 6% of the male subjects in the first experiment and 10% of the male subjects in the second experiment chose to show the distracting but least explicit erotic slides, and only 27% of the male subjects chose the nonerotic categories of slides in the third experiment. Despite the same demand characteristics as in the first three experiments, only 43% of female subjects chose to show erotic slides in the fourth experiment (Hall et al., 1992).

That 43% of female subjects showed erotic slides in the fourth experiment (vs. 73% of men in the third experiment) is consistent with our prediction that women are less likely than men to show erotic slides to an unwilling confederate. In laboratory studies of physical aggression, women have been less aggressive than men (Eagly & Steffen, 1986). Although few women are perpetrators of extreme forms of sexually aggressive behaviors (e.g., rape), not surprisingly, women, as well as men, perpetrate milder but serious forms of sexually aggressive behaviors (Rich, 1980; Sandberg, Jackson, & Petretic-Jackson, 1987; Sarrel & Masters, 1982; Struckman-Johnson, 1988, 1991). Common in vivo examples of mild but serious forms of sexually aggressive behavior, which could be perpetrated by both genders knowingly or unknowingly, are unwanted sexually oriented jokes, same-gender peer pressure to engage in heterosexual sex, and sexual harassment.

Conceivably, male and female subjects simply chose to show the category of slides that they most preferred. However, ad lib viewing times before subjects selected a slide category to show generally did not differ among slide categories; and although subjects viewed the autopsy slides longer than the other slides in the third experiment, less than one fourth of the subjects chose to show the autopsy slides. Only three subjects in the second experiment and one subject in the third experiment stated that they chose the slide category because of personal preference. All other subjects chose the slide category that they believed would be most effective in accomplishing the distraction task. Moreover, in the fourth experiment, in which female subjects rated the erotic and autopsy slides as approximately equally repulsive, 55% of the female subjects chose to show the autopsy slides and none chose the least explicit erotic slide category.

Subjects in the Hall et al. (1992) experiments did not know that they were participating in an experiment on sexual imposition, and, as mentioned earlier, may not have intended to be sexually impositional (i.e., they may have believed that showing erotic pictures to a woman who dislikes pornography does not constitute sexually imposing behavior) (Hall et al., 1992). However, discrepancies in perpetrator and victim perceptions of sexual aggression (Koss et al.,

1987; Scully & Marolla, 1984) suggest that many men who are sexually aggressive do not consider their behavior to be sexually aggressive. Moreover, the knowledge that showing erotic pictures to a woman who dislikes pornography may constitute a mild form of sexually impositional behavior may have alerted subjects that it was socially desirable not to show the erotic pictures.

CURRENT RESEARCH USING THE NEW LABORATORY METHODOLOGY

The Hall et al. (1992) procedure lends itself to experimental investigation of variables hypothesized to be motivational precursors of sexually aggressive behavior. More specifically, we used the procedure to examine the primary motivational precursors (physiological, cognitive, affective, and developmental) from our quadripartite model (Hall & Hirschman, 1991). The model is treatment driven because it limits the number of precursors so that classification schemes and consequent treatments derived from the precursors are manageable in scope for clinician use. We considered the model to be broader than univariate models (e.g., Abel et al., 1977; Groth & Birnbaum, 1979), but not as broad or reductionistic as those based on multidimensional classification schemes (e.g., Malamuth, Sockloskie, Koss, & Tanaka, 1991; Prentky & Knight, 1991). In the model, we sacrificed some comprehensiveness for potentially more clinical usefulness, and we hope that the laboratory paradigm described in this chapter provides data supporting this approach.

Cognitive Distortions

As an example of an experimental manipulation of one of the motivational precursors, Shondrick, Hall, and Hirschman (1992) investigated the cognitive component of the model using the slide showing paradigm. Evidence from past studies suggests that individuals may misperceive others' sexual intentions based on cognitive appraisals or distortions (Burt, 1980). Both men and women may experience such misperceptions, although this may be more common among men (Abbey, 1987). Men may also attribute more sexuality (e.g., sexiness, seductiveness) to women based on the degree to which a woman's clothing is revealing (Abbey, Cozzarelli, McLaughlin, & Harnish, 1987).

Shondrick et al. (1992) examined men's cognitive distortions with respect to the way a woman is dressed. Fifty male and 50 female undergraduates selected and showed, under the guise of a problem-solving task, neutral, childbirth, autopsy, or erotic slides to a female confederate who was depicted as strongly disliking pornography. A possible weakness of the previous experiments was that more erotic slide categories were presented to choose from than nonerotic categories (Hall et al., 1992). Subjects could have interpreted this to mean that the experimenters condoned choosing the erotic categories to show to the confederate (Freedman, 1988). Shondrick et al. (1992) used only one erotic slide category to reduce this apparent demand characteristic. Before selecting the slide category to show, half of the subjects were introduced to a female confederate who was dressed provocatively (i.e., short skirt, red blouse) and the other half was introduced to the same confederate who was dressed conservatively (i.e., long skirt, white blouse, glasses).

Twenty-two percent (22%) of the men showed the erotic slides, whereas only 14% of the women did so, suggesting that a single erotic slide category created lower demand characteristics to show erotic slides than in the previous studies. Self-reported sexual aggression, or likelihood of engaging in sexual aggression if impunity were guaranteed, did not correspond with erotic slide showing among the men (Shondrick et al., 1992). Although this result may be interpreted as undermining the external validity of the laboratory results, self-report cannot be used as a gold standard of the actual frequency of sexually aggressive behavior for reasons of social desirability discussed earlier. Presenting erotic stimuli to an unwilling confederate constitutes sexually imposing behavior. Thus, despite their behavior outside the laboratory, some men are willing to engage in mild forms of sexually aggressive behavior given the right conditions, which in this case is a laboratory experiment.

Eighteen percent (18%) of the men in the Shondrick et al. (1992) study showed erotic slides to the provocatively dressed confederate, versus only 4% to the conservatively dressed confederate. Women's showing of the erotic slides was just the opposite: only 2% showed the erotic slides to the provocatively dressed confederate, whereas 12% showed the erotic slides to the conservatively dressed confederate. These results suggest that men may interpret women's appearance as an excuse to be sexually imposing.

Future Research

Other studies currently in progress involve the investigation of the effects of sexual arousal or anger provocation on slide showing and the effects of confederate resistance. The physical aggression that is a component of some forms of sexual aggression has not been represented in the current laboratory procedure (Hall et al., 1992). However, most sexual aggression does not involve physical force, but involves imposition of unwanted sexual activity as a function of repeated arguments or other psychological pressure (Byers, 1988; Koss et al., 1987). Thus, the current laboratory procedure may be representative of the most common forms of sexual aggression. Nevertheless, we intend to combine the sexually imposing components of the current paradigm with the physical aggression analogue (i.e., shock) that has been used in other research.

As with other complex psychological problems such as depression, sexually aggressive behavior may have multiple etiological precursors, but only one primary precursor (such as in functional or organic depression) that catalyzes the expression of the behavior. With this idea in mind, and given the heterogeneity of sexually aggressive men, we believe that each primary motivational precursor (physiological arousal, cognitive, affective dyscontrol, and personality problems) helps to define a particular subgroup and points to the core treatment element for that subgroup. The precursor for a particular subgroup is primary to the extent that it uniquely causes a person in that subgroup to overcome antagonistic and inhibitory tendencies (e.g., psychological defenses, moral convictions, and environmental constraints) to commit a sexually aggressive act. A particular precursor may be sufficiently strong for members of a particular subgroup of sexual aggressors to overcome their inhibitory tendencies to act, but not strong enough for members of another subgroup to overcome their inhibitory tendencies to act. For example, the cognition that all women enjoy being raped may be the necessary precursor for one male to commit a sexually aggressive act, but not another male who may be from a different subgroup defined by a different motivational precursor. This other male may have a similar or equally strong irrational cognition, but for him the primary driving force necessary to counteract his inhibitory tendencies to commit a sexually aggressive act may be a different primary motivational precursor (e.g., affective dyscontrol, personality, or physiological arousal).

Not only may the differential call to action be uniquely determined by the strength of the subgroup-specific precursor, but it also may be partially determined by the inhibitory makeup of the perpetrator. For example, the type of motivational precursor necessary to overwhelm an inhibitory environmental constraint (e.g., the fear of getting caught) may be very different from the kind of motivational precursor necessary to overwhelm the inhibitory constraint of a concern for the potential victim's well-being. Implicit in this latest addition to our quadripartite model is the idea that primary motivational precursors interact dynamically with different types and gradients of a limited number of inhibitory forces, producing different threshold gradients for action in different subgroups of sexual aggressors.

Not only may the primary precursors vary from subpopulation to subpopulation of sexual aggressors, but the level of threshold for the sexually aggressive act to occur may also vary. If the same potentially motivational conditions (i.e., physiological sexual arousal, cognitive distortions, affective dyscontrol, or developmentally related personality problems) exist in two males with equal potency, but only one commits a sexually aggressive act, then possibly the threshold for action is lower in the acting-out male. Therefore, we propose that what may distinguish subpopulations or sexual aggressors from each other and from nonaggressive men is not the compelling behavioral-drive aspect of the primary precursor only, but also psychological mechanisms that determine thresholds for acting on socially unacceptable but compelling internal psychological forces. That many nonaggressive men experience the same potentially motivational conditions (e.g., physiological sexual arousal, cognitive distortions, affective dyscontrol, developmentally related personality problems) as sexually aggressive men also suggests that what distinguishes these groups may not only be the compelling quality of the precursor, but also the ability to keep it below threshold (i.e., not act on it). From this perspective, understanding the interactions of primary precursors and inhibitory threshold gradients of sexually aggressive behavior is critical. We believe that our laboratory model will aid us in doing it.

At the risk of being overly simplistic in our thinking about sexual aggressors, we intentionally limited the number of primary motivational precursors and inhibitory factors in our model to reflect what we believe to be the most salient dynamic processes and antecedent factors necessary to create different foci for treatments of various subgroups. Like most other behaviors reflecting psychological disturbance, sexually aggressive behaviors probably result from infinite levels of psychological complexity. Yet the value of restricting a model to a particularly lower level of complexity, as we did, reflects our purpose of developing easily disseminated treatments. Complex models lend themselves most directly to the development of comprehensive classification schemes or assessment tools (e.g., see the elegant and complex model building of Malamuth et al., 1991; Prentky & Knight, 1991) that may or may not be easy for other clinicians to utilize in day-to-day practice. Typically, treatment-driven models in other areas of psychological disturbance are constructed with a limited number of variables or processes in mind. Although these models may not fully account for all or most of the etiological factors of the disturbance in question, presumably they account for the most important ones and, as such, are potentially useful for the typical practitioner. This has been our intent as well, particularly given the lack of well-documented, systematized, and successful treatment approaches for sexual aggressors that lend themselves to dissemination.

CONCLUSION

A method of assessing sexually impositional behavior that is less susceptible to social desirability and less inferential than previous methods is needed. We have reviewed the development of a laboratory model of what we consider to be a mild but serious form of sexually aggressive behavior. This model involves the presentation of erotic stimuli to an unwilling female confederate. This method does not appear susceptible to social desirability, because 90% of men have chosen to show erotic slides to the unwilling female confederate. After establishing that men would show erotic slides to an unwilling female confederate, we attempted to reduce the demand to show erotic slides by providing fewer erotic slide categories from which to select. When only one of four slide categories was erotic, 22% of the men selected the erotic category to show to the unwilling female confederate. This rate of slide showing closely corresponds to actual rates of self-reported sexual aggression (Koss et al., 1987). However, we do not consider self-report to be a gold standard of the actual frequency of sexually aggressive behavior, because of social desirability demands. Rather than rely on self-report or inferential assessments of sexual arousal patterns, the current laboratory procedure allows the direct measurement of a mild but serious form of sexually impositional behavior and examination of the conditions, which might generalize to other forms of sexual aggression.

REFERENCES

Abbey, A. (1987). Misperceptions of friendly behavior as sexual interest: A survey of naturally occurring incidents. *Psychology of Women Quarterly, 11,* 173–194.

Abbey, A., Cozzarelli, C., McLaughlin, K., & Harnish, R. J. (1987). The effects of clothing and dyad sex composition on perceptions of sexual intent: Do women and men evaluate these cues differently? *Journal of Applied Social Psychology, 17,* 108–126.

Abel, G. G., Barlow, D. H., Blanchard, E. B., & Guild, D. (1977). The components of rapists' sexual arousal. *Archives of General Psychiatry, 34,* 895–903.

Avery-Clark, C. A., & Laws, D. R. (1984). Differential erection response patterns of sexual child abusers to stimuli describing activities with children. *Behavior Therapy, 15,* 71–83.

Barbaree, H. E., & Marshall, W. L. (1991). The role of male sexual arousal in rape: Six models. *Journal of Consulting and Clinical Psychology, 59,* 621–630.

Barbaree, H. E., Marshall, W. L., & Lanthier, R. D. (1979). Deviant sexual arousal in rapists. *Behavior Research and Therapy, 17,* 215–222.

Blader, J. C., & Marshall, W. L. (1989). Is assessment of sexual arousal in rapists worthwhile? A critique of current methods and the development of a response compatibility approach. *Clinical Psychology Review, 9,* 569–587.

Blader, J. C., Marshall, W. L., & Barbaree, H. E. (1988, June). *The inhibitory effect of coercion on sexual arousal in men and disinhibition by provocation.* Paper presented at the meeting of the Canadian Psychological Association, Montreal.

Burt, M. R. (1980). Cultural myths and support for rape. *Journal of Personality and Social Psychology, 38,* 217–230.

Byers, E. S. (1988). Effects of sexual arousal on men's and women's behavior in sexual disagreement situations. *The Journal of Sex Research, 25,* 235–254.

Dermen, K. H. (1990). *Against her will: The effect of alcohol expectancy set on male "sexual aggression" toward a female target.* Unpublished doctoral dissertation, State University of New York, Buffalo.

Eagly, A. H., & Steffen, V. J. (1986). Gender and aggressive behavior: A meta-analytic review of the social psychological literature. *Psychological Bulletin, 100,* 309–330.

Ellis, L. (1989). *Theories of rape: Inquiries into the causes of sexual aggression.* New York: Hemisphere.

Freedman, J. L. (1988). Keeping pornography in perspective. *Contemporary Psychology, 33,* 858–860.

Freund, K. R., Blanchard, R. (1989). Phallometric diagnosis of pedophilia. *Journal of Consulting and Clinical Psychology, 57,* 100–105.

Geen, R. G., & Donnerstein, E. I. (1983). *Aggression: Theoretical and empirical reviews: Vol. 2. Issues in research.* New York: Academic Press.

George, W. H., & Marlatt, G. A. (1986). The effects of alcohol and anger on interest in violence, erotica, and deviance. *Journal of Abnormal Psychology, 95,* 150–158.

Groth, A. N., & Birnbaum, A. H. (1979). *Men who rape: The psychology of the offender.* New York: Plenum.

Hall, G. C. N. (1989). Self-reported hostility as a function of offense characteristics and response style in a sexual offender population. *Journal of Consulting and Clinical Psychology, 57,* 306–308.

Hall, G. C. N. (1990). Prediction of sexual aggression. *Clinical Psychology Review, 10,* 229–245.

Hall, G. C. N. (1991). Sexual arousal as a function of physiological and cognitive variables in a sexual offender population. *Archives of Sexual Behavior, 20,* 359–369.

Hall, G. C. N., & Hirschman, R. (1991). Towards a theory of sexual aggression: A quadripartite model. *Journal of Consulting and Clinical Psychology, 59,* 662–669.

Hall, G. C. N., Hirschman, R., & Oliver, L. L. (1992, August). *Direct measurement of sexually aggressive behavior in the laboratory.* Paper presented at the meeting of the American Psychological Association, Washington, DC.

Hall, G. C. N., Proctor, W. C., & Nelson, G. M. (1988). Validating of physiological measures of pedophilic sexual arousal in a sexual offender population. *Journal of Consulting and Clinical Psychology, 56,* 118–122.

Hall, G. C. N., Shondrick, D. D., & Hirschman, R. (in press). The role of sexual arousal in sexually aggressive behavior: A meta-analysis. *Journal of Consulting and Clinical Psychology.*

Koss, M. P., Gidycz, C. A., & Wisniewski, N. (1987). The scope of rape: Incidence and prevalence of sexual aggression and victimization in a national sample of higher education students. *Journal of Consulting and Clinical Psychology, 55,* 162–170.

Lang, A. R., Searles, J., Lauerman, R., & Adesso, V. (1980). Expectancy, alcohol, and sex guilt as determinants of interest in and reaction to sexual stimuli. *Journal of Abnormal Psychology, 89,* 644–653.

Lanyon, R. I., & Lutz, R. W. (1984). MMPI discrimination of defensive and nondefensive felony sex offenders. *Journal of Consulting and Clinical Psychology, 52,* 841–843.

Lisak, D., & Roth, S. (1988). Motivational factors in nonincarcerated sexually aggressive men. *Journal of Personality and Social Psychology, 55,* 795–802.

Lopez, P. A., & George, W. H. (1992, August). *Effects of female presence and erotophilia on male pornography-viewing behavior.* Paper presented at the meeting of the American Psychological Association, Washington, DC.

Malamuth, N. M. (1986). Predictors of naturalistic sexual aggression. *Journal of Personality and Social Psychology, 50,* 953–962.

Malamuth, N. M. (1988) A multidimensional approach to sexual aggression: Combining measures of past behavior and present likelihood. In R. A. Prentky & V. L. Quinsey (Eds.), *Human sexual aggression: Current perspectives* (pp. 123–132). New York: New York Academy of Sciences.

Malamuth, N. M., Sockloskie, R. J., Koss, M. P., & Tanaka, J. S. (1991). Characteristics of aggressors against women: Testing a model using a national sample of college students. *Journal of Consulting and Clinical Psychology, 59,* 670–681.

Marshall, W. C., Barbaree, H. E., & Christopher, D. (1986). Sexual offenders against female children: sexual preferences for age of victims and type of behaviour. *Canadian Journal of Behavioural Science, 18,* 424–439.

McGovern, F. J., & Nevid, J. S. (1986). Evaluation apprehension on psychological inventories in a prison-based setting. *Journal of Consulting and Clinical Psychology, 54,* 576–578.

Milgram, S. (1963). Behavioral study of obedience. *Journal of Abnormal and Social Psychology, 67,* 371–378.

Muehlenhard, C. L., & Linton, M. A. (1987). Date rape and sexual aggression in dating situations: Incidence and risk factors. *Journal of Counseling Psychology, 34,* 186–196.

Murphy, W. O., Haynes, M. R., Stalgaitis, S. J., & Flanagan, B. (1986). Differential responding among four groups of sexual offenders against children. *Journal of Psychopathology and Behavioral Assessment, 8,* 339–353.

Prentky, R. A., & Knight, R. A. (1991). Identifying critical dimensions for discriminating among rapists. *Journal of Consulting and Clinical Psychology, 59,* 643–661.

Pryor, J. B. (1987). Sexual harassment proclivities in men. *Sex Roles, 17,* 269–290.

Quinsey, V. L. & Chaplin, T. C. (1988). Penile responses of child molesters and normals to descriptions of encounters with children involving sex and violence. *Journal of Interpersonal Violence, 3,* 259–274.

Quinsey, V. L., Chaplin, T. C., & Upfold, D. (1984). Sexual arousal to nonsexual violence and sadomasochistic themes among rapists and non-sex-offenders. *Journal of Consulting and Clinical Psychology, 52,* 651–657.

Quinsey, V. L., Chaplin, T. C., & Varney, G. (1981). A comparison of rapists' and non-sex offenders' sexual preferences for mutually consenting sex, rape, and physical abuse of women. *Behavioral Assessment, 3,* 127–135.

Rapaport, K., & Burkhart, B. R. (1984). Personality and attitudinal characteristics of sexually coercive college males. *Journal of Abnormal Psychology, 93,* 216–221.

Rich, A. (1980). Compulsory heterosexuality and lesbian existence. *Signs: Journal of Women in Culture and Society, 5,* 631–660.

Sandberg, G. G., Jackson, T. L., & Petretic-Jackson, P. (1987). College dating attitudes regarding sexual coercion and sexual aggression: Developing education and prevention strategies. *Journal of College Student Personnel, 28,* 302–310.

Sarrel, P. M., & Masters, W. H. (1982). Sexual molestation of men by women. *Archives of Sexual Behavior, 11,* 117–131.

Scully, D., & Marolla, J. (1984). Convicted rapists' vocabulary of motive: Excuses and justifications. *Social Problems, 31,* 530–544.

Shondrick, D. D., Hall, G. C. N., & Hirschman, R. (1992, August). *Laboratory sexual aggression as a function of perceived provocation.* Paper presented at the meeting of the American Psychological Association, Washington, DC.

Shotland, R. L. (1992). A theory of the causes of courtship rape: Part 2. *Journal of Social Issues, 48,* 127–143.

Struckman-Johnson, C. (1988). Forced sex on dates: It happens to men, too. *Journal of Sex Research, 24,* 234–241.

Struckman-Johnson, C. (1991). Male victims of acquaintance rape. In A. Parrot & L. Bechhofer (Eds.), *Acquaintance rape: The hidden crime* (pp. 192–214). New York: Wiley.

Taylor, S. P. (1986). The regulation of aggressive behavior. In R. Blanchard & C. Blanchard (Eds.), *Advances in the study of aggression* (vol. 2, pp. 91–119). New York: Academic Press.

Zuckerman, M. (1971). Physiological measures of sexual arousal in the human. *Psychological Bulletin, 25,* 297–327.

II

TREATMENT

8

INTRODUCTION: TREATMENT OF SEXUAL AGGRESSION

Lori Boone Wills
Kent State University

The identification of etiological factors and reliable and valid methods of assessment are essential for the subsequent development of effective treatment interventions for sex offenders. In this second section of the book, the emphasis is on treatment issues related to sex offenders. The authors of the following chapters take into account current theories and research on sexual aggression as they discuss the continuing development of treatment programs.

Marshall (chapter 9) begins his chapter with a brief review of the different types of treatment techniques that have been used with sex offenders and their reported effectiveness. Within the past 20 years, there has been increased emphasis on the use of cognitive–behavioral approaches to treat sex offenders. Marshall states that many of the early behavioral interventions focused primarily on the reduction of deviant sexual arousal. However, although this continues to be an important component of treatment, it has since been recognized that treatment needs to address a broader range of problems commonly found among sex offenders. According to Marshall, recent reviews of research on treatment efficacy have indicated that comprehensive cognitive behavioral programs, especially those that incorporate relapse prevention methods, appear to be the most consistently effective. However, Marshall goes on to state that these programs may be more effective for child molesters and exhibitionists than for rapists.

Based on current research as well as his own clinical experiences in both outpatient and correctional settings, Marshall discusses considerations for treatment that may be particularly useful in working with rapists. He states that whereas both child molesters and rapists exhibit some similar characteristics (e.g., cognitive distortions, tendency to blame external factors for their deviant behavior, lack of victim empathy), additional characteristics that may be more unique to rapists need to be identified and addressed, because they may impact treatment effectiveness.

The attitudes of sexual offenders toward treatment are especially significant, and Marshall indicates that it is essential for therapists to maintain a noncondemnatory attitude toward the offenders with whom they work. It is also necessary to emphasize the personal benefits of participating in treatment to rapists as a means of engaging them in the treatment process, because they are likely to be less responsive to moral arguments for changing their behavior. Another factor to consider is that of deviant sexual arousal. As do other authors in this book, Marshall cites data that suggest rapists are a heterogeneous group, particularly in the extent to which deviant sexual arousal acts as a motivating factor in their behavior. Therefore, assessment of how deviant sexual arousal or alternative motives (e.g., a need for power) contribute to the individual offender's behavior is important in specifying treatment needs.

Marshall also addresses issues related to the lack of victim empathy and the inappropriate attitudes often exhibited by sex offenders, and he provides detailed suggestions as to how to address these issues in treatment. Furthermore, he describes how difficulties with social skills, intimacy, low self-esteem, and a lack of confidence in masculinity may be related to sex offending, and need to be dealt with in treatment. Finally, Marshall emphasizes the importance of assessing the presence of drug or alcohol abuse and a general criminal lifestyle.

Marshall finishes chapter 9 with a description of a three-tiered comprehensive treatment program for rapists, some elements of which have already been instituted in the Canadian Penitentiary Services system. In this program, sex offenders graduate through three levels. They begin the program in a restricted prison setting in which they receive extensive treatment (i.e., 3 hours per day for 5 months). Based on the sex offenders' progress in treatment, they may move to a less restricted prison setting and eventually to a community placement, where they continue to receive treatment and ongoing supervision. Different components of treatment are emphasized to varying degrees at each of these three levels. Marshall also emphasizes that, in addition to continued research and work on the treatment of rapists, therapists and researchers have a social responsibility to advocate for greater changes in public policy and societal attitudes that would discourage the subjugation of women.

In chapter 10, Pithers begins by examining past research on treatment efficacy, and offers a case for why reviews of past research may not adequately represent the current state of treatment effectiveness for sex offenders. Pithers argues that some effective components of treatment may be overlooked in larger studies, and specific interventions designed for the unique needs of a given offender may indeed prove useful. As in earlier chapters of this book, Pithers cautions against the uniformity myth of sex offenders, stating that not all sex offenders have identical problems. Therefore, it is important to distinguish between child molesters and rapists and also to examine possible subcategories of these two groups. As did Marshall, Pithers cites research indicating that treatment appears to reduce recidivism rates in sex offenders. Although data indicate that treated rapists exhibit lower recidivism rates than untreated rapists, reduction in recidivism rates is significantly greater overall for child molesters than for rapists. Thus, Pithers notes that, in terms of treatment, "substantial room for improvement exists."

In developing more effective treatments for rapists, it is important to examine the variables that may differentiate child abusers and rapists. Pithers provides an examination of these potential differences. He proposes that the presence of a history of general criminality is one variable to assess, because it raises the issue of whether the rapist's behavior is more likely a product of aggressive antisocial behavior or sexual maladjustment. Pithers suggests that for sex offenders with an extensive criminal history, treatment directed at deviant sexual arousal may be less relevant than interventions that address the wider range of antisocial attitudes and general impulsivity that are likely to be present. Furthermore, Pithers argues that acts of sexual aggression may lie on a trait–state continuum (i.e., the obsessional quality of pedophilia may be viewed as more of an enduring trait), whereas the behavior of rapists may fall on a wider range of the continuum. He also proposes that a distinction be made between rape as "planned impulsivity" and a genuine impulsive act. Such distinctions would be especially useful because one goal of treatment is to assist the rapist in identifying the sequence of events that can lead to relapse and how to cope with these events differently in the future.

According to Pithers, attention should also be directed toward examining the prodromal period leading to sexual abuse. Although there may be some similarity in the type of precursors leading to abuse among child abusers and rapists, it is important to assess the number of precursors involved in the relapse process and the rapidity with which the offender moves through the relapse process. Pithers notes that rapists may move rapidly through their relapse process, and this may increase their risk for reoffending in the future. Precursors specifically related to deviant sexual arousal also are very important to examine, and Pithers endorses the use of the penile plethysmograph in both the initial assessment of the offender and ongoing measurement of treatment progress. Pithers also states that societal attitudes may differentially impact child abusers and rapists. Whereas societal attitudes strongly condemn sexual behavior with children, messages related to the sexual exploitation and objectification of women are seen more commonly within society.

After identifying some of the differences that appear to exist among sex offender subtypes, Pithers discusses a variety of treatment interventions that may be applied to sex offenders. Modifications are clearly indicated for the treatment of all types of rapists, whether their sexual aggression is more paraphilic in nature or a product of a general criminal lifestyle. Pithers offers suggestions for how to address issues such as reducing arousal to abusive sexual fantasies, increasing empathetic skills, and increasing general recognition of the offender's own emotions. He also describes methods for addressing the personal victimization that rapists may have experienced in their lives. Attributional style and the cognitive distortions often displayed by offenders also are an important part of any treatment program, and these too are discussed by Pithers.

In chapter 11, Marques, Day, Nelson, and West provide a detailed description of the research being conducted in an experimental treatment program for sex offenders at Atascadero State Hospital in California. As these authors discuss the development of their program and the methods they have employed to assess its efficacy, they provide added perspective on important issues to consider in the treatment of rapists. The Sex Offender Treatment and Evaluation Project (SOTEP) described by Marques et al. was created in 1985 and is a controlled, longitudinal study of the effectiveness of a comprehensive, intensive treatment program for both convicted rapists and child molesters who are in the California State Penitentiary system.

According to Marques et al., in the initial developmental stages of SOTEP, the California State Legislature mandated that the program utilize a valid experimental design that would allow its treatment methods to be tested rigorously. As a result, every effort was made to instill appropriate experimental controls and add a strong evaluative component to the program. Three groups of convicted sex offenders are being examined as part of SOTEP. Members of two of these groups are sex offenders who volunteered to participate in treatment. These volunteers are assigned randomly to either a treatment (i.e., treatment group) or no-treatment (i.e., volunteer group) condition. The third group of offenders is a nonvolunteer control group. All subjects are screened based on specific selection criteria and are matched on identified variables.

Marques et al. report that for the treatment group, the initial phase of SOTEP involves an intensive 2-year inpatient program that primarily utilizes a relapse prevention model. Included in this program are specific treatment interventions designed to address the multiple factors (e.g., difficulties with anger management, social skill deficits, cognitive distortions) that are believed to contribute to a sexually deviant pattern of behavior. The program also incorporates a 1-year aftercare phase that provides ongoing treatment to the offenders after they are paroled and returned to a community setting. Offenders from all three groups are then followed for a period of 5 years after parole to determine their rates of recidivism.

Marques et al. provide a thorough summary of the methods they use to evaluate treatment effects at various stages in the program. In addition to outlining the types of psychometric measures used, they describe the range of data to be collected and the time periods during which assessments are made. Unfortunately, given that this program is relatively new, longitudinal data on reoffense rates are still limited. However, Marques et al. provide preliminary findings. They cite data related to reoffense rates of the different groups of offenders and also report on initial findings related to specific variables that may be predictive of reoffense.

In the last part of chapter 11, Marques et al. present views on the current status of sex offender treatment and offer recommendations for future directions of research. In terms of treatment issues, Marques et al. maintain that the primary goal of treatment of sex offenders has become one of management rather than cure. This has occurred because of the increased recognition that offenders are continually faced with risk factors or "triggers" with which they must cope. Therefore, offenders must assume lifelong responsibility for appropriately managing their sexual behavior. Also, as did Marshall and Pithers, Marques et al. state that comprehensive programs for offenders are essential to address the multiple factors that contribute to sexual deviance. However, they emphasize that, due to the heterogeneity within the sex offender population, it is important that treatment programs be flexible enough to include interventions that address each individual's particular combination of risk factors. Other important treatment considerations discussed by Marques et al. are the importance of strong aftercare/community supervision, the revision of programs to meet the differing needs of offender subtypes, and understanding social policy and its continuing impact on the development of treatment programs.

Marques et al. finish chapter 11 with a discussion of methodological issues related to research on treatment effectiveness. Based on their experience with SOTEP, they provide a number of beneficial suggestions regarding the development and assessment of treatment programs. In particular, they emphasize that evaluators should not rely solely on "rapsheet" data when determining recidivism, because they may not adequately represent violations and high-risk behaviors exhibited by offenders after they are paroled. Finally, Marques et al. offer some thought-provoking comments related to the idea of "treatment success" and how it may need to be redefined in work with sex offenders.

Although this volume is on adult perpetrators of sexual aggression, much adult sexual aggression has developmental antecedents. Becker, Harris, and Sales (chapter 12) conclude the treatment section of this book by focusing on the lack of empirical research that has been conducted with adolescent sex offenders. Becker et al. point out that adolescents account for a significant percentage of sexually related crimes, and that sex offending is considered a chronic disorder that has early origins. Thus, these authors offer a strong argument for the need for increased research directed toward understanding and treating adolescent sex offenders. Toward this end, Becker et al. review much of the research that has previously been conducted on adolescent sex offenders and provide suggestions as to the continuing work that needs to be done with this population.

Although Becker et al. classify types of sex offenses into three categories (i.e., "hands off," "hands on," and pedophilic offenses), they report that the classification of offenders is a much more difficult task. As did Marshall, Pithers, and Marques et al., Becker et al. emphasize that sex offenders are a heterogeneous group and, thus, it is useful to identify subcategories of offenders. They cite one classification system that categorizes rapists into nine types based on the primary motivation related to sexual deviance and the degree of social competence exhibited by the offender. They also provide descriptions of two separate models that attempt to explain the etiology of sexual deviance.

A number of studies have also been conducted on the characteristics often associated with adolescent offenders, their families, and their social environments. Summarizing the results of these studies, Becker et al. report that certain individual characteristics have been shown to be prevalent among adolescent sex offenders. These characteristics include a lack of social skills, a history of nonsexual delinquency, poor academic performance, impulsivity, depression, and lack of appropriate sex education. However, Becker et al. also state that these characteristics are not specific to adolescent sex offenders, because they have also been found among other types of juvenile offenders. Furthermore, they caution that results of this research cannot be used to assume that a specific profile of adolescent sex offenders exists.

Following a review of the content, reliability, and validity of several instruments used in the assessment of adolescent sex offenders, Becker et al. discuss the current literature on treatment. In the past 10 years, the number of treatment programs developed for adolescent offenders has increased significantly. The goals for treatment appear to be quite similar despite the diversity of the programs. These goals include increasing social competence, developing victim empathy and nondeviant sexual interests, and cognitive restructuring. According to Becker et al., the two types of programs most often described in the research literature are either cognitive/behavioral or multisystemic. They offer examples of both types of treatment approaches and some outcome data for each. As Marques et al. did in chapter 11, Becker et al. comment on the primary goal for sex offender treatment, stating that "although the hope is to cure, the aim is to control." They also briefly review data that have been collected regarding variables believed to be predictive of recidivism among adolescent sex offenders.

Becker et al. end chapter 12 with a summary and critique of the research conducted to date. They state that, although some models seem intuitively useful, the relative lack of empirical validation of these models may limit their utility. Also, in the area of treatment efficacy, there has been relatively little well-controlled research, thereby limiting confidence in these treatments.

Taken together, the authors in all four chapters of this section offer many relevant and practical ideas to consider as treatment approaches for rapists (both adult and adolescent) are reevaluated and modified. Although Becker et al.

report that data on treatment of adolescent sex offenders are still very limited, Marshall, Pithers, and Marques et al. cite evidence indicating that effective treatment programs for adult sex offenders do exist and such programs provide a good foundation on which to build. All of the authors in this section advocate the development of comprehensive treatment approaches that address the multiple factors believed to be involved in the etiology of sexually aggressive behavior. Furthermore, all of these authors note that rapists appear to be a heterogeneous group, and that identifying subtypes of rapists has implications for treatment interventions that need to take such differences into account. It is the interplay of ideas related to theory, research, and clinical practice that contributes to increased knowledge and understanding of sexual aggression. The authors of these chapters effectively synthesize theoretical ideas, current research findings, and their own clinical observations to provide recommendations for the treatment of rapists that potentially can be useful to clinicians, researchers, and policymakers.

9

A REVISED APPROACH TO THE TREATMENT OF MEN WHO SEXUALLY ASSAULT ADULT FEMALES

W. L. Marshall
Queen's University

We recently completed extensive reviews of the literature (Marshall & Barbaree, 1990a; Marshall, Jones, Ward, Johnston, & Barbaree, 1991; Marshall, Ward, Johnston, Jones, & Barbaree, 1991) concerned with the effectiveness of treatment with sex offenders. These reviews revealed a number of things. Contrary to the earlier gloomy conclusions of Furby, Weinrott, and Blackshaw (1989), we observed what we took to be clear indications that treatment of sex offenders can be effective. Certainly, some studies have found either negative effects for treatment (J. J. Peters Institute, 1980; Rice, Harris, & Quinsey, 1991) or no apparent benefits for the treated offenders (Leger, 1989; Massachusetts Post Audit Bureau, 1979; Saylor, 1979); however, there are also clear demonstrations of treatment effectiveness.

The history of the evaluation of treatment for sex offenders is quite short, with the earliest reasonably substantive reports dating from the 1960s. Some of the early reports indicated what seems to be clear benefits for treatment. Pacht, Halleck, and Ehrmann (1962) found that only 6.3% of 414 treated sex offenders, followed for up to 20 years beyond discharge, had reoffended. Because these offenders were selected carefully after extensive observation as those most "deviated," and therefore presumably at greatest risk to reoffend, this quite low recidivism rate strongly suggests that treatment was effective. Similarly, Prendergast (1978) reported a recidivism rate of only 9.3% in treated sex offenders who appeared to have been a problematic and reasonably high-risk group. Treatment programs by both Pacht et al. (1962) and Prendergast (1978) appeared to have been based on psychodynamic, or at least precognitive/behavioral, approaches to therapy.

PHYSICAL TREATMENT APPROACHES

There are also numerous reports of the effectiveness of various physical intervention procedures. For example, physical castration has been demonstrated to reduce the number of sexual offenses subsequently committed by castrates (Bradford, 1990), although this procedure produces disabling side effects (Heim, 1981; Heim & Hursch, 1979) and may increase the subsequent frequency of nonsexual crimes (Sturup, 1968). In any event, physical castration is unlikely to be adopted in North America as a standard of treatment for sex offenders. On the other hand, antiandrogens seem clearly valuable and can be routinely administered without much problem if their use is monitored carefully. Several studies have shown benefits for antiandrogens (Berlin & Meinecke, 1981; Bradford & Pawlak, 1987, in press; Cooper, 1987a; Laschet & Laschet, 1975; Walker & Meyer, 1981; Walker, Meyer, Emory, & Rubin, 1984); but it seems likely that these effects do not include changes in preferred sexual outlets (Cooper, 1987b; Cordoba & Chapel, 1983), but rather reflect an overall nonspecific reduction in sexual interests and activities (Money, 1972). Antiandrogens have rarely been used alone and are typically offered as part of an overall program that includes either extensive counseling (Gagne, 1981; Money, 1972) or a carefully constructed cognitive/behavioral treatment program (Bloom, Bradford, & Kofoed, 1988). Therefore, it is difficult, given the evidence available at the moment, to determine the actual contribution that the administration of antiandrogen medication makes to the outcome reported in the studies.

Marshall et al. (1991) suggested that the value of antiandrogen medications may be in reducing the relatively immediate risk presented by those offenders who are in the community and who have frequent and strong urges to offend. However, there are other ways to deal with this risk. Hospitalization is a reasonable alternative, and recently there have been developments in the use of anticompulsive drugs to control these pressing urges. These medications have been shown to produce benefits with Obsessive-Compulsive Disorder (Pearse, 1988) and with Impulse Control Disorders (Swedo et al., 1989), and a clear formulation has been offered to suggest that they may be similarly effective with some sex offenders (Pearson, 1990). There is now available evidence in support of this claim (Bianchi, 1990; Cesnik & Coleman, 1989; Fedoroff, 1988; Kafka, 1991; Pearson, Marshall, Barbaree, & Southmayd, in press).

CURRENT COGNITIVE/BEHAVIORAL APPROACHES

Over the past 20 years, behavioral and, more latterly, cognitive/behavioral approaches to the treatment of sex offenders have been developed. Some early behavioral clinicians (Bond & Evans, 1967) considered that simply reducing deviant sexual arousal would be sufficient to change the aberrant behavior of sex deviants, and unfortunately this naive assumption lives on tod. al., 1991). However, early on this simplistic approach was replace grams that targeted a broader range of problems in sex offenders. For Marshall (1971) argued that it was necessary to reduce deviant arou enhance appropriate sexual responding and also to provide skill training so that offenders could act on this changed sexual orientation. Throughout the 1970s, behavioral approaches continued to extend the range of problematic functioning that was given attention in treatment (Abel, Blanchard, & Becker, 1976; Marshall & Williams, 1975). By the following decade, the cognitive processes of sex offenders entered into treatment considerations (Abel, Becker, & Skinner, 1986; Marshall, Earls, Segal, & Darke, 1983), and relapse prevention procedures were introduced into these, by now, comprehensive cognitive/behavioral programs (Marques, 1988; Marshall, Hudson, & Ward, 1992; Pithers, Martin, & Cumming, 1989).

We concluded from our reviews that these comprehensive cognitive/ behavioral programs, particularly those with an explicit relapse prevention component, appeared to be the most consistently effective approaches to the treatment of sex offenders (Marshall et al., 1991; Marshall et al., 1992). However, we also observed that these programs were not as effective with men who sexually assaulted adult females (hereafter referred to as *rapists*) as they were with child molesters and exhibitionists. For example, an evaluation of our early program (Marshall & Williams, 1975) for incarcerated sex offenders revealed that we were more effective with nonfamilial child molesters than we were with rapists (Davidson, 1984). Similarly, Maletzky's (1991) excellent results with his outpatient child molesters and exhibitionists were not matched by corresponding successes with rapists. Finally, the Vermont State Corrections program was also less successful with rapists than with child molesters (Pithers & Cumming, 1989). Obviously, we have to reconsider our approach to the treatment of rapists.

PROPOSED CHANGES TO THE COGNITIVE/
BEHAVIORAL APPROACH

First, let me dismiss any idea that the fault lies with rapists. Although it is tempting to suggest that we fail with these men because certain features that may characterize them (e.g., they are typically more youthful than child molesters, they may be more psychopathic, more generally rejecting of help, less motivated, too "macho" to admit problems, etc.) seriously stand in the way of doing effective therapy, we should see it rather as our task to overcome these obstacles. In fact, if we consider the literature describing the features of rapists, and our own clinical experience in working with them, it seems to me there are obvious features about them that we have failed to systematically address so far. Indeed, it is fair to say that an examination of the content of most treatment programs reveals that the targets in treatment focus essentially on those features that characterize child molesters. That is not to say that all of the components in present treatment programs are irrelevant to rapists. Clearly, some target common problems. For example, sex offenders of all types engage in denial, minimization, and distortion; all attribute responsibility to persons or facts outside themselves; all lack victim empathy; and all need relapse prevention training. No doubt all have social deficits of one kind or another, but the emphasis in this aspect of treatment has been more on the deficits of child molesters (e.g., underassertiveness). Perhaps the area that most emphasizes child molester problems is the focus on sexually deviant interests. However, there are several other areas that need emphasizing if we are to improve our treatment of rapists.

Attitudes Toward Treatment

The main problems here are those already mentioned. For instance, many rapists refuse treatment or fail to effectively participate because it threatens their sense of masculinity (which is typically rather fragile) to admit they have problems. Similarly, their more general lack of motivation to change and their overall psychopathic disposition (Langevin, 1983) make it a difficult task to persuade rapists to enter and properly participate in treatment. All of these need to be kept in mind when initially contacting rapists for treatment and in attempting to secure their full participation in treatment. It is essential for the therapist to maintain a nonthreatening, noncondemnatory attitude in dealing with all sex offenders, but particularly with rapists. It is also essential to get rapists to recognize the value to them of participating in treatment. Depending on where they are in the judicial process, it can be shown that entering effectively into treatment may make the courts, a parole board, or a prison transfer board (with a possible move to lower security status) look more favorably on them. Similarly, treatment may make them feel more self-confident, may make them more socially impressive, and may give them skills that will allow them to get greater enjoyment out of life.

These suggestions are meant to be just that: suggestions. Each treatment program needs to develop its own approach, but it is very important to have in place some strategy for getting rapists to both enter, and effectively participate in, treatment. Whatever tactics are used at this stage, it is important to remember that arguments based on moral reasoning rarely persuade anyone to change their behavior, whereas making clear the personal benefits (and the personal costs of not changing) is typically a more effective strategy.

Focus on Deviant Arousal

Although comprehensive cognitive/behavioral programs cover a broad range of problems in treatment and do not simply focus on deviant sexuality, the fact that they retain a concern for deviant arousal indicates that the designers of these programs still adhere, at least to some degree, to the notion that sexual offending is an expression (albeit a deviant expression) of sexual desire. The emphasis placed on modifying deviant arousal varies somewhat from program to program, but most report that this is a critical feature of treatment (Knopp, 1984).

Our treatment programs for child molesters (Marshall & Barbaree, 1987, 1988) include a significant component aimed at changing the direction of sexual desires and inhibiting deviant sexual thoughts. However, we have also described evidence indicating a low incidence of deviant sexuality among rapists (Baxter, Barbaree, & Marshall, 1986; Marshall & Barbaree, 1992; Marshall, Barbaree, Laws, & Baxter, 1986). We (Marshall & Eccles, 1991) took these data to mean that sexual motives may not be preeminent in rape. In this view, of course, we are not alone, nor by any means are we the first. Groth (1979) has claimed for many years that rape is a pseudo-sexual act, serving motives of power and aggression through the means of sex; and feminist writers have long since claimed that rape has little to do with sex and more to do with the intimidation of women (Brownmiller, 1975; Russell, 1984).

In opposition to these views is the position advocated by several behaviorally oriented theorists (Abel & Rouleau, 1990; Freund, 1990; Quinsey & Earls, 1990). These authors hold that rape is understood best as sexually motivated and that sexual aggression against adult females is but one manifestation of a more generally deviant sexual disposition (Abel, Becker, Cunningham-Rathner, Mittelman, & Rouleau, 1988; Freund & Blanchard, 1986). In this view, rape may be seen as the result of conditioning processes entrenching an attraction to forced, nonconsenting sex (Laws & Marshall, 1990), or rape may be simply an evolutionarily entrenched option for deprived males (Quinsey, 1984). We have provided data that seem at odds with the notion of a more generally deviant disposition among sex offenders (Marshall, Barbaree, & Eccles, 1991), and we (Marshall & Eccles, in press) could find little support in the literature for a conditioning view of sexual deviance. Similarly, scholarly examinations of the sociobioloical (i.e., evolutionary) accounts of rape have found them lacking in compelling evidence and based on dubious comparisons of so-called forced sex in infrahuman species and rape in humans (Fausto-Sterling, 1985; Gould, 1974). Nevertheless, within the field of treatment of sex offenders, theories emphasizing the preeminence of sexual motives have had a very significant influence. So much so, in fact, that most programs treating rapists have set about convincing these patients that, whether they recognize it or not, they are sexually attracted by the combination of a woman's nonconsent and their own use of force.

The evidence that we (Marshall & Barbaree, 1992) obtained from laboratory evaluations of 60 rapists indicated that only 30% of them were either equally or more aroused by depictions of coercive sex than they were by consenting sex. In this study, 26.8% of nonrapist, nondeviant males also displayed either equal or greater arousal to rape than consenting sex. Clearly, if we are to take these data seriously, rapists do not differ from nonrapists in terms of their arousal to forced sex. Therefore, it will be hard to maintain that the reason these men rape is because they are driven to commit their offenses as a result of being strongly sexually aroused by the prospect of forcing a noncompliant woman to have sex with them. If this is so, then other motives must be considered and our treatment focus must shift to dealing with these other motives.

However, obviously some rapists do display deviant arousal, and among these offenders there appear to be those who are sadistic. Quinsey, Chaplin, and Upfold (1984) found that the rapists in their study were more aroused by descriptions of rather vicious rapes than they were by consenting sex depictions. Subjects in this study included an overrepresentation of sadists, and Langevin, Paitich, and Russon (1985) found that only the sexual sadists among their rapists displayed deviant arousal. Unfortunately, Barbaree (1990) was unsuccessful in his attempts to modify the deviant arousal of a sadist. At present, the evidence concerning the efficacy of procedures for modifying sadistic sexual arousal is not encouraging. However, the procedures employed by Barbaree (1990) involved electric aversive therapy, and physical punishment may not be the most appropriate method to use with sadists. Masturbatory reconditioning (see Laws & Marshall, 1991, for a review of these techniques) may be more effective, and we (Johnston, Hudson, & Marshall, 1992) have recently demonstrated the value of one particular version of this approach, which combined the techniques of directed masturbation and satiation.

Lack of Empathy

Numerous studies have demonstrated that rapists score higher on psychopathy scales than do either nonoffenders or nonassaultive sexually anomalous offenders (Armentrout & Hauer, 1978; Langevin, 1983; Panton, 1978; Rada, 1978). Such measures reflect poor empathy, among other features. Clinicians (Becker, Skinner, & Abel, 1983; Maletzky, 1991; Salter, 1988) and theoreticians (Marshall & Barbaree, 1990b) also have pointed to specific deficits in empathy, but they have not provided data to support their claim as yet. Recent research in a treatment center in New Zealand (Jones et al., 1992) suggested that sex offenders may not lack general empathy (i.e., toward all people), but rather they may be specifically deficient in empathy toward either their own victims or to the victims of sexual assault in general. Obviously, as long as a rapist feels no empathy toward his victims he can continue to abuse them without feeling the distress that would prevent such abuse.

Empathy appears to involve four processes: recognition of the other person's feelings, the evocation in the observer of those same feelings, the recognition of these states by the observer, and the acceptance of the shared feelings. We have some tentative data suggesting that rapists may be deficient in the first process (i.e., in their ability to recognize emotions in others) (Hudson, Wales, Bakker, McLean, & Marshall, 1991). In any case, empathy training is essential, and although some attention has been given to this in the treatment of rapists, it has not been as extensive as seems necessary.

Maletzky (1991) outlined his empathy training program that involves a clear description of the known harmful effects on victims of sexual abuse, having the offender write a letter of apology to the victim explaining his responsibility for the offense, and having the offender read victim reports or view videotapes of victims describing their hurt. We add several features to this.

Initially, we have each member of the group of offenders describe all of the harmful effects he thinks are likely to follow from sexual assault. These are listed on a flip chart until all members of the group have described their estimated effects. Then the therapist adds, from a list of known effects, those missed by the group. In this process, we have the offenders distinguish the evident effects at the time of the assault, those expected over the subsequent several weeks and throughout the trial, and the long-term harm. The therapist also outlines the harm resulting to others; for instance, to the victim's present and possible future family, and to the offender's own family.

We then attempt to personalize the effects of sexual victimization. We do this because it has been shown (Bandura, Underwood, & Fromson, 1975) that the more another person is seen as different from ourselves, the easier it is to aggress against them. We attempt to do this in two ways. First, we either have one of the members of the group (if available) who was sexually abused as a child describe how this affected him, or we have the offender imagine that he is sexually assaulted by several tough fellow inmates in a prison, or we ask them to imagine it was their mother, sister, or daughter who was raped. Second, we have the group either watch an emotionally provocative videotape or listen to a similar story. An example of this type of scenario might be a film clip of the growth of a relationship between a boy and his pet where the pet is eventually killed and the boy's distress is graphically depicted. The offenders are asked to imagine they are the boy, and at the end of the story they are asked to describe how they felt. Invariably this produces some degree of upset in the offenders, and they are told that this is empathy: they recognized the boy's distress and they experienced his feelings. We then have them reexposed to the story and, immediately after it ends, we show them a videotape depicting a victim relating the dreadful impact on her or him of being sexually abused. If a videotape is not available, simply reading the offender a similar description, in a victim's own words, seems to have equally beneficial effects.

Finally, we not only have the offender write (but not send) a letter to the victim, we also have him write an imaginary letter from the victim. Both these letters are then presented to the treatment group for open discussion, at which time the offender may be challenged for presenting his and the victim's views in a self-serving way.

All of these procedures seem valuable, but specifically training offenders in the recognition of emotional states in both themselves and others has been all but neglected in the treatment of rapists. Exactly how we might go about this is not presently clear, but obviously a start must be made.

Inappropriate Attitudes

Related to the lack of empathy for victims are the attitudes held by rapists concerning the status of women and the use of aggression toward women, as well as their acceptance of a variety of rape myths and their distorted views of sexual relations between men and women (Segal & Stermac, 1990; Stermac, Segal, & Gillis, 1990). These beliefs, attitudes, and distortions, like lack of empathy, serve to both justify the acts of rape and to dehumanize women in a way that Bandura et al. (1975) have shown disinhibits aggression.

Attitude change procedures have not been very well developed in the treatment of sexual aggression, and have, for the most part, relied on some variant of cognitive restructuring and the use of role-play to facilitate group challenges (Murphy, 1990). These procedures run something like the following: (a) identifying the inappropriate beliefs, attitudes, or distortions, and clarifying the thoughts underpinning them; (b) demonstrating the role these views play in offending; (c) pointing out that these views are contradicted by the evidence; (d) pointing to the costs to the offender of holding these views; (e) having the offender role-play the expression of his current distorted views in interaction with a female; (f) offering (or having the group generate) alternative, more positive views; (g) demonstrating the value to the offender of these alternative views; and (h) having the offender role-play the expression of these changed views. There is, of course, an extensive body of experimental literature on attitude change procedures demonstrating clear benefits for particular approaches (Cialdini, Petty, & Cacioppo, 1981; McGuire, 1985). However, therapists working with sex offenders remain essentially ignorant of this literature.

Feminists have long claimed that the sexual assault of women satisfies power motives (Brownmiller, 1975; Clark & Lewis, 1977; Griffin, 1971; Medea & Thompson, 1974) and that rape may have the effect of extending the power of all males over females. Groth (1979) and Groth and Burgess (1977) claimed that rape serves to give power to a male who otherwise has little or none in his life. In Groth's view, rapists lack confidence in their masculinity and consequently feel angry toward women whom they blame for their low self-confidence and for the lack of power and control they feel over their lives. In attempting to express this anger through rape, these men engage in unnecessary aggression during their assaults, and they attempt to humiliate and degrade their victims. Indeed, from this perspective, the sexual aspects of rape are seen simply as one means of humiliating the victim. Darke (1990) pointed out that because rapists appear to be sexually prudish (Marshall, Christie, & Lanthier,

1979), forcing their victims into engaging in various sexual acts can be construed as attempts by the rapist to humiliate the woman rather than (or perhaps in addition to) satisfying eccentric sexual desires.

There are obviously a number of intertwined features of this general view. Rapists should lack power or control in their lives and they should lack confidence in their masculinity. If this is so, then they should also have low self-esteem. Rapes should be characterized by aggression and various acts that are meant to humiliate the victim. Rapists should also be hostile toward women, and anger should be a precipitant in most rapes.

Although there are few studies directly testing hypotheses concerning the experience of power and control in rapists' lives, there are studies addressing their sense of masculinity and self-esteem, and these features may be seen as reciprocally related to the presence of power and control. Revitch (1965) and Groth (1979) both found rapists to be characterized by insecurities about their masculinity. We (Marshall & Marshall, 1981; Marshall & Turner, 1985) found that rapists tend to score either excessively low or excessively high (almost two standard deviations above or below the mean) on a measure of social self-esteem (Lawson, Marshall, & McGrath, 1979). For those rapists who scored well above the mean of nonoffenders, we had prison staff who were well acquainted with them provide their evaluations of the offenders using the same scale. These staff reported that high-scoring offenders were low in self-esteem, but compensated for that with a bravado style that reflected a hyperidentification with the traditional male role. These were the more difficult rapists to work with, at least in part because they needed constant reassurance whenever we addressed any problem, even their low self-esteem.

There is clear evidence that rapists use more aggression in the commission of their offenses than is necessary to coerce a woman into having vaginal intercourse with them (Amir, 1971; Christie, Marshall, & Lanthier, 1979; Groth & Burgess, 1977; Quinsey, Chaplin, & Varney, 1981). We (Christie et al., 1979) perused victim reports, police reports, court records, and medical examinations of the victims of rape and found clear evidence of physical aggression and injuries (apart from vaginal damage) in over 75% of the offenses. Of these particular victims, over 50% required comprehensive medical attention for their injuries. Darke (1990) and Darke, Marshall, and Earls (1982) examined victim reports and descriptions by the offenders of their intentions when raping a woman, as well as reports of the offenders' actual behavior during rapes. They found that in over 60% of cases there was a clear intent to humiliate and degrade the victim. These observations—that excessive aggression and attempts to humiliate victims characterize rape—have typically been taken to indicate that rapists are hostile toward women, or perhaps hostile in general.

Stille, Malamuth, and Schallow (1987) reported that, among nonoffender males, the likelihood that they would use force in a sexual encounter was dependent on the degree of hostility they felt toward women. In evaluating various aspects of sex offenders, Marshall and Seidman (1992) found that rapists expressed specific hostility toward women. Rada, Kellner, Laws, and Winslow (1978) not only found that rapists scored high on a measure of general hostility, but these hostility scores were predictive of the degree of violence in their rapes. Related to these issues is the consistent observation that rapes are frequently preceded by an incident where the offender was angered by a woman (Day, Miner, Nafpaktisi, & Murphy, 1987). Also, Garlic (1991), in an examination of deficiencies in intimacy, found that rapists blamed women for their feelings of loneliness; no doubt this is part of their general anger or hostility toward women. In a similar vein, Yates, Barbaree, and Marshall (1984) found that nonoffender males angered by a woman prior to assessment showed greater sexual arousal to rape than to consenting sex, whereas nonangered males displayed the opposite profile (i.e., lower arousal to rape than to consenting sex).

Obviously the related and intertwined issues of power, anger, hostility, aggression, and attempts to humiliate victims, as well as low self-esteem and a lack of confidence in their masculinity, among rapists are all issues that must be addressed in treatment. Although these issues are mentioned repeatedly in the literature by clinicians and theoreticians alike, no one has proposed a set of procedures for modifying these problematic features of rapists, and yet they seem very much to be the core factors in the sexual assault of women. Anger, it is true, has been given attention in treatment, and, for the most part, therapists have followed Novaco's (1975) approach. There is every reason to suppose that this will reduce anger and provide effective controls over its expression. However, it is not at all clear that such changes will affect hostility, particularly that directed toward women, or have any effect on self-confidence or feelings of power and control. All of these need to be targeted specifically in treating rapists.

In a series of studies (Marshall & Christie, 1982; Marshall, Christie, Lanthier, & Cruchley, 1982; Marshall & Khana, 1979), effective procedures were developed to enhance self-esteem. The client is assisted in producing a list of 10 features of himself that are positive and about which he should be proud. This is not always easy, but it can be achieved with determined effort. These features are then written on pocket-sized cards that the client carries at all times. He reads each of these 10 positive statements at least three times each day in circumstances where he either feels positive/happy or where he is about to engage in a positive experience. Similarly, the client is assisted in scheduling an increase in positive or rewarding experiences (particularly social experiences) in his daily life. The combination of increased enjoyment and repetitions of positive self-statements gradually leads to an enhancement of self-confidence.

Skill training of various kinds, depending on the offender's particular deficits (e.g., conversational skills, assertiveness, job-search-and-secure skills, self-care, financial management, hobby pursuits, etc.), will also enhance both self-confidence and feelings of power and control in the lives of these offenders, as well as increasing their daily enjoyment. In assertiveness training, it is particularly important with rapists to clarify the distinction (and the costs–benefits ratio) between degrees of aggression and appropriate assertiveness. Increases in control over their lives and enhanced self-respect should reduce general and specific hostility, but one cannot simply assume that to be the case. Therefore, we need to deal directly with hostility. Here the procedures suggested earlier for attitude change would seem to be appropriate, although specific procedures for reducing hostility have not been developed yet.

Intimacy

I (Marshall, 1989, 1991) claimed that intimacy is not only deficient in rapists, but is importantly related to their offensive behavior. A desire for intimacy (albeit inappropriately expressed) is said to be part of the multiply motivated basis for sexual assault. It has been observed that intimacy's reciprocal—emotional loneliness—leads to a marked increase in aggression of various kinds (Check, Perlman, & Malamuth, 1985). Evidence suggesting that adult intimacy derived primarily from the effectiveness or otherwise of child–parent attachments (Marshall, Hudson, & Hodkinson, in press) also was reviewed.

In some degree of confirmation of these claims, it has been found that rapists are severely deficient in intimacy (Garlic, 1991; Marshall & Seidman, 1992) and that they blame women for this deficit (Garlic, 1991). Rapists adopt the position that they do not want love or intimacy (Marshall & Seidman, 1992). The latter position (i.e., avoidance of intimacy) has been shown to be one consequence of poor child–parent attachments, particularly when the parent has rejected the child (Ainsworth, Blehar, Waters, & Wall, 1978). Although Marshall, Payne, Barbaree, and Eccles (1991) found evidence of rejection in the child–parent bonds of exhibitionists, they have not extended this research to rapists yet. Nevertheless, given other evidence regarding their childhood experiences (Marshall & Barbaree, 1990b), rapists presumably will be shown to have had disruptive child–parent bonds.

Two things need to be addressed in treatment to correct the problems associated with intimacy. An exploration of the attitudes of rapists toward their parents, particularly of their childhood experiences of rejection, needs to be a focus in treatment to assist the offenders to resolve these issues so that they can begin to develop intimacy skills. No doubt disruptive child–parent bonds are related to the lack of self-confidence evident in rapists, hence helping them resolve these conflicts may contribute to an enhancement of their sense of self-worth; indeed, it may be necessary to do this before working on their self-esteem directly.

The enhancement of intimacy skills can only be approached once the offender has overcome his fear of intimacy and expresses a desire to achieve intimacy. Standard procedures exist to overcome various fears (Marshall &

Segal, 1988), and these can readily be adapted to reducing fear of intimacy. A desire for intimacy may be instilled by exploring the costs of emotional loneliness and the benefits derived from achieving intimacy (Marshall, 1991). However, in a more general sense, most of the procedures used to enhance relationship fulfillment (Jacobson & Dallas, 1981) are relevant to improving intimacy skills. Most of these procedures not only produce enhanced intimacy, but they can be expected to facilitate the resolution of other problems displayed by rapists. For instance, conflict resolution skills are important to intimacy and to avoid one of the main precursors of sexual offending (Marques & Nelson, 1989). Similarly, dating skills and communication skills not only make the attainment of intimacy possible and enhance whatever level already exists, they also help reduce other social interactive problems. Certainly the constructive use of shared leisure activities is one of the most effective paths to intimacy, and it helps to reduce the risk to relapse by having these men avoid boredom.

General Criminal Lifestyle

It has been consistently observed that rapists are more generally criminal (Christie et al., 1979; Gebhard, Gagnon, Pomeroy, & Christensen, 1965; Langevin, 1983; Rada, 1978) in their behavior, and that they are impulsive and psychopathic in disposition (see Langevin 1983, for a summary of this evidence). Marshall, Turner, and Barbaree (1989) showed that men with these features can be effectively changed by procedures aimed at reducing their identification with the criminal subculture, enhancing their empathy and self-confidence, and helping them recognize both the costs of impulsive actions and the corresponding benefits of more thoughtfully guided behavior.

Essentially, the treatment efforts aimed at changing the criminal disposition of rapists present a cost–benefit analysis of remaining a criminal, followed by identifying and challenging their present procriminal views, and suggesting more profitable attitudes. Of course, throughout all phases of treatment, procriminal attitudes are identified and challenged, but also specific focus is placed on these issues. Similar approaches (identifying and challenging their views, cost–benefit analyses, and offering alternative strategies) are used when attempting to reduce impulsiveness, and the empathy training outlined earlier is the approach used to overcome psychopathic tendencies.

Alcohol Abuse

Alcohol use has been implicated in well over 70% of sexual assaults against adult women (Christie et al., 1979; Langevin, 1983; Rada, 1978). It has been shown that alcohol intoxication releases inhibitions over arousal to rape in nonoffender males (Barbaree, Marshall, Yates, & Lightfoot, 1983). Treatment aims in this respect are, for most offenders, to get them to learn to control their use of intoxicants and to develop strategies so that they are not at risk when intoxicated (e.g., always drink with someone who is aware of the problem). However, some offenders may abuse alcohol (or some other drug) so seriously that an abstinence program is the only sensible route. In these cases, the offender is referred to specialized drug/alcohol programs that are available to patients in both prison and community settings. When such a specialized program is not available as a referral possibility, the need to design and implement one, although absolutely essential, places special burdens on treatment staff. However, relapse prevention approaches, which are familiar to therapists dealing with sex offenders, present an appropriate program for alcohol or drug use.

General Issues

None of the above remarks is meant to dismiss all the other features that presently characterize treatment attempts with rapists. Certainly, I have intended to diminish the present importance placed on deviant sexuality in treatment, but procedures to deal with denial, minimization, and acceptance of responsibility for offending (Barbaree, 1991) are essential to effective treatment as are stress management and treatment of social problems. Perhaps most important of all is the attempt to instill the principles and practices of relapse prevention, and to provide the external supervision necessary on discharge from treatment to ensure that these practices are carried out by the rapists (Pithers, 1990).

In addition to the specific treatment components, it is necessary to develop a more general plan for treating rapists to maximize likely effectiveness. Marshall, Eccles, & Barnes (1992) envisaged an overall treatment approach with sex offenders, within which rapists are definitely meant to be included. This plan involves three tiers of treatment, and is approximately in place (at least in its skeletal structure) in the Canadian Penitentiary Services system. Tier 1 is provided in maximum or medium security institutions and involves extensive treatment. Most, but not yet all, of the above mentioned procedures are included in Tier 1 treatment, which is conducted in groups of 12–14 offenders and one or two therapists meeting for 3 hours each working day for approximately 5 months. If reassessment reveals that the offender has made the required progress, he is moved on to Tier 2 or he may go directly to Tier 3. If he has not made sufficient progress, he will be recycled through whatever components of Tier 1 are deemed necessary. Tier 2 involves less extensive treatment than Tier 1, and focuses primarily on modifying cognitive factors and developing release and relapse prevention plans. The Tier 2 program, which not only includes graduates from Tier 1 but also those offenders whose criminal history reveals very limited involvement in sex offending and whose assessment results indicate few problems, is conducted in a minimum security institution. Tier 3 involves a move to the community, which may be to a halfway house or full release, but involves both treatment in a community program and relapse prevention supervision.

This comprehensive program, involving extensive and continuous treatment and gradual release with supervision, is ideally suited to dealing with rapists. However, given that I have suggested an extensive revision and reemphasis on certain elements of present programs, it may be that we have to offer separate programs for child molesters and rapists. Up to now, our programs (Barbaree & Marshall, in press; Marshall & Eccles, 1991) have included mixed groups of sex offenders. Although this has worked well from the viewpoint of actually operating the program, and has, indeed, had beneficial effects on the attitudes of superiority often displayed by rapists toward other sex offenders, it may be difficult to attend to all the changes suggested in treating rapists while still effectively dealing with the child molesters within the same group. On the other hand, rapists tend to encourage one another to believe that rape is not all that bad (it does after all, so they tell one another, involve an adult woman rather than a male or a child), so the gains derived from having them in a separate group from other sex offenders may be offset by the difficulties their cohesiveness presents to therapists. Only practice will answer this question.

I believe the utilization of the above program will produce far greater benefits in the rehabilitation of rapists than have been achieved heretofore. However, we will have to wait considerable time for a proper evaluation to be available. In the meantime, we can make greater research efforts to more precisely specify the problems that beset those men who sexually assault adult females. However, no research or treatment efforts directed toward changing rapists will have any impact on the sociocultural features that encourage the subjugation of women and make them vulnerable to assaults of various kinds. We must take to heart what we know of the factors that cause rape and work toward changing those social and cultural structures that institutionalize the oppression of women, and we must personally present models to others of gender egalitarian behavior if the intolerably high frequency of sexual assault is to be reduced. Therapists and researchers often seem to believe that their social contribution ends with treating offenders or publishing research; I believe it does not. We, along with those who treat victims, know better than almost anyone else the extent and nature of sexual assaults. Therefore, it falls on us to publicly advocate for changes that will make life as free from fear for women and children as it is for most men.

REFERENCES

Abel, G. G., Becker, J. V., Cunningham-Rathner, J., Mittelman, M. S., & Rouleau, J. L. (1988). Multiple paraphilic diagnoses among sex offenders. *Bulletin of the American Academy of Psychiatry and the Law, 16,* 153–168.
Abel, G. G., Becker, J. V., & Skinner, L. J. (1986). Behavioral approaches to

treatment of the violent sex offender. In L. H. Roth (Ed.), *Clinical treatment of the violent person* (pp. 100–123). New York: Guilford.

Abel, G. G., Blanchard, E. B., & Becker, J. V. (1976). Psychological treatment of rapists. In M. J. Walker & S. L. Brodsky (Eds.), *Sexual assault: The victim and the rapist* (pp. 99–115). Lexington, MA: D. C. Heath.

Abel, G. G., & Rouleau, J. L. (1990). The nature and extent of sexual assault. In W. L. Marshall, D. R. Laws, & H. E. Barbaree (Eds.), *Handbook of sexual assault: Issues, theories, and treatment of the offender* (pp. 9–21). New York: Plenum.

Ainsworth, M. D. S., Blehar, M. C., Waters, E., & Walls, S. (1978). *Patterns of attachment: A psychological study of the strange situation.* Hillsdale, NJ: Lawrence Erlbaum.

Amir, M. (1971). *Patterns in forcible rape.* Chicago: University of Chicago Press.

Armentrout, J. A., & Hauer, A. I. (1978). MMPIs of rapists of adults, rapists of children, and nonrapist sex offenders. *Journal of Clinical Psychology, 34,* 330–332.

Bandura, A., Underwood, B., & Fromson, M. E. (1975). Disinhibition of aggression through diffusion of responsibility and dehumanization of victims. *Journal of Research in Personality, 9,* 253–269.

Barbaree, H. E. (1990). Stimulus control of sexual arousal: Its role in sexual assault. In W. L. Marshall, D. R. Laws, & H. E. Barbaree (Eds.), *Handbook of sexual assault: Issues, theories, and treatment of the offender* (pp. 115–142). New York: Plenum.

Barbaree, H. E. (1991). Denial and minimization among sex offenders: Assessment and treatment outcome. *Forum on Corrections Research, 3,* 30–33.

Barbaree, H. E., Marshall, W. L., Yates, E., & Lightfoot, L. (1983). Alcohol intoxication and deviant sexual arousal in male social drinkers. *Behavior Research and Therapy, 21,* 365–373.

Barbaree, H. E., & Marshall, W. L. (in press). Treatment of the sexual offender. In R. M. Wettstein (Ed.). *Treatment of the Mentally Disordered Offender.* New York: Guilford Press.

Baxter, D. J., Barbaree, H. E., & Marshall, W. L. (1986). Sexual responses to consenting and forced sex in a large sample of rapists and nonrapists. *Behavior Research and Therapy, 24,* 513–520.

Becker, J. V., Skinner, L. J., & Abel, G. G. (1983). Sequelae of sexual assault: The survivor's perspective. In J. G. Greer & I. R. Stewart (Eds.), *The sexual aggressor: Current perspectives on treatment* (pp. 240–266). New York: Van Nostrand Reinhold.

Berlin, F. S., & Meinecke, C. F. (1981). Treatment of sex offenders with antiandrogenic medication: Conceptualization, review of treatment modalities and preliminary findings. *American Journal of Psychiatry, 138,* 601–607.

Bianchi, M. D. (1990). Floxetine treatment of exhibitionism. *American Journal of Psychiatry, 147,* 1089–1090.

Bloom, J. D., Bradford, J. M. W., & Kofoed, L. (1988). An overview of psychiatric treatment approaches to three different groups. *Hospital and Community Psychiatry, 39,* 151–158.

Bond, I., & Evans, D. (1967). Avoidance therapy: Its use in two cases of underwear fetishism. *Canadian Medical Association Journal, 96,* 1160–1162.

Bradford, J. M. W. (1990). The antiandrogen and hormonal treatment of sex offenders. In W. L. Marshall, D. R. Laws, & H. E. Barbaree (Eds.), *Handbook of sexual assault: Issues, theories, and treatment of the offender* (pp. 297–310). New York: Plenum.

Bradford, J. M. W., & Pawlak, A. (1987). Sadistic homosexual pedophilia: Treatment with cyproterone acetate. A single case study. *Canadian Journal of Psychiatry, 32,* 22–31.

Bradford, J. M. W., & Pawlak, A. (in press). Double-blind placebo crossover study of cyproterone acetate in the treatment of sexual deviation—Phase I. *Archives of Sexual Behavior.*

Brownmiller, S. (1975). *Against our will: Men, women, and rape.* New York: Bantam Books.

Cesnik, J. A., & Coleman, E. (1989). Use of lithium carbonate in the treatment of autoerotic asphyxia. *American Journal of Psychotherapy, 63,* 277–286.

Check, J. V. P., Perlman, D., & Malamuth, N. M. (1985). Loneliness and aggressive behavior. *Journal of Social and Personal Relationships, 2,* 243–252.

Christie, M. M., Marshall, W. L., & Lanthier, R. D. (1979). *A descriptive study of incarcerated rapists and pedophiles.* Report to the Solicitor General of Canada, Ottawa.

Cialdini, R. B., Petty, R. E., & Cacioppo, J. T. (1981). Attitude and attitude change. *Annual Review of Psychology, 32,* 357–404.

Clark, L., & Lewis, D. (1977). *Rape: The price of coercive sexuality.* Toronto: Women's Educational Press.

Cooper, A. J. (1987a). Medroxyprogesterone acetate (MPA) treatment of sexually acting out in men suffering from dementia. *Journal of Clinical Psychiatry, 48,* 368–370.

Cooper, A. J. (1987b). Sadistic homosexual pedophilia treatment with cyproterone acetate. *Canadian Journal of Psychiatry, 32,* 738–740.

Cordoba, O. A., & Chapel, J. L. (1983). Medroxyprogesterone acetate antiandrogen treatment of hypersexuality in a pedophilic sex offender. *American Journal of Psychiatry, 140,* 1036–1039.

Darke, J. L. (1990). Sexual aggression: Achieving power through humiliation. In W. L. Marshall, D. R. Laws, & H. E. Barbaree (Eds.), *Handbook of sexual assault: Issues, theories, and treatment of the offender* (pp. 55–72). New York: Plenum.

Darke, J. L., Marshall, W. L., & Earls, C. M. (1982, April). *Humiliation and rape: A preliminary inquiry.* Fourth National Conference on the Evaluation and Treatment of Sexual Aggressors, Denver, Colorado.

Davidson, P. (1984, March). *Outcome data for a penitentiary-based treatment program for sex offenders.* Paper presented at the Conference on the Assessment and Treatment of the Sex Offender, Kingston, Ontario.

Day, D. M., Miner, M. H., Nafpaktitis, M. K., & Murphy, J. F. (1987). *Development of a situational competency for sex offenders.* Unpublished transcript.

Fausto-Sterling, A. (1985). *Myths of gender: Biological theories about women and men.* New York: Basic Books.

Fedoroff, J. P. (1988). Buspirone hydrochloride in the treatment of transvestic fetishism. *Journal of Clinical Psychiatry, 49,* 408–409.

Freund, K. (1990). Courtship disorder. In W. L. Marshall, D. R. Laws, & H. E. Barbaree (Eds.), *Handbook of sexual assault: Issues, theories, and treatment of the offender* (pp. 195–207). New York: Plenum.

Freund, K., & Blanchard, R. (1986). The concept of courtship disorder. *Journal of Sex & Marital Therapy, 12,* 79–92.

Furby, L., Weinrott, M. R., & Blackshaw, L. (1989). Sex offender recidivism: A review. *Psychological Bulletin, 105,* 3–30.

Gagne, P. (1981). Treatment of sex offenders with medroxyprogesterone acetate. *American Journal of Psychiatry, 138,* 644–646.

Garlic, Y. (1991). *Intimacy failure, loneliness and the attribution of blame in sexual offending.* Unpublished masters thesis, University of London.

Gebhard, P., Gagnon, J., Pomeroy, W., & Christensen, C. (1965). *Sex offenders: An analysis of types.* New York: Harper & Row.

Gould, S. J. (1974). *Ever since Darwin: Reflections in natural history.* New York: W. W. Norton.

Griffin, S. (1971). Rape: The all-American crime. *Ramparts, 10,* 26–35.

Groth, A. N. (1979). *Men who rape: The psychology of the offender.* New York: Plenum.

Groth, A. N., & Burgess, A. W. (1977). Rape: A sexual deviation. *American Journal of Orthopsychiatry, 47,* 400–406.

Heim, N. (1981). Sexual behavior of castrated sex offenders. *Archives of Sexual Behavior, 10,* 11–19.

Heim, N., & Hursch, C. J. (1979). Castration for sex offenders: Treatment or punishment? A review and critique of recent European literature. *Archives of Sexual Behavior, 8,* 281–304.

Hudson, S. M., Wales, D., Bakker, L. W., McLean, A., & Marshall, W. L. (1991). *Recognition of emotional expression by male prisoners.* Unpublished manuscript.

Jacobson, N. S., & Dallas, M. (1981). Helping married couples improve their relationships. In W. E. Craighead, A. E. Kazdin, & M. J. Mahoney (Eds.), *Behavior modification: Principles, issues and applications* (2nd ed., pp. 379–398). Boston: Houghton Mifflin.

Johnston, P., Hudson, S. M., & Marshall, W. L. (1992). The effects of masturbatory reconditioning with nonfamilial child molesters. *Behaviour Research and Therapy, 30,* 559–561.

Jones, R., Hudson, S. M., & Marshall, W. L. (1992). *Empathy in child molesters.* Unpublished manuscript.

Kafka, M. P. (1991). Successful antidepressant treatment of nonparaphilic sexual addictions and paraphilias in men. *Journal of Clinical Psychiatry, 52,* 60–65.

Knopp, F. H. (1984). *Retraining adult sex offenders: Methods and models.* Syracuse, NY: Safer Society Press.

Langevin, R. (1983). *Sexual strands: Understanding and treating sexual anomalies in men.* Hillsdale, NJ: Lawrence Erlbaum.

Langevin, R., Paitich, D., & Russon, A. (1985). Are rapists sexually anomalous, aggressive, or both? In R. Langevin (Ed.), *Erotic preference, gender identity, and aggression in men: New research studies* (pp. 13–38). Hillsdale, NJ: Lawrence Erlbaum.

Laschet, U., & Laschet, L. (1975). Antiandrogens in the treatment of sexual deviations of men. *Journal of Steroid Biochemistry, 6,* 821–826.

Laws, D. R., & Marshall, W. L. (1990). A conditioning theory of the etiology and maintenance of deviant sexual preference and behavior. In W. L. Marshall, D. R. Laws, & H. E. Barbaree (Eds.), *Handbook of sexual assault: Issues, theories, and treatment of the offender* (pp. 209–229). New York: Plenum.

Laws, D. R., & Marshall, W. L. (1991). Masturbatory reconditioning with sexual deviates: An evaluative review. *Advances in Behaviour Research and Therapy, 13,* 13–25.

Lawson, J. S., Marshall, W. L., & McGrath, P. (1979). The Social Self-Esteem Inventory. *Educational and Psychological Measurement, 39,* 803–811.

Leger, G. (1989). Research on sex offenders: Regional Treatment Centre (Ontario). *Forum on Corrections Research, 1,* 21.

Maletzky, B. M. (1991). *Treating the sex offender.* Newbury Park, CA: Sage.

Marques, J. K. (1988). *The Sex Offender Treatment and Evaluation Project: First report to the legislature in response to PC1365.* Sacramento, CA: California State Department of Mental Health.

Marques, J. K., & Nelson, C. (1989). Elements of high-risk situations for sex offenders. In D. R. Laws (Ed.), *Relapse prevention with sex offenders* (pp. 35–46). New York: Guilford.

Marshall, W. L. (1971). A combined treatment method for certain sexual deviations. *Behaviour Research and Therapy, 9,* 292–294.

Marshall, W. L. (1989). Intimacy, loneliness and sexual offenders. *Behaviour Research and Therapy, 27,* 491–503.

Marshall, W. L. (1991, November). *Loneliness and intimacy issues among sex offenders.* Paper presented at the 10th Annual Research and Treatment Conference of the Association for the Treatment of Sexual Abusers, Fort Worth, Texas.

Marshall, W. L., & Barbaree, H. E. (1987). A manual of the treatment of child molesters. *Social and Behavioral Sciences Documents, 17,* 57.

Marshall, W. L., & Barbaree, H. E. (1988). The long-term evaluation of a behavioral treatment program for child molesters. *Behavioural Research and Therapy, 26,* 499–511.

Marshall, W. L., & Barbaree, H. E. (1990a). Outcome of comprehensive cognitive–behavioral treatment programs. In W. L. Marshall, D. R. Laws, & H. E. Barbaree (Eds.), *Handbook of sexual assault: Issues, theories, and treatment of the offender* (pp. 363–385). New York: Plenum.

Marshall, W. L., & Barbaree, H. E. (1990b). An integrated theory of the etiology of sexual offending. In W. L. Marshall, D. R. Laws, & H. E. Barbaree (Eds.), *Handbook of sexual assault: Issues, theories, and treatment of the offender* (pp. 257–275). New York: Plenum.

Marshall, W. L., & Barbaree, H. E. (1992). *Erectile preference profiles among rapists and nonrapists.* Unpublished manuscript.

Marshall, W. L., Barbaree, H. E., Eccles, A., & Barbaree, H. E. (1991). Early onset and deviant sexuality in child molesters. *Journal of Interpersonal Violence, 6,* 323–336.

Marshall, W. L., Barbaree, H. E., Laws, D. R., & Baxter, D. (1986, September). *Rapists do not have deviant sexual preferences: Large scale studies from Canada and California.* Paper presented at the 12th Annual Meeting of the International Academy of Sex Research, Amsterdam.

Marshall, W. L., & Christie, M. M. (1982). The enhancement of social self-esteem. *Canadian Counsellor, 16,* 82–89.

Marshall, W. L., Christie, M. M., & Lanthier, R. D. (1979). *Social competence, sexual experience and attitudes to sex in incarcerated rapists and pedophiles.* Report to the Solicitor General of Canada, Ottawa.

Marshall, W. L., Christie, M. M., Lanthier, R. D., & Cruchley, J. (1982). The nature of the reinforcer in the enhancement of social self-esteem. *Canadian Counsellor, 16,* 90–96.

Marshall, W. L., Earls, C. M., Segal, Z. V., & Darke, J. L. (1983). A behavioral program for the assessment and treatment of sexual aggressors. In K. Craig, & R. McMahon (Eds.), *Advances in clinical behavior therapy* (pp. 148–174). New York: Brunner/Mazel.

Marshall, W. L., Eccles, A., & Barbaree, H. E. (1991). Issues in clinical practice with sex offenders. *Journal of Interpersonal Violence, 6,* 68–93.

Marshall, W. L., & Eccles, A. (1992). *A three-tier approach to the rehabilitation of incarcerated sex offenders.* Unpublished manuscript.

Marshall, W. L., & Eccles, A. (in press). Pavlovian conditioning processes in adolescent sex offenders. In H. E. Barbaree, W. L. Marshall, & S. M. Hudson (Eds.), *The assessment and treatment of the juvenile sex offender.* New York: Guilford.

Marshall, W. L., Hudson, S. M., & Hodkinson, S. (in press). The importance of attachment bonds in the development of juvenile sex offending. In H. D. Barbaree, W. L. Marshall, & S. M. Hudson (Eds.), *The assessment and treatment of the juvenile sex offender.* New York: Guilford.

Marshall, W. L., Hudson, S. M., & Ward, T. (1992). Sexual deviance. In P. H. Wilson (Ed.), *Principles and practice of relapse prevention* (pp. 235–254). New York: Guilford.

Marshall, W. L., Jones, R., Ward, T., Johnston, P., & Barbaree, H. E. (1991). Treatment outcome with sex offenders. *Clinical Psychology Review, 11,* 465–485.

Marshall, W. L., & Marshall, P. (1981). *Social functioning in penitentiary inmates.* Unpublished manuscript.

Marshall, W. L., & Khana, A. (1979). *Programmed increases in social behavior and its effect on social self-esteem.* Unpublished manuscript.

Marshall, W. L., Payne, K., Barbaree, H. E., & Eccles, A. (1991). Exhibitionists: sexual preferences for exposing. *Behaviour Research and Therapy, 29,* 37–40.

Marshall, W. L., & Segal, Z. V. (1988). Behavior therapy. In G. C. Last & M. Hersen (Eds.), *Handbook of anxiety disorders* (pp. 338–361). New York: Pergamon.

Marshall, W. L., & Seidman, B. (1992). *Intimacy and emotional loneliness in various groups of sex offenders and nonoffenders.* Unpublished manuscript.

Marshall, W. L., & Turner, B. A. (1985). *Life skills training of penitentiary inmates in Canada.* Report to the Solicitor General of Canada, Ottawa.

Marshall, W. L., Turner, B. A., & Barbaree, H. E. (1989). An evaluation of Life Skills Training for penitentiary inmates. *Journal of Offender Counselling, Services & Rehabilitation, 14,* 41–59.

Marshall, W. L., Ward, T., Johnston, P., Jones, R., & Barbaree, H. E. (1991). An optimistic evaluation of treatment outcome with sex offenders. *Violence Update, March,* 1–8.

Marshall, W. L., & Williams, S. (1975). A behavioral approach to the modification of rape. *Quarterly Bulletin of the British Association for Behavioural Psychotherapy, 4,* 78.

Massachusetts Post Audit Bureau. (1979). *Report of the Committee on Post Audit and Oversight.* Bridgewater, MA: Author.

McGuire, W. J. (1985). The nature of attitude and attitude change. In G. Lindzey & E. Aronson (Eds.), *Handbook of social psychology* (3rd ed., vol. 2, pp. 45–76). New York: Random House.

Medea, A., & Thompson, K. (1974). *Against rape: A survival manual for women.* New York: Farrar, Straus & Giroux.

Money, J. (1972). The therapeutic use of androgen-depleting hormone. *International Psychiatry Clinic, 8,* 165–174.

Murphy, W. D. (1990). Assessment and modification of cognitive distortions in sex offenders. In W. L. Marshall, D. R. Laws, & H. E. Barbaree (Eds.), *Handbook of sexual assault: Issues, theories, and treatment of the offender* (pp. 331–342). New York: Plenum.

Novaco, R. W. (1975). *Anger control: The development and evaluation of an experimental treatment.* Lexington, MA: D. C. Heath.

Pacht, A. R., Halleck, S. L., & Ehrmann, J. C. (1962). Diagnosis and treatment of the sexual offender: A nine year study. *American Journal of Psychiatry, 118,* 802–808.

Panton, J. H. (1978). Personality differences appearing between rapists of adults, rapists of children and non-violent sexual molesters of female children. *Research Communication in Psychology, Psychiatry, and Behavior, 3,* 385–393.

Pearse, T. (1988). Obsessive–compulsive disorder: A treatment review. *Journal of Clinical Psychiatry, 49,* 48–55.

Pearson, H. J. (1990). Paraphilias, impulse control and serotonin. *Journal of Clinical Psychopharmacology, 10,* 133–134.

Pearson, H. J., Marshall, W. L., Barbaree, H. E., & Southmayd, S. E. (in press). Treatment of a compulsive paraphiliac with buspirone. *Annals of Sex Research.*

Peters, J. J., Institute. (1980). *A ten-year follow-up of sex offender recidivism.* Philadelphia: Author.

Pithers, W. D. (1990). Relapse prevention with sexual aggressors: A method for maintaining therapeutic gain and enhancing external supervision. In W. L. Marshall, D. R. Laws, & H. E. Barbaree (Eds.), *Handbook of sexual assault: Issues, theories, and treatment of the offender* (pp. 343–361). New York: Plenum.

Pithers, W. D., & Cumming, G. F. (1989). Can relapses be prevented? Initial outcome data from the Vermont Treatment Program for Sexual Aggressors. In D. R. Laws (Ed.), *Relapse prevention with sex offenders* (pp. 313–325). New York: Guilford.

Pithers, W. D., Martin, G. R., & Cumming, G. F. (1989). Vermont Treatment Program for Sexual Aggressors. In D. R. Laws (Ed.), *Relapse prevention with sex offenders* (pp. 292–310). New York: Guilford.

Prendergast, W. E. (1978). *RORE: Re-education of attitudes and repressed emotions.* Avenell, NJ: Adult Diagnostic and Treatment Centre Intensive Group Therapy Program.

Quinsey, V. L. (1984). Sexual aggression: Studies of offenders against women. In D. Weisstub (Ed.), *Law and mental health: International perspectives* (vol. 1, pp. 84–121). New York: Pergamon.

Quinsey, V. L., Chaplin, T. C., & Upfold, D. (1984). Sexual arousal to nonsexual violence and sadomasochistic themes among rapists and non-sex offenders. *Journal of Consulting and Clinical Psychology, 52,* 651–657.

Quinsey, V. L., Chaplin, T. C., & Varney, G. (1981). A comparison of rapists' and non-sex offenders' sexual preferences for mutually consenting sex, rape, and physical abuse of women. *Behavioral Assessment, 3,* 127–135.

Quinsey, V. L., & Earls, C. M. (1990). The modification of sexual preferences. In W. L. Marshall, D. R. Laws, & H. E. Barbaree (Eds.), *Handbook of sexual assault: Issues, theories, and treatment of the offender* (pp. 279–295). New York: Plenum.

Rada, R. T. (1978). *Clinical aspects of the rapist.* New York: Grune & Stratton.

Rada, R. T., Kellner, R., Laws, D. R., & Winslow, W. W. (1978). Drinking, alcoholism, and the mentally disordered sex offender. *Bulletin of the American Academy of Psychiatry and the Law, 6,* 296–300.

Revitch, E. (1965). Sex murder and the potential sex murderer. *Diseases of the Nervous System, 26,* 640–646.

Rice, M. E., Harris, G. T, & Quinsey, V. L. (1991). Evaluation of an institution-based treatment program for child molesters. *Canadian Journal of Program Evaluation, 6,* 111–129.

Russell, D. E. H. (1984). *Sexual exploitation: Rape, child sexual abuse and workplace harassment.* Newbury Park, CA: Sage.

Salter, A. C. (1988). *Treating child sex offenders and victims: A practical guide.* Newbury Park, CA: Sage.

Saylor, M. (1979, September). *A guided self-help approach to treatment of the habitual sexual offender.* Paper presented at the 12th Cropwood Conference, Cambridge, England.

Segal, Z. V., & Stermac, L. E. (1990). The role of cognition in sexual assault. In W. L. Marshall, D. R. Laws, & H. E. Barbaree (Eds.), *Handbook of sexual assault: Issues, theories, and treatment of the offender* (pp. 161–174). New York: Plenum.

Stermac, L. E., Segal, Z. V., & Gillis, R. (1990). Social and cultural factors in sexual assault. In W. L. Marshall, D. R. Laws, & H. E. Barbaree (Eds.), *Handbook of sexual assault: Issues, theories, and treatment of the offender* (pp. 143–159). New York: Plenum.

Stille, R. G., Malamuth, N., & Schallow, J. R. (1987, August). *Prediction of rape proclivity by rape myth attitudes, and hostility toward women.* Paper presented at the Annual Meeting of the American Psychological Association, New York.

Sturup, G. K. (1968). Treatment of sexual offenders in Herstedvester, Denmark: The rapists. *Acta Psychiatrica Scandinavica, 44* (Suppl. 204), 8–63.

Swedo, S. E., Leonard, H. L., Rapoport, J. L., Lenane, M. C., Goldberger, E. L., & Cheslow, D. L. (1989). A double-blind comparison of clomipramine and desipramine in the treatment of trichotillomania (hair pulling). *New England Journal of Medicine, 321,* 497–501.

Walker, P. A., & Meyer, W. J. (1981). Medroxyprogesterone acetate treatment of paraphiliac sex offenders. In J. R. Hays, T. K. Roberts, & K. S. Solway (Eds.), *Violence and the violent individual* (pp. 353–373). New York: SP Medical & Scientific Books.

Walker, P. A., Meyer, W. J., Emory, L. E., & Ruben, A. L. (1984). Antiandrogen treatment of the paraphilias. In H. C. Stancer, P. E. Garfinkel, & V. M. Rakoff (Eds.), *Guidelines for use of psychotropic drugs: A clinical handbook* (pp. 427–443). New York: SP Medical & Scientific Books.

Yates, E., Barbaree, H. E., & Marshall, W. L. (1984). Anger and deviant sexual arousal. *Behavior Therapy, 15,* 287–294.

10

TREATMENT OF RAPISTS: REINTERPRETATION OF EARLY OUTCOME DATA AND EXPLORATORY CONSTRUCTS TO ENHANCE THERAPEUTIC EFFICACY

William D. Pithers
Center for Prevention and Treatment of Sexual Abuse, Waterbury, Vermont

INTRODUCTION

The efficacy of sex offender treatment has been the topic of research and debate for as long as sex offender treatment has existed. According to some authors, the quality of debates regarding this topic surpasses the quality of most of the research. In a review of controlled outcome studies, Furby, Weinrott, and Blackshaw (1989) specified that only tentative conclusions could be made because every investigation contained significant methodological flaws. They concluded,

Nevertheless, we can at least say with confidence that there is no evidence that treatment effectively reduces sex offense recidivism. Treatment models have been evolving constantly, and many of those evaluated in the studies reviewed here are now considered obsolete. Thus, there is always the hope that more current treatment programs are more effective. That remains an empirical question. (p. 25)

A Reinterpretation

Furby et al. (1989) were correct in asserting that many of the treatment models they reviewed were obsolete. In fact, the major treatment programs based on early theoretical constructs about the origins of sex offenses, such as "sexual psychopathy," no longer existed when the review was published. Among the casualties were Metro State Hospital (California), Atascadero State Hospital (California), the Massachusetts Treatment Center at Bridgewater, Western State Hospital (Washington), and the Sex Crime Facility (Wisconsin).

Thirty treatment outcome studies are included in the review by Furby et al. (1989). However, one program at Atascadero State Hospital, extinct before publication of the review, accounted for more than one third of all the subjects considered in the review.

The treatment program at Atascadero State Hospital began in 1954 and ended in 1981. Sex offenders were civilly committed to Atascadero as mentally disordered sex offenders under the sexual psychopath statutes then prevalent in the United States. Treatment provided at Atascadero between 1954 and 1981 bore little resemblance to modern therapeutic practices. Patients returning to the community from Atascadero State Hospital received no follow-up treatment. Current philosophy maintains that transitional and follow-up services are essential to maintenance of therapeutic change. Modern programs endorse the use of behavioral interventions with offenders who manifest excessive arousal to abusive fantasies. At Atascadero, fewer than 10% of the patients participated in behavioral assessment or treatment. Although Atascadero provided more than one third of the data considered by Furby et al. (1989), another 25% of the data came from four other programs (Bridgewater, Massachusetts; Avenel, New Jersey; Western State Hospital, Washington; and the Sex Crime Facility, Wisconsin) that appear to have followed treatment paradigms similar to that of Atascadero.

Offenders Treated as Early as 1935

A brief review reveals the relative antiquity of much of the information considered by Furby et al. (1989). Fifty-five primary and secondary studies are cited in their review, 15 of which were published after 1978. Twelve of these 15 studies looked at the recidivism rates of treated sex offenders; three studies reported recidivism rates for untreated offenders. The 12 treatment outcome studies published after 1978 involved an average follow-up duration of 49.69 months, with a median follow-up of 33 months. Follow-up durations of treated offenders ranged from 2 years since the beginning of treatment (Gagne, 1985) to 20 years after release from an institutional program (Massachusetts Post Audit Bureau, 1979).

The year during which offenders in each study left treatment can be estimated by subtracting the follow-up duration from the year of the publication (disregarding the inevitable delay between acceptance and appearance of a journal article). The subtraction reveals that some offenders in the 12 most recent treatment outcome articles cited by Furby et al. (1989) exited treatment in 1959. Subtracting follow-up durations from publication dates provides only a crude estimate of the epoch during which offenders were treated. At least 1 of the 12 most recently published treatment outcome studies involved offenders who entered therapy in 1955 (Saylor, 1979). Since institution-based sex offender treatment programs are estimated to have begun in 1954 in the United States (Freeman-Longo & Wall, 1986), therapeutic interventions employed in 1955 probably were not very specialized. Unquestionably, treatment approaches of 1955 (e.g., milieu therapy, nondirective group therapy) bear little similarity to those employed today (e.g., olfactory aversive conditioning, relapse prevention, structured victim empathy building). Thus, it is reasonable to surmise that differences exist in the therapeutic efficacy of nonspecific interventions employed in pioneering programs and the specialized interventions considered essential to current programs.

Some early outcome studies included in the review bear even less similarity to current treatment practices. Sturup (1953) examined the recidivism rates of 117 sex offenders who were castrated as early as 1935. Although his data were impressive, the intervention appears ethically unacceptable and holds little relevance to modern sex offender treatment.

The conclusions of Furby et al. (1989) accurately reflect that little evidence existed to demonstrate the effectiveness of very early, unspecialized approaches to sex offender treatment. Due to the significant changes in the nature of sex offender treatment during the last 35 years, their conclusions about the early treatment programs have little relevance to more modern, highly specialized intervention and management strategies.

"One-component" outcome studies

Some studies reviewed by Furby et al. (1989) examined the effect of a single-treatment component. One of these studies (Prendergast, 1978) reported a 10-year follow-up of 324 sex offenders who had participated in up to 10 years of "emotional release therapy." In other studies, offenders received only individual therapy (Hackett, 1971), assisted covert sensitization (Maletzky, 1980a, 1980b), or a combination of medroxyprogesterone acetate and assertion training or assertion training alone (Langevin et al., 1979).

Evaluation of specific treatment components is critical to the evolution of effective treatment programs. This research can be used to validate a variety of therapeutic components that, together, constitute an integrated treatment program. However, studies evaluating single interventions cannot be expected to generate outcome data as favorable as that emerging from comprehensive, integrated programs involving multiple treatment components. A single intervention, even when implemented by the most highly skilled practitioners, cannot be considered optimal treatment for most sex offenders. Using a single intervention to address behaviors resulting from the convergence of multiple factors (e.g., emotional management, sexual and aggressive fantasies, interpersonal isolation) logically will not be associated with highly favorable treatment outcome.

Potential cultural bias against treatment effect

Of the 30 treatment outcome studies reviewed by Furby et al. (1989), 24 involved programs located in the United States. An additional 12 studies examined the recidivism of untreated sex offenders. Only 1 of these 12 studies took place in the United States (in Pennsylvania); 10 were conducted in Europe and 1 was performed in Canada. The United States is widely considered to have the highest rate of interpersonal violence and criminal activity in the world. Therefore, the disproportionate representation of recidivism studies of treated sex offenders in America and untreated sex offenders in Europe may have introduced a subtle bias against identifying therapeutic effectiveness.

In addition, interventions (e.g., registration and parole supervision) were used with some sex offenders considered "untreated" by Furby et al. (1989). Although parole supervision cannot be considered a traditional mental health intervention, it is an essential component of the comprehensive treatment strategies employed in modern programs. This category of interventions has been referred to as the "external, supervision dimension" of the relapse prevention model (Pithers, Cumming, Beal, Young, & Turner, 1989).

Redundant data

Finally, a large number of offenders were included in at least two different outcome studies (which Furby et al. [1989] acknowledged). Many of the 402 subjects in a study of sex offenders treated at Western State Hospital between December 1967 and May 1979 (Saylor, 1979) also were included in a study of 342 sex offenders treated at the same institution between 1970 and 1980 (Hall & Proctor, 1986).

In the same manner, many of the 475 subjects treated at Wisconsin's Sex Crime Facility between 1951 and 1960 (Pacht, Halleck, & Ehrmann, 1962) also appeared in another publication concerning 461 offenders treated in the same program between 1951 and 1963 (Pacht & Roberts, 1968). Some of the 224 subjects appearing in Peters and Roether (1971) were included among the 231 subjects in a second study based at the same treatment facility (J. J. Peters Institute, 1980). Of the 215 offenders in Serrill (1974), some also appeared in Prendergast's (1978) study involving 324 offenders treated in the same program at Avenel, New Jersey. Some of Frisbie's (1969) offenders treated at Atascadero State Hospital may have been included in Dix's (1976) report.

At least 10 of the 30 treatment outcome studies considered in the review involved overlapping populations. These studies were generated by the immense treatment programs that contributed nearly 60% of the 7,000 subjects included in the review.

Given the number of problems with the review, another conclusion of Furby et al. (1989) appears fitting: "Many of the recidivism studies reviewed here were, unfortunately, not very informative. It is time that we give this issue the resources and attention it deserves" (pp. 27–28).

SUGGESTIONS FOR SEX OFFENDER OUTCOME STUDIES

Avoid the Limitations Inherent in "Overcontrolled" Outcome Research

Carefully controlled investigations of treatment efficacy are important. Highly structured approaches to outcome research can demonstrate whether a specific intervention has the desired effect and yield information about the characteristics of clients that derive the greatest benefit from a treatment component. However, such studies necessarily result in an underestimation of actual treatment efficacy.

In clinical practice, selection of interventions responsive to the client's changing needs over time is an essential element of maximally effective therapy. Highly structured outcome studies requiring clients to take part in time-limited, inflexibly sequenced interventions will underestimate the potential effectiveness of treatment. This research strategy neglects the reality that clients change at different rates of speed, because of differences in motivation, problem severity, and personal resources (e.g., cognitive skills, emotional access, etc.). For example, individuals who are cognitively impaired or are from cultures different than the individual who developed the treatment program may need more time in each treatment component than more gifted or culturally similar individuals. In contrast, clients who function with greater cognitive and personal skills may need less treatment exposure. Potentially, outcome studies requiring clients to participate in interventions addressing areas in which they already possess skills may attenuate treatment effects by fostering the clients' expectations that treatment is irrelevant to their problems.

Examine Treatment Efficacy Across Sex Offender Subtypes

Much of the early outcome research seemingly subscribed to the uniformity myth within which all sex offenders have identical problems and should benefit equally from similar treatments. This has occurred even though most researchers and practitioners readily agree that subtypes of sex offenders exist. Less agreement is found regarding what these subtypes are.

Many taxonomies have been proposed. Some of the taxonomies show great promise (Knight & Prentky, 1990), yet room for improvement exists. For example, no system accounts adequately for individuals who victimize both children and adults. Despite the limitations of existing taxonomic systems, with few exceptions, treatment outcome investigations have neglected to employ subtypes beyond *rapist* and *pedophile*. Thus, although a reasonable body of evidence suggests that specialized treatment is more effective than no treatment (and more effective than traditional mental health interventions), little data exist about what kind of treatment works best with various offender subtypes. Murphy (1990) noted, "All of these approaches provide some understanding of sex offenders, although they do not always clearly translate into specific treatment programs" (p. 331). Relevance to treatment interventions or prognosis needs to be demonstrated before taxonomic systems will become utilized widely.

Examine Treatment Programs Representing the Standard of Practice

Therapeutic interventions for sex offenders have evolved rapidly during recent years, and the number of practitioners working with sex offenders has escalated dramatically. A survey conducted in 1986 identified 643 providers of sex offender treatment (Knopp & Stevenson, 1986). Their 1992 survey reported that 1,500 treatment professionals are working in the field (Knopp, Freeman-Longo, & Stevenson, 1992). Between 1986 and 1992, there was a 133% increase in the number of professionals working with sex offenders. This rapid increase reflects a dramatic influx of energy into this field.

Comparing the results of their 1988 and 1990 surveys of interventions used with sex offenders, Knopp and Stevenson (1990) found the greatest growth in utilization of thinking errors treatment groups, penile plethysmography, aversive conditioning, and psychohormonal interventions. These data suggest that treatment of sex offenders is becoming increasingly specialized.

To be meaningful to practitioners, treatment outcome studies need to employ therapeutic procedures currently recognized as the standard of practice. The treatment providers' adherence to prescribed treatment protocols should be monitored. By following these procedures, research will be relevant to current practices and produce treatment protocols that can be implemented easily by providers.

RECENT REPORTS OF TREATMENT EFFICACY WITH SEX OFFENDERS

Several studies have evaluated the efficacy of sex offender programs that employ modern interventions developed specifically for sexual abusers (Cumming & Pithers, 1992; Marshall & Barbaree, 1990; Marshall, Jones, Ward, Johnston, & Barbaree, 1991; Pithers & Cumming, 1989). Although these studies vary greatly in methodological sophistication, they converge on the conclusion that sex offenders who have engaged in specialized treatment reoffend at considerably lower rates than offenders who have not participated in treatment.

Beyond evaluating therapeutic efficacy generally, some studies have investigated the differential efficacy of specialized interventions with broadly defined subtypes of sex offenders. Although delineation of offender subtypes remains inadequate in these investigations, the data simultaneously demonstrate the general efficacy of treatment and the need to modify existing approaches for some subgroups.

Although specialized treatment programs result in diminished recidivism rates for child abusers and rapists in comparison with untreated samples, the reduction in recidivism rates is significantly greater for child abusers than rapists in some studies (Cumming & Pithers, 1992; Hildebran & Pithers, 1992; Maletzky, 1987; Marshall et al., 1991; Pithers & Cumming, 1989). Specialized treatment appears to have a greater influence on child abusers than on rapists. These data allude to the importance of identifying the functional characteristics of child abusers and rapists that are associated with differential outcome. If functional differences are discerned, treatment methods may be modified or developed to address the characteristics of rapists associated with less favorable outcome.

It is important to emphasize that existing interventions result in lower recidivism rates for both child abusers and rapists relative to their untreated counterparts. The treatment effect appears to be smaller for rapists than child abusers.

DIFFERENTIAL FACTORS IN CHILD ABUSERS AND RAPISTS

History of General Criminality

Alder (1984) asked whether convicted rapists are sexual or violent offenders. She noted that an increasing number of theorists are asserting that rape is part of a pattern of aggressive antisocial behavior and not an act of sexual maladjustment (Bart, 1975; Gager & Schurr, 1976; Gibbens, Way, & Soothill, 1977; Greer, 1973; Griffin, 1977; Russell, 1975). Looking at a variety of demographic and criminal factors in several samples of incarcerated offenders, Alder (1984) concluded, "There is little difference between rapist and either property or violent offenders. . . . The offender group with which rapists differed most were the other sex offenders" (pp. 165, 173).

Implications of general criminality for sex offender treatment

In the search for factors distinguishing child abusers from rapists, general criminality may be important to examine. One hypothesis for the differential efficacy of specialized interventions with child abusers and rapists would postulate that some rapists may be more likely than child abusers to have a history of frequent general criminal activity. Although child abusers may repeatedly engage in sexual violations, they may be less likely to follow a lifestyle of general criminality or psychopathy.

This hypothesis might predict that untreated child abusers would have a higher recidivism rate for sex offenses than rapists, whereas at least a subset of rapists would have a higher rate of recidivism for nonsexual offenses. Child abusers, particularly those who meet the diagnostic criteria for pedophilia, have an unwavering sexual attraction to children and therefore seek out children for sexual gratification. On the other hand, some rapists may be less attracted to sexualized violence than to a lifestyle involving intermittent and generic criminal acts offering relief from boredom. Within this framework, child abusers would be considered "sex offenders," whereas some rapists would represent general criminals.

The smaller reduction in recidivism rates for rapists than child abusers could reflect the relative ineffectiveness of treating general criminals with techniques designed specifically for individuals experiencing problems such as a preponderance of abusive sexual fantasies. Some of the more specialized interventions for sex offenders attempt to minimize the frequency and strength of abusive sexual fantasies (e.g., covert sensitization, olfactory aversive conditioning, masturbatory satiation) or heighten interest in adult sexuality (e.g., orgasmic reconditioning). Such procedures address one of the significant factors predisposing child abusers' behaviors. With rapists who have an extensive history of nonsexual criminal offenses, efforts to decrease excessive arousal to sexualized violence may be less relevant to their core problem. Sexually abusive fantasies of rapists may be only one manifestation of a constellation of highly varied thoughts and impulses about violating others' rights, persons, and properties.

Implications of general criminality for self-maintenance strategies

Some therapeutic approaches commonly employed with sex offenders, such as relapse prevention (Pithers, Marques, Gibat, & Marlatt, 1983) or offense cycles (Isaac & Lane, 1990), propose that sex offenders experience negative feelings when they lapse into a precursor associated with past abusive behaviors. In relapse prevention, this experience is called the abstinence violation effect. Concepts such as the abstinence violation effect may not apply to general criminal offenders who find antisocial behaviors to be more ego-syntonic than a prosocial lifestyle. Anecdotal information supports this notion. Several rapists with extensive nonsexual criminal histories reoffended after receiving treatment in the Vermont Treatment Program for Sexual Aggressors (VTPSA). Interviewed after reconviction, some of these individuals poignantly depicted their failed efforts to maintain a prosocial lifestyle. One person commented,

I started out using what I learned in the program. It helped a lot some of the time. I kept out of trouble. I felt good at first. People treated me differently. Even though I felt good, it took a lot of work. . . . Eventually, I got tired of all the work. Trying to live a good life started to wear me down. I found myself thinking about my old ways, how much more fun I had then. The new ways were [hard work] and boring. My old ways were easy and felt good. When I thought about my old ways, it almost felt like I was going home again. When I've been away from home a long time and I open the door to my place and step back in, it feels really good. Thinking about my old ways felt like that. I felt like going home again, like a breath of fresh air.

Rather than experiencing distress at the return of criminogenic thinking (as in the abstinence violation effect), this individual actually found comfort in his "lapse." Similar experiences have been reported by other rapists who had extensive nonsexual criminal histories. Given these self-reports, existing treatment models for sex offenders may require modification for use with a subset of rapists. Alternately, entirely new treatment models may need to be devised.

Although some rapists may resemble career criminals, others do not. From the perspective of specialized treatment, the important matter may be finding a reliable way to tell the difference. The ultimate challenge, from a societal and scientific perspective, is to develop effective treatment interventions and supervision strategies for both groups.

Trait (Obsessionality)–State (Disinhibition) Characteristics

Pedophilia as a trait

As conceptualized in DSM-III-R (American Psychiatric Association, 1987), pedophiles experience an enduring sexual attraction to children that exceeds their attraction to adults. Pedophiles often choose occupations, avocations, and residences on the basis of the access afforded to children. Remarkable creativity and persistence may be evidenced as pedophiles begin to groom children and their caregivers, establishing the trust and intimacy that often is a precursor to victimization. It takes time to establish trust in any relationship, whether it involves an adult couple or a pedophile initiating the grooming of a child.

The consistency of the pedophiles' interests resembles a trait. The interest is present across time and situations. This makes pedophiles' behaviors relatively stable, predictable, and, therefore, more tractable.

Rapists: Potential subgroups of trait and state offenders

Some theorists have suggested that rapes are impulsive acts. However, others have suggested that many rapists' behaviors may not be impulsive, but planned.

In our analysis of precursors to assaults, more than half of all offenders . . . left a hostile interaction without expressing anger. Over time, as they brooded about the incident, their animosity grew. Some offenders . . . had harbored hatred from a single event for a decade. . . . Eventually their continual amplification of emotion led to a later explosive release. Since this outburst, or assault, was temporally so far removed from the instigating event, the behavior might appear situationally noncontingent, or "impulsive." In reality, however, the act was not impulsive at all, but motivated by a delayed emotional response. (Pithers, Kashima, Cumming, Beal, & Buell, 1988, p. 246)

For some rapists, these theorists propose, premeditation allows the offender to minimize the possibility of apprehension and, if caught, to appear exculpable. In relapse prevention terminology, this premeditated behavior has been called *planned impulsiveness.*

Several examples of planned impulsiveness may help to clarify the distinction between "planned" and "lifestyle" impulsivity. Some rapes occur during the course of other criminal activities such as burglaries (Amir, 1971; Chappell & Singer, 1977; Scheff, 1979). In treatment some of these burglar/rapists have disclosed that they entered the house with the hope of finding a woman alone whom they might rape. If more than one person was found in the house, these offenders considered it "too dangerous" to rape and elected to take only property. This represents a blending of planned and lifestyle impulsivity. The offender planned to enter houses with the hope of finding someone to rape. Failing that, he engaged in a nonsexual type of criminal activity. Often these individuals appear motivated by the desire to escape boredom.

In other cases, rape has been the topic of sexual fantasies for years, but victim selection was opportunistic. Even though chance determined victim selection, the acts performed during the rape had been contemplated for some time. In the absence of a potential rape victim, the offender was unlikely to engage in nonsexual criminal activity. This offense pattern typifies planned impulsiveness.

Other rapes appear genuinely impulsive. It is my clinical impression that impulsive rapes are performed most often by generic criminals whose histories are marked by lifestyle impulsivity (Prentky & Knight, 1986). The type of criminal act this individual performs seems to be determined by rolling dice, with the specific act being defined by the resulting number. Regardless of the type of offense, there often is evidence that it has been poorly planned. Such offenders occasionally leave evidence at the crime scene that reveals their identity.

Thus, type of impulsivity may be a critical feature in distinguishing rapist subtypes. Differential therapeutic outcomes may be observed for rapists whose acts entailed planned versus lifestyle impulsivity. One example of the implications on recidivism of lifestyle and planned impulsivity is provided by Prentky (1990). He divided 106 rapists into low (or planned) and high (or lifestyle) impulsivity groups on the basis of historical data (e.g., behavior management problems during childhood, instability in employment, interpersonal relationships, and residence). Because his subjects had been released from a maximum security treatment facility 25 years earlier, Prentky (1990) was able to determine the relationship between degree of impulsivity and treatment outcome. High impulsivity rapists were approximately three times more likely than low impulsivity rapists to have been convicted of new sex offenses during the follow-up period.

One may speculate that lifestyle impulsivity functions as a trait. Across time and situations, lifestyle impulsive offenders may be predisposed to engage in abusive acts regardless of their environmental circumstances. In contrast, planned impulsivity functions more as a state-dependent factor. Individuals engaging in planned impulsivity may fantasize frequently about engaging in sexually abusive acts, but likely engage in abusive behaviors only when the external environment contains a vulnerable person and a low likelihood of apprehension, or when their fantasies are disinhibited by anger, alcohol, or other factors.

Precursors to Sexual Abuse: Observability, Number, and Velocity

Observability of the relapse process

Regardless of whether a rape results from planned or lifestyle impulsivity, many rapists abuse people with whom they have no familiarity. Unlike pedophilic child abusers, who generally need to establish some measure of trust and intimacy with a child and his or her caregivers prior to abuse, many rapists employ advantages of larger physical stature and threats of harm to overwhelm their victims.

However, it is essential to acknowledge that not all rapes involve strangers. An unknown number of acquaintance, date, and marital rapes occur each year. It is highly unlikely that an accurate estimate of the number of acquaintance, date, and marital rapes will ever be established as a result of several factors. Rapes performed within intimate relationships are far less likely to be reported than rapes committed by nonintimates. Russell (1984) found that 30% of stranger rapes, 1% of the date rapes, and none of the marital rapes in her sample had been reported. Other research indicated that only 12% of all rapes were committed by a stranger, with 88% being performed by someone the victim knows (Koss, Dinero, Siebel, & Cox, 1988). Koss et al. (1988) noted that 21% of stranger rapes and only 1% of acquaintance rapes were reported to police. Even in acquaintance rapes, assaultive violence may be used to force the victim's submission; however, there may be more instances where psychological rapes are indiscernible to the victim. In these cases, the rape exists in the angry and abusive fantasies of an individual whose partner has no means of detecting the violence that exists within the thoughts of their apparently affectionate lover. An accurate estimation of rapes within relationships can be made only by gaining access to the abuser's inner fantasies, feelings, thoughts, and memories.

One may question whether stranger and acquaintance rapes are generally committed by different offender subtypes. Perhaps rapists of strangers would be high in lifestyle impulsivity, whereas acquaintance rapists would adhere to a planned impulsivity. Thus, acquaintance rapists may engage in psychological rapes on many occasions, with the true abusiveness of their intent becoming observable only when their behaviors have been disinhibited by anger, substance use, or other factors.

Number and velocity of offense precursors

Specific precursors to offenses are observable in both child abusers and rapists (Pithers et al., 1988). Although categories of precursors to sexual abuse assaults can be identified, and can serve as useful warning signs of future assaults, their utility in treatment and supervision may differ across child abusers and rapists.

At least two aspects of offense precursors may affect their ability to be used to enhance maintenance of change and facilitate supervision: (a) the number of precursors involved in the relapse process, and (b) the velocity with which the precursors occur. Although considerable variability exists across offenders, clinical experience suggests that the number of risk factors does not differ significantly between rapists and child abusers as groups. However, the velocity of offense precursors appears greater for rapists than child abusers.

Velocity is intended to convey the strength and directionality of offense precursors. The strength or power of offense precursors varies. Some are relatively weak distractions; others have a magnetic influence of nearly magical proportions. Some offense precursors are followed by additional lapses; others lead directly to high-risk situations where offenses are imminent. One may hypothesize that rapists' offense precursors have greater velocity than child abusers'. The first year after release contains the highest frequency of rape relapses (Frisbie, 1969; Pithers & Cumming, 1989; Sturgeon & Taylor, 1980). This finding may reflect the influence of anger and power as the predominant motivations for sexual violence. Eruptions of anger and feelings of disempowerment have precipitous onsets and are essential precursors to rape. In the face of these precursors, loss of behavioral control can take place rapidly. Because rapists may progress through offense precursors within an extremely short time frame, maintenance strategies relying on rapists' and their prevention teams' (Gray & Pithers, in press) ability to detect and respond to risk factors may be less effective with rapists than child abusers.

Because most paraphilic child abusers establish relationships prior to abusing, their precursors may entail a longer time period. This provides greater opportunity for the child abuser to report to treatment providers or probation officers that he has engaged in behaviors related to offending. Others on his prevention team also have increased opportunity to witness these precursive behaviors and intervene. In addition, once the trusting relationship has been established, additional precursors (e.g., loneliness, depression, fear of rejection) may need to be experienced before an offense occurs. Given this difference in velocity of precursors, relapse prevention programs may find more favorable treatment outcomes with child abusers than rapists.

Offense precursors to general criminality

As described earlier, factors associated with career criminality contributing to a poor treatment prognosis include lifestyle impulsivity and the futility of attempting to address general criminality with therapeutic interventions designed specifically for sex offenders. If an individual engages in a lifestyle of crime, offense precursors may not be related to any specific type of illegal act. In individuals who engage in a wide variety of crimes, precursors unique to rape may not be identified. Offense precursors would suggest that criminal activity was imminent, but not allow one to determine the type of crime that would follow.

Precursors to Measurable Sexual Arousal Disorders

A recent survey of sex offender treatment providers (Knopp & Stevenson, 1990) found that assessment of sexual arousal patterns by means of the penile plethysmograph has become increasingly common. The plethysmograph permits clinicians to: (a) identify individuals who manifest excessive arousal to stimuli depicting sexual abuse, (b) spot lack of arousal to stimuli of consenting sex, (c) note offenders whose arousal disorder necessitates specialized behavioral therapies, (d) confront misrepresentations evident in self-reported levels of arousal, (e) evaluate therapeutic efficacy, and (f) enhance certain forms of behavioral therapy (Pithers & Laws, 1989).

Disordered sexual arousal: State versus trait?

Concern is growing that phallometry may be less applicable to rapists than pedophiles. Plethysmography does not differentiate rapists and nonrapists sufficiently. In contrast, plethysmography appears quite useful in distinguishing pedophiles and nonpedophiles, and may even assist differentiation among child abuser subtypes (Barbaree & Marshall, 1989).

The arousal patterns of pedophiles resemble traits, whereas rapists' arousal patterns may be state dependent. By definition, pedophiles experience strong and enduring sexual attraction toward children. The pedophile's sexual desire for children may be altered to some degree by various emotional states, but across emotional states the pedophile's strongest sexual interest remains focused on children. When pedophiles are happy, their strongest sexual desire is for children; when they feel angry, their strongest sexual desire is for children.

If feeling calm or affectionate, rapists' arousal patterns may be highly similar to those of nonabusers. However, arousal patterns may be altered dramatically by different emotional and cognitive states (Barbaree, 1990). The abusive interests of some rapists emerge only after an activating event occurs. Only in the presence of these factors does a latent abusive belief system become evident in arousal to sexually violent stimuli. The activating events differ across rapists. Among the influences that have been shown to activate sexual arousal to stimuli depicting rape are victim blame due to clothing and location (Barbaree, 1990), anger (Yates, Barbaree, & Marshall, 1984), alcohol intake (Barbaree, Marshall, Yates, & Lightfoot, 1983), and exposure to aggressive pornography shortly before assessment (Seidman, Marshall, & Barbaree, 1989). Professional ethics constrain clinicians' and researchers' freedom to create the circumstances that might activate sexually abusive interests and enable their identification via plethysmography. Therefore, information about the mechanisms activating the abusive interests of an individual rapist needs to be gained in another manner.

Discovery of emotional and cognitive factors that disinhibit abusive sexual arousal demonstrates that the penis is connected to the brain and is, at least on some occasions, influenced by it. Identification of disinhibitors signifies that inhibitory influences also can be discovered. Behavioral therapies conducted in the presence of disinhibiting influences and followed by interventions focused on cognitive distortions can decrease abusive interests. Although not subjected to empirical scrutiny, clinical practice demonstrates that behavioral skills gained through other interventions can diminish arousal to abusive fantasies. Among these skills are enhanced empathy for sexual abuse victims, resolution of personal victimization, and increased ability to cope with emotions through their constructive expression.

If the disordered arousal of pedophiles resembles a trait and that of rapists is state dependent, rapists' disordered arousal patterns will be more difficult to identify than those of pedophiles. This difficulty is exacerbated by clinicians' inability to use known disinhibitors of disordered arousal in rapists. Thus, plethysmographic assessments are more likely to miss the disordered arousal of rapists than pedophiles. The implications of this are twofold. First, some rapists will not take part in behavioral therapies even though they need and could benefit from these treatments. Second, plethysmographic evaluations conducted as part of exit evaluations may fail to detect rapists' disordered arousal patterns. The inability to detect and treat a predisposing risk factor of rape may be associated with a worse outcome for rapists than child abusers.

Social Proscription Versus Social Mediation

Although Western society overtly condemns the acts of child abusers and rapists, considerable evidence implies the existence of social proscriptions concerning child sexual abuse and acceptance of attitudes predisposing abuse of women. Sexually explicit photographs of children are illegal and the subject of sting operations by Postal Inspectors. In contrast, degrading and violent acts against women are commonly seen in highly successful commercial films. Objectification of women seems to be the essence of advertising for automobiles, alcoholic beverages, and other products whose manufacturers target male consumers. Perhaps the difference in prevalence of abuse-predisposing messages makes it more difficult for rapists than pedophiles to maintain treatment-induced behavioral change.

Beliefs predisposing rape exist in all segments of the population, including police, factory workers, rapists, judges, and students (Burt, 1980, 1983; Feild, 1978; Malamuth, 1981; Russell, 1975; Salter, 1988). In contrast, far fewer members of society subscribe to beliefs promoting child sexual abuse. Many theorists and researchers have attempted to account for the pervasiveness of these beliefs. Stock (1991) offered "the principle of hegemonic control," commenting, "the class in power will use all means available to control the less powerful class—force, coercion, intimidation, propaganda, and institutional and ideological control—to maintain its advantage, without necessarily conscious intent or design" (p. 61). Thus, if distorted beliefs, objectified images in the media, unequal status in the workplace, and messages imparted in some educational programs cannot maintain male superiority, sexualized violence represents the ultimate weapon. Other authors see less of struggle for control between genders, viewing rape as "cultural spillover" within a society that legitimizes many manifestations of violence (Baron, Straus, & Jaffe, 1988).

It is interesting to speculate that Stock (1991) and Baron et al. (1988) referred to different subtypes of rapists. Perhaps those captured by Stock's (1991) formulation are "state" rapists who do not have extensive criminal histories. They may be individuals who assault whenever they see no other way of "staying in control," "getting their way," or "seeing whether she really means 'no'." Baron et al. (1988) may have captured the criminally oriented "trait" rapist who sees little difference in performing an aggravated or a sexual assault.

TREATMENT

At this time, existing treatment approaches do not apply equally well to all sex offenders, appearing less effective with rapists than pedophiles. Part of the reason for this differential efficacy may be explained by career criminality manifested by more rapists than pedophiles. However, this would not appear to account for all the discrepancy, because programs that do not admit career criminals still identify this finding. It appears that modifications of existing interventions are needed to respond adequately to the needs of rapists.

If the absence of relevant data, creativity may be exercised in devising a comprehensive treatment approach to rapists. The following portion of this chapter presents observations based on assessment data and clinical experiences accumulated during the operation of a residential treatment program for adult sex offenders. Some of the interventions proposed have been subjected to process evaluation and appear to enable offenders to create significant personal changes; others are pure speculation. Whether these interventions will result in favorable treatment outcome is therefore unknown.

Because rape is a multiply determined act, a credible treatment design must be able to address issues such as personal victimization, cognitive distortions, behavioral treatment to attenuate excessive arousal to sexually abusive fantasies, victim empathy, emotional recognition and modulation, and attributional processes. The relevance of these interventions is outlined in the next section. These suggestions are made for treatment of rapists whose acts are not representative of a career criminal orientation.

Behavioral Therapies to Alter Arousal to Abusive Sexual Fantasies

Use when activating stimuli are present

One group of interventions that may require modification is the behavioral therapies used to modify sexual arousal patterns. Because sexual arousal to rape stimuli appears to be disinhibited by a variety of conditions that are idiosyncratic to each offender (Barbaree, 1990), some behavioral therapies may be most effective if offenders invoke them when activating influences are present. If performed in the absence of disinhibitors, and therefore in the absence of deviant sexual arousal, the interventions may seem irrelevant. Under such conditions, distorted beliefs that frequently accompany deviant fantasies may not be observed. Behavioral therapies would fail to break the intertwined associations between sexual arousal, distorted beliefs, and interpersonal violence. In the same manner, interventions involving sexual fantasies depicting sexual communication of intimacy may be completed most effectively while the rapist is experiencing relatively positive emotional and attitudinal states. An acutely angry rapist attempting to complete a masturbatory satiation session may only reinforce a fusion between sexuality and aggression, potentially predisposing additional sexual assaults (Table 1).

Use olfactory and gustatory aversion

Depending on the sensory modality of the noxious stimulus, aversive therapies may have a beneficial or exacerbating effect. Olfactory and gustatory aversion, conducted when disordered arousal has been disinhibited, may diminish abusive sexual interests temporarily.

To reinforce decreased arousal to sexually violent themes, concentrated efforts to assist change in belief systems must take place during the window of opportunity opened by behavioral therapy. The vehemence with which distorted cognitions are usually defended appears to dissipate when behavioral therapies have reduced the strength and frequency of abusive interests. If cognitive

TABLE 1   Proposed Time of Use for Maximal Efficacy of Behavioral
Therapies

Behavioral intervention	Proposed time of use
Covert sensitization	Abusive arousal disinhibited
Olfactory/gustatory aversion	Abusive arousal disinhibited
Masturbatory satiation	Positive emotional state
Orgasmic reconditioning	Positive emotional state

changes do not accompany behavioral changes, excessive interest in sexually abusive fantasies will return.

In contrast to olfactory and gustatory aversion, faradic stimulation may exert a counterproductive effect and heighten abusive interests. Olfactory and gustatory aversion can involve truly disgusting sensory experiences, but they generally do not evoke pain and anger. Faradic aversive stimuli can be painful and elicit anger. Faradic aversion may produce diminution of abusive arousal during treatment sessions, but self-monitoring of deviant interests may reveal increased frequency and strength outside the treatment setting.

An additional advantage of olfactory aversion is that it may be performed in vivo. Clients can be required to keep a vial of the aversive stimulus with them at all times. In addition to enhancing generalization of behavioral change, this procedure also provides parole officers supervising rapists with another way to verify the clients' adherence to treatment plans.

Emotional Recognition and Empathetic Skill

Expand knowledge of emotional terms

Whether the result of victimization, extreme beliefs about "gender-appropriate" behaviors, or other factors, some rapists have little awareness of a full range of emotions. In a treatment group entitled "Emotional Recognition," therapists begin by requesting clients to prepare a list of all of the emotions that they experience personally. They are not permitted to discuss this assignment with others or to rely on reference books. Across several groups, rapists reported significantly fewer names of emotions than child abusers. One 19-year-old who had raped on five occasions had four emotions on his list: "anger, rage, fury, and depressed." As in this individual's case, many of the emotions listed by rapists defined various types of anger. Some of the words listed by rapists conveyed emotions that were not defined precisely (e.g., hurt) or which represented cognitive states rather than emotions (e.g., confused). In comparison, child abusers' lists contained a greater range of affect states. Although the child abusers' most commonly identified emotion was "anxious," their lists contained more "sensitive" emotions (e.g., compassion, fondness) than the rapists.

Emotional awareness essential to empathy

The finding that rapists have less emotional awareness than pedophiles may be related to the higher levels of empathetic skills observed in pedophiles. Using the Interpersonal Reactivity Index (Davis, 1980, 1983) as a process measurement to validate a structured victim empathy-building treatment group, pretreatment scores revealed that incarcerated pedophiles surpassed rapists on three of the four subscales (Pithers, Cumming, & Martin, 1992). Pedophiles obtained higher scores than rapists on subscales measuring perspective taking (cognitive ability to look at another's point of view), empathic concern (affective ability to feel compassion for others encountering negative experiences), and fantasy (imaginal capacity to place oneself in the role of a character). In contrast, rapists attained a higher score than pedophiles on personal distress, which reflects the degree to which one shares the negative emotions of another. Some evidence suggests that personal distress also may be correlated with an inability to cope with negative feelings (Salter, 1988).

These data were derived from incarcerated sex offenders, few of whom were acquaintance rapists. Additional research needs to be performed to determine whether group differences exist between pedophiles, acquaintance rapists, "state" rapists, career criminals (or "trait rapists"), and a control sample.

The fact that pedophiles have greater emotional access and higher levels of empathy than rapists should not be surprising. Because most pedophiles must be sufficiently functional human beings to be able to establish trusting relationships with children and their parents, these fundamental skills may be essential to grooming. One might speculate that the pedophiles' ability to "take the role of the other" might be related to their tendency to projectively identify with the child.

Emotional awareness and modulation

The challenge with rapists is heightening their awareness of emotional states other than anger, fostering a belief system that gives them freedom to be emotionally aware, and assisting modulated expression of emotions. Because many rapists in the emotional recognition groups appear to be aware of an extremely constricted range of feelings, a second homework assignment requires them to use all the reference sources available to prepare as thorough a list as possible of emotional states and to define the emotions. The goal of this assignment is to have the rapist simply gain labels for emotions he is not aware of experiencing. The availability of definitions may begin the sometimes subtle process of emotional differentiation. Each person presents his homework to the group.

Once a reasonable list of emotions has been developed, offenders watch a series of movies that evoke various emotional responses (e.g., *A Christmas Story, The Great Santini, Star 80, To Kill a Mockingbird*). Offenders are requested to describe the character with whom they most closely identified. They are asked to indicate the emotions that this character experienced, and then to describe the emotion with which they most closely identified. When strong elements of relationships and family life are depicted, offenders are requested to describe which emotions were evident in their relationships, which emotions were not permitted expression, which felt most comfortable, which felt most uncomfortable, which feelings they fear experiencing and expressing, and which they wish they could experience but feel unable. The clients' responses typically lead the group into discussion of personal victimization, grief over lost experiences, disclosure of unreported offenses, concern about gender identity, or any number of long-held secrets that individuals now feel the courage to disclose. Recognizing the support that an individual risking such disclosures receives, other clients begin to venture into a world of uncertain emotions.

The existence of "chronic" anger

In this group, the type of anger recollected differs from that seen in many anger management groups. Rather than addressing anger elicited by interpersonal or situational provocation, clients begin to disclose "chronic anger," or archival events about which they remain enraged. Different from "state anger," chronic anger resembles a personality trait, functioning as a distorted lens that warps perceptions of life events and reinforces existing thinking errors. Because affect and cognition are related, emotional recognition groups sometimes must delve into correctives for distorted beliefs.

Liberal use of role-plays can assist practice in emotional expression. Situations recalled during discussion of the movies often provide ample stimuli for rehearsal of skills. Videotapes of role-plays in which clients demonstrate constructive and destructive expression of emotion in these situations facilitates differentiation; humor, that encourages clients to take part in an inherently scary process; and helps clients to gain perspective about their behaviors.

Personal Victimization

Numerous publications document the extent to which sex offenders have been victims of various types of abuse. A substantial percentage of pedophiles appear to have been sexually abused, most often prior to puberty. Many rapists report having been physically abused during early development. Although there is general agreement that many sex offenders have been victims, the role that victimization plays in the etiology of sexual abuse remains uncertain. Some researchers propose that sexual abuse victims may evolve into perpetrators as a result of abuse-induced cognitive distortions. Ryan (1989) took this position to its extreme, stating, "Simplistically, the etiology of sexual offending may be in the offender's attempt to 'master' his/her own helplessness by taking the agressor's role" (p. 328). This single-factor theory neglects numerous aspects of one's personal history and social environment that mitigate or amplify the impact of abuse.

Subjective definitions of victimization

It is not surprising that many sex offenders regard themselves as victims of some type of abuse. For better or worse, nearly all members of modern society regard themselves as having been abused in some significant manner (Sykes, 1992). Some feel abused because their first lover exited their relationship in a callous way, they perceive themselves as having received less parental attention than their siblings, a teacher graded them unfairly, the car dealer sold them a defective vehicle, or they were beaten consistently by a parent. In informal polls of professional groups I have trained, there has yet to be one person who does not believe that they have been victimized in some fashion. The critical issue may not be whether someone has been abused, but the way in which their perception of others has been affected by their interpretation of the abuse.

Certainly, from an objective viewpoint, not all forms of abuse are equal. Unfortunately, objective viewpoints exert less influence over an individual's behaviors than their own subjective interpretation of an event. Regardless of the abuse type, the affected individual interprets the victimization in a unique manner. One individual may consider physical abuse to symbolize an unsafe, uncaring, victimizing world and develop a system of beliefs that endorses taking whatever one can get from the world. Another person may experience an identical level of physical abuse, yet develop an aversion to violence and advocate for programs to prevent victimization.

Offenders' responses to perceived victimization

Clinical experience suggests that rapists experience responses common to victims including emotional numbing and conversion of vulnerable emotions into invulnerable emotions. One functional effect of these responses is constricted emotional experience. Sometimes emotional constriction serves as a coping response that allows an individual to survive a crisis, but that eventually can create other problems.

The sequence of emotional constriction as both a coping and a dysfunctional response can be seen in one client's recollection of "deciding to die emotionally" when, as a fourth grade student, he was taunted daily by a female peer about his poor clothing. His choice to die was prompted by a recognition that he could not do well in school if he continued to feel deeply embarrassed and shamed. Yet 30 years later, while in a chronic anger treatment group, the child abuser recalled this as the earliest life event about which he still remained angry. After processing his anger at the perceived abuse, the client was able to articulate the helpless feeling of his initial embarrassment. By slowing his reexamination of an emotional response, the client acknowledged the vulnerability he had experienced initially and became aware that his anger was a mask for humiliation and vulnerability. Over time, his angry response had assumed the qualities of an "automatic emotion." Whenever he recalled the event, he immediately felt angry, which impeded his ability to process the memory. The client had lost the perception that he had initially felt shamed and humiliated. Processing perceived victimizations allow rapists to awaken vulnerable emotions that have long felt dead and to gain enhanced modulation of emotions that once seemed beyond all control.

Linkage of shame and rage

The client's response to shame, converting the emotional energy into a smoldering, resentful anger, is not unique. Bowlby (1982) observed that shame, as distinct from transitory guilt, functions as a personality trait associated with withdrawal and hostile outbursts. The linkage to interpersonally abusive behaviors is clear:

> *The link between shame reactions and externalization of blame is consistent with Lewis (1971) and Sheff's (1987) description of rage or the humiliated fury that often accompanies shame. A person suffering from a painful shame experience may be part motivated to make use of hostile or defensive maneuvers somewhat akin to externalization. This projection outward may lessen the pain of shame in the short run, but it's likely to be pretty irrational and destructive to our interpersonal relationships. (Tangney, 1989)*

If therapy is to have long-term effects, facilitating rapists' emotional access, particularly to feelings heightening perceived vulnerability, is essential. If rapists do not have access to a full range of their own emotions, it is impossible to establish empathy for victims of sexual abuse. To attach emotions to others in a realistic fashion, rapists first must be able to accept the existence of these emotions within themselves. Rapists need to perceive their own emotions accurately in order to understand, in any meaningful way, how their actions may affect others. Only then does the possibility of establishing victim empathy exist. This may be a key component of assisting change in rapists.

Attributional Style

Things are what we think of them

Regardless of the objective nature of an event, an individual's cognitive interpretation of the event mediates its ultimate effects. Beliefs promoting sexual victimization are influenced by the individual's attributions. By facilitating attributional change, the process of treatment and maintenance of behavioral change may be enhanced.

Abramson, Seligman, and Teasdale (1978) formulated an attributional model of learned helplessness depression. They proposed that several dimensions of an individual's attributions affect the severity of one's depressive state. These authors also suggested that the focus of treatment might vary in accordance with the individual's attributions.

Abramson et al. (1978) defined three attributional dimensions: (a) internality–externality, (b) specific–general, and (c) acute–chronic. Each of these dimensions represents a continuum, rather than a binary classification. Each dimension holds different implications for the severity of one's distress and for the steps one might take toward alleviation of distress.

The internality–externality dimension identifies the extent to which individuals consider themselves to be personally responsible for their state of being (internality) versus their status being determined by factors outside their control (externality). The specific–general dimension reflects the extent to which someone can delimit the circumstances creating their distress (specific) versus those circumstances encompassing numerous variables (general). The acute–chronic dimension taps one's expectation about the duration of the distress, ranging from short-term effects that will dissipate without intervention to long-term effects that may never lessen regardless of the intervention.

Attributions about victimization that promote abuse

The attributional model can be modified to assist offenders in redefining the role that their victimization played in the etiology of their self-image and abusive patterns. Individuals who use their own victimization to fuel abuse of others may have assigned responsibility for how they feel to a vicious world (external and general) that will never change (chronic). This attributional style may either give rise to, or help to justify, cognitive distortions that promote many kinds of interpersonal violence, including rape.

Attributions about treatment that affect outcome

Attributional styles also may be associated with different degrees of behavioral change and maintenance of change. One may hypothesize that offenders who attribute therapeutic change to external sources (e.g., magical therapists, law enforcement), who believe their change process should only address global issues (e.g., self-esteem), and who believe in acute, curative therapies (e.g., no maintenance needed) may be less likely to derive benefit from treatment than offenders who are more flexible in their attributional style.

Cognitive Distortions

Cognitive distortions "refer to self-statements made by offenders that allow them to deny, minimize, justify, and rationalize their behavior. . . . The cognitive factors are not seen as the direct causes of deviant sexual behavior, but as steps offenders go through to justify their behaviors which serve to maintain their behavior" (Murphy, 1990, p. 332). Scully and Marolla (1984, 1985) documented some of the justifications rapists use to excuse their acts and deny harm to victims.

Cognitive distortions can be difficult to change when approached directly through aggressive confrontations. Similar to Kelly's (1957) comments in regard to individuals' efforts to integrate discrepant information within their existing personal constructs, a rapist will engage "in frantic efforts to make data fit his hypotheses, sometimes resorting to vigorous measures" (p. 278).

Analyzing Distortions with an Attributions Approach

The structure of the attributional framework (Abramson et al., 1978) may foster rapists' abilities to analyze their cognitive distortions. The following examples may help to clarify how some distorted beliefs can be processed within an attributional framework: "You always do that to me"—externality, specific, chronic; "It is my fault that I will never be able to have a healthy relationship with a woman"—internality, general, chronic; "My victim led me on"—externality, specific, acute; "All women are whores at heart"—externality, general, chronic. Using this structure to analyze cognitive distortions can create the sense of a game, allowing the offender sufficient distance from his distorted thinking so that he is able to examine it more closely.

Murphy (1990) reviewed approaches used to affect cognitive change in sex offenders. He noted that these techniques provide:

(1) patients with a rationale for the role cognitions have in maintaining sexual abuse, (2) corrective information and education to the patient usually around such issues as victim impact, (3) ways of helping subjects identify their specific distortions, and (4) exercises to assist patients in challenging and exploring their distortions. (p. 336)

Readers are referred to Murphy's (1990) review for additional information about most of these strategies. The importance of one of these approaches, building empathy for sexual abuse survivors, is discussed in the next section.

Victim Empathy

Empathy is derived from the Greek word *Empatheia,* or *passion. Empathy* can be defined as the capacity to cognitively perceive another's perspective, to recognize affective arousal within oneself, and to base compassionate behavioral responses on the motivation induced by these precepts. Empathetic responses involve an interplay of cognitive, affective, and behavioral domains. Intellectual understanding alone does not constitute empathy. Empathy is not equivalent to feeling guilt or feelings focused on oneself; rather empathy is a process of feeling for another. Absorption in guilt can evolve into shame, which may be externalized as aggression. Empathy is externalized as compassionate understanding.

The Importance of Empathy

Empathy can exert profound influences in human interactions. In subjects who have undergone empathy training, empathy induced by oneself or by experimenters' interventions has been demonstrated to replace acts of aggression with nonviolence (Feshbach, 1978; Iannotti, 1978; Tangney, 1989). The implications for sex offender work are obvious. Establishing empathy for victims of sexual abuse can provide motivation for behaviorial change and maintenance that endures beyond the fabricated self-concerns induced by fear of incarceration. If empathy can be established, significant effects may be observed in sexual arousal, cognitive distortions, intimacy within interpersonal relationships, realistic self-esteem, and motivation to change and maintain change.

> *Victim empathy gives [the rapist] the pivotal reason for not reoffending, for, with empathy, he can no longer not perceive his victim's pain. Unless he experiences this shift of consciousness, he will manage to dismiss the logical consequences of moving farther into his relapse process. The farther into the process that he moves, the less he can count on logic to pull him back. (Hildebran & Pithers, 1989, p. 238)*

Detailed information on a process evaluation-validated approach to building offender empathy for victims of sexual abuse is available in other sources (Freeman-Longo & Pithers, 1992; Hildebran & Pithers, 1989).

CONCLUSION

This chapter began by critiquing the widely distributed review article by Furby et al. (1989), which called into question the efficacy of early efforts to treat sex offenders. Although this study sometimes has been considered to reflect badly on sex offender treatment, the conclusions of that review were largely irrelevant to modern, specialized, sex offender treatment programs. Among the factors permitting this conclusion were: (a) nearly 60% of the 7,000 subjects included in the review were treated in one of five institutions that based their programs on a premise widely recognized as ill conceived (i.e., "sexual psychopathy"); (b) several studies in the review used only one treatment component in an effort to alter a behavior associated with multiple determinants; (c) the most recently published studies in the review included some offenders who had entered treatment in 1955, an era when treatment programs employed traditional mental health interventions with sex offenders; (d) the review included one study that examined the recidivism status of offenders castrated as early as 1935; (e) at least 10 of the 30 treatment outcome studies involved many of the same clients; and (f) some of the interventions used with offenders considered untreated by Furby et al. (1989) (e.g., registration and parole supervision) currently are considered an essential component of comprehensive treatment.

An accumulating body of evidence demonstrates that current cognitive–behavioral approaches to sex offender treatment are associated with reduced recidivism rates. In most research, the reduced recidivism rates are greater for pedophiles than rapists. Among the hypotheses for this differential treatment efficacy are: (a) more rapists than pedophiles have a lengthy history of nonsexual criminal acts, suggesting the greater presence of lifestyle impulsivity among rapists; (b) the prodromal period for rape may be shorter than that for child sexual abuse, affording less opportunity for rapists to interrupt their progression toward offending or for others to observe and disrupt the course of the rapists' behaviors; (c) the effect of disinhibitors that appear to be precursors to some rapists' assaults (e.g., intoxication, anger) cannot be evaluated ethically, and, as a result, some rapists do not receive treatments addressing these precursors and their disordered arousal; (d) the prevalence of social attitudes and stimuli condoning violence against women may erode treatment effects in rapists; and (e) rapists appear to have less access than pedophiles to a broad range of emotions, resulting in a greater impairment in empathetic skills among rapists.

Developing a taxonomy or, alternately, an assessment procedure that specifies the fundamental excesses and deficits of various subtypes of rapists and, accordingly, delineates treatment components that may be employed to address these excesses and deficits appears essential to the evolution of this field. In its absence, the ability to devise specialized interventions to address the narrowly defined problems of rapists will continue to be compromised.

REFERENCES

Abramson, L. Y., Seligman, M. E. P., & Teasdale, J. D. (1978). Learned helplessness in humans: Critique and reformulation. *Journal of Abnormal Psychology, 87,* 49–74.

Alder, C. (1984). The convicted rapist: A sexual or violent offender? *Criminal Justice and Behavior, 11,* 157–177.

American Psychiatric Association. (1987). *Diagnostic and statistical manual of mental disorders* (3rd. ed. rev.). Washington, DC: Author.

Amir, M. (1971). *Patterns of forcible rape.* Chicago: University of Chicago Press.

Barbaree, H. E. (1990). Stimulus control of sexual arousal. In W. Marshall, D. R. Laws, & H. E. Barbaree (Eds.), *The handbook of sexual assault:*

Issues, theories, and treatment of the offender (pp. 115–142). New York: Plenum.

Barbaree, H. E., & Marshall, W. L. (1989). Erectile responses amongst heterosexual child molesters, father-daughter incest offenders and matched nonoffenders: Five distinct age preference profiles. *Canadian Journal of Behavioral Science, 21,* 70–82.

Barbaree, H. E., Marshall, W. L., Yates, E., & Lightfoot, L. O. (1983). Alcohol intoxication and deviant sexual arousal in male social drinkers. *Behavior Research and Therapy, 21,* 365–373.

Baron, L., Straus, M. A., & Jaffee, D. (1988). Legitimate violence, violent attitudes, and rape: A test of the cultural spillover theory. In R. A. Prentky and V. L. Quinsey (Eds.), *Human sexual aggression: Current perspectives. Annals of the New York Academy of Sciences* (Vol. 528, pp. 79–110). New York: New York Academy of Sciences.

Bart, P. G. (1975). Rape doesn't end with a kiss. *Viva, 2,* 39–42, 100–101.

Bowlby, J. (1982). *Attachment and loss* (Vol. 3). *Loss: Sadness and depression.* New York: Basic Books.

Burt, M. R. (1980). Cultural myths and supports for rape. *Journal of Personality and Social Psychology, 38,* 217–230.

Burt, M. R. (1983). Justifying personal violence: A comparison of rapists and the general public. *Victimology, 8,* 131–150.

Chappell, D., & Singer, S. (1977). Rape in New York City: A study of material in the police files and its meaning. In D. Chappell, R. Geis, & G. Geis (Eds.), *Forcible rape: The crime, the victim, and the offender* (pp. 245–271). New York: Columbia University Press.

Cumming, G. F., & Pithers, W. D. (1992). *Evaluation of the Vermont Treatment Program for Sexual Aggressors: 1982–1992.* Waterbury, VT: Vermont Department of Corrections.

Davis, M. H. (1980). A multidimensional approach to individual differences in empathy. *JSAS Catalog of Selected Documents in Psychology, 10,* 85.

Davis, M. H. (1983). The effects of dispositional empathy on emotional reactions and helping: A multidimensional approach. *Journal of Personality, 51,* 67–184.

Dix, G. E. (1976). Determining the continued dangerousness of psychologically abnormal sex offenders. *Journal of Psychiatry and the Law, 3,* 327–344.

Feild, H. S. (1978). Attitudes toward rape: A comparative analysis of police, rapists, crisis counselors, and citizens. *Journal of Personality and Social Psychology, 36,* 156–179.

Feshbach, N. D. (1978). Studies of empathetic behavior in children. In B. A. Mahler (Ed.), *Progress in experimental personality research* (Vol. 8, pp. 1–47). New York: Academic Press.

Freeman-Longo, R. E., & Pithers, W. D. (1992). *A structured approach to preventing relapse: A guide for offenders.* Orwell, VT: Safety Society Program.

Freeman-Longo, R. E., & Wall, R. V. (1986). Changing a lifetime of sexual crime. *Psychology Today, 20,* 58–64.

Frisbie, L. (1969). *Another look at sex offenders in California* (Research Monograph No. 12). Sacramento, CA: California Department of Mental Hygiene.

Furby, L., Weinrott, M. R., & Blackshaw. L. (1989). Sex offender recidivism: A review. *Psychological Bulletin, 105,* 3–30.

Gager, N., & Schurr, C. (1976). *Sexual assault: Confronting rape in America.* New York: Grosset & Dunlap.

Gagne, P. (1985, July). *Pretreatment prognosis predictors in sexual deviants.* Paper presented to the 1985 Congress on Criminal Justice, Vancouver, British Columbia, Canada.

Gibbens, T. C. N., Way, C. K., & Soothill, K. L. (1977). Behavior types of rapes. *British Journal of Psychiatry, 130,* 32–44.

Gray, A. S., & Pithers, W. D. (in press). Relapse prevention with sexually abusive adolescents: Three applications to treatment and supervision. In H. E. Barbaree, W. L. Marshall, & S. M. Hudson (Eds.), *Juvenile sex offending.* New York: Guilford.

Greer, G. (1973). Seduction is a four-letter word. *Playboy, 20* (January), 80–82, 164, 178, 224–228.

Griffin, S. (1977). Rape: The all-American crime. In D. Chappell, R. Geis, & G. Geis (Eds.), *Forcible rape: The crime, the victim and the offender* (pp. 47–66). New York: Columbia University Press.

Hackett, T. P. (1971). The psychotherapy of exhibitionists in a court clinic setting. *Seminars in Psychiatry, 3,* 297–306.

Hall, G. C. N., & Proctor, W. C. (1986, February). *Criminological predictors of recidivism in a sexual offender population.* Paper presented at the National Institute of Mental Health Conference on the Assessment and Treatment of Sex Offenders, Tampa, FL.

Hildebran, D., & Pithers, W. D. (1989). Enhancing offender empathy for sexual abuse victims. In D. R. Laws (Ed.), *Relapse prevention with sex offenders* (pp. 236–243). New York: Guilford.

Hildebran, D., & Pithers, W. D. (1992). Relapse prevention: Application and outcome. In W. T. O'Donohue & J. H. Geer (Eds.), *The sexual abuse of children: Critical issues* (pp. 365–393). New Jersey: Lawrence Erlbaum.

Iannotti, L. A. (1978). Effect of role-taking experiences on role-taking, empathy, altruism, and aggression. *Developmental psychology, 41,* 119–124.

Isaac, C., & Lane, S. (1990). *The sexual abuse cycle in the treatment of adolescent sexual abusers.* Orwell, VT: Safer Society Press.

J. J. Peters Institute. (1980, June). *A ten-year follow-up of sex offender recidivism.* Philadelphia, PA: Author.

Kelly, G. (1957). *Hostility.* Presidential address to the Clinical Division, American Psychological Association.

Knight, R. A., & Prentky, R. A. (1990). Classifying sexual offenders. The development and corroboration of taxonomic models. In W. Marshall, D. R. Laws, & H. E. Barbaree (Eds.), *The handbook of sexual assault: Issues, theories, and treatment of the offender* (pp. 23–52). New York: Plenum.

Knopp, F. H., Freeman-Longo, R., & Stevenson, W. F. (1992). *Nationwide survey of juvenile and adult sex-offender treatment programs.* Orwell, VT: Safer Society Press.

Knopp, F. H., & Stevenson, W. F. (1986). *Nationwide survey of juvenile and adult sex-offender treatment programs.* Orwell, VT: Safer Society Press.

Knopp, F. H., & Stevenson, W. F. (1990). *Nationwide survey of juvenile and adult sex-offender treatment programs.* Orwell, VT: Safer Society Press.

Koss, M. P., Dinero, T. E., Seibel, C. A., & Cox, S. L. (1988). Stranger and acquaintance rape: Are there differences in the victim's experience? *Psychology of Women Quarterly, 12,* 1–24.

Langevin, R., Paitich, D., Hucker, S., Newman, S. Ramsay, G., Pope, S., Geller, G., & Anderson, C. (1979). The effect of assertiveness training, provera and sex of therapist in the treatment of genital exhibitionism. *Journal of Behavior Therapy and Experimental Psychiatry, 10,* 275–282.

Malamuth, N. M. (1981). Rape proclivity among males. *Journal of Social Issues, 37,* 138–157.

Maletzky, B. M. (1980a). Assisted covert sensitization. In D. J. Cox & R. J. Daitzman (Eds.), *Exhibitionism: Description, assessment and treatment* (pp. 187–251). New York: Garland.

Maletzky, B. M. (1980b). Self-referred versus court-referred sexually deviant patients: Success with assisted covert sensitization. *Behavior Therapy, 11,* 306–314.

Maletzky, B. M. (1987, May). *Data generated by an outpatient sexual abuse clinic.* Paper presented at the First Annual Conference on the Assessment and Treatment of Sexual Abusers, Newport, OR.

Marshall, W. L., & Barbaree, H. E. (1990). Outcome of comprehensive cognitive–behavioral treatment programs. In W. Marshall, D. R. Laws, & H. E. Barbaree (Eds.), *The handbook of sexual assault: Issues, theories, and treatment of the offender.* New York: Plenum.

Marshall, W. L., Jones, R., Ward, T., Johnston, P., & Barbaree, H. E. (1991). Treatment outcome with sex offenders. *Clinical Psychology Review, 11,* 465–485.

Massachusetts Post Audit Bureau. (1979, August). *Report of the committee on post-audit and oversight.* Bridgewater, MA: Author.

Murphy, W. D. (1990). Assessment and modification of cognitive distortions in sex offenders. In W. L. Marshall, D. R. Laws, & H. E. Barbaree (Eds.),

Handbook of sexual assault: Issues, theories, and treatment of the offender (pp. 331–342). New York: Plenum.

Pacht, A. R., Halleck, S. L., & Ehrman, J. C. (1962). Diagnosis and treatment of the sexual offender: A nine-year study. *American Journal of Psychiatry, 118,* 802–808.

Pacht, A. R., & Roberts, L. M. (1968). Factors related to parole experience of the sexual offender: A nine-year study. *Journal of Correctional Psychology, 3,* 8–9.

Peters, J. J., & Roether, H. A. (1971). *Success and failure of sex offenders.* Philadelphia: American Association for the Advancement of Science.

Pithers, W. D., & Cumming, G. F. (1989). Can relapses be prevented? Initial outcome data from the Vermont Treatment Program for Sexual Aggressors. In D. R. Laws (Ed.), *Relapse prevention with sex offenders* (pp. 313–325). New York: Guilford.

Pithers, W. D., Cumming, G. F., Beal, L. S., Young, W., & Turner, R. (1989). Relapse prevention. In B. Schwartz (Ed.), *A practitioner's guide to treating the incarcerated male sex offender* (pp. 123–140). Washington, DC: National Institute of Corrections.

Pithers, W. D., Cumming, G. F., & Martin, G. (1992). [Validation of a treatment model for enhancing offender empathy for sexual abuse victims]. Unpublished raw data.

Pithers, W. D., Kashima, K. M., Cumming, G. F., Beal, L. S., & Buell, M. M. (1988). Relapse prevention of sexual aggression. In R. A. Prentky & V. L. Quinsey (Eds.), *Human sexual aggression: Current perspectives.* Annals of the New York Academy of Sciences (Vol. 528, pp. 244–260). New York: New York Academy of Sciences.

Pithers, W. D., & Laws, D. R. (1989). The penile plethysmograph. In B. K. Schwartz (Ed.), *A practitioner's guide to treating the incarcerated male sex offender* (pp. 85–94). Washington, DC: U.S. Department of Justice.

Pithers, W. D., Marques, J. K., Gibat, C. C., & Marlatt, G. A. (1983). Relapse prevention: A self-control model of treatment and maintenance of change for sexual aggressives. In J. Greer & I. R. Stuart (Eds.), *Sexual aggression: Current perspectives on treatment* (pp. 214–239). New York: Van Nostrand Reinhold.

Prendergast, W. E. (1978). *ROARE; Re-education of attitudes (and) repressed emotions.* Avenel, NJ: Adult Diagnostic and Treatment Center Intensive Group Therapy Program.

Prentky, R. A. (1990). *Sexual violence: A review.* Paper presented at the Ninth Annual Clinical and Research Conference on the Assessment and Treatment of Sexual Abusers, Their Families and Victims, Toronto, Canada.

Prentky, R. A., & Knight, R. A. (1986). Impulsivity in the lifestyle and criminal behavior of sexual offenders. *Criminal Justice and Behavior, 14,* 403–426.

Russell, D. E. H. (1984). *Sexual exploitation*. Beverly Hills, CA: Sage.

Russell, D. E. H. (1975). *The politics of rape: The victim's perspective*. New York: Stein & Day.

Ryan, G. (1989). Victim to victimizer: Rethinking victim treatment. *Journal of Interpersonal Violence, 4*, 325–341.

Salter, A. S. (1988). *Treating child sex offenders and victims: A practical guide*. Newbury Park, CA: Sage.

Saylor, M. (1979, December). *A guided self-help approach to treatment of the habitual sex offender*. Paper presented at the 12th Cropwood Conference, Cambridge, England.

Scheff, A. F. (1979). Statistical trends in rape. *Journal of the Forensic Science Society, 19*, 95–106.

Scully, D., & Marolla, J. (1984). Convicted rapists vocabulary of motive: Excuses and justifications. *Social Problems, 31*, 530–544.

Scully, D., & Marolla, J. (1985). Rape and vocabularies of motive: Alternative perspectives. In A. W. Burgess (Ed.), *Rape and sexual assault: A research handbook* (pp. 294–312). New York: Garland.

Seidman, B. T., Marshall, W. L., & Barbaree, H. E. (1989). *Male sexual arousal to rape depictions following exposure to forced and consenting sexual stimuli*. Manuscript submitted for publication.

Serrill, M. S. (1974). Treating sex offenders in New Jersey: The ROARE program. *Corrections Magazine, 1*, 13–24.

Stock, W. E. (1991). Feminist explanations: Male power, hostility, and sexual coercion. In E. Grauerholz & M. A. Koralewski (Eds.)., *Sexual coercion: A sourcebook on its nature, causes, and prevention* (pp. 61–73). Lexington, MA: Lexington books.

Sturgeon, V. H., & Taylor, J. (1980). Report of a five-year follow-up study of mentally disordered sex offenders released from Atascadero State Hospital in 1973. *Criminal Justice Journal, 4*, 31–63.

Sturup, G. K. (1953). Sexual offenders and their treatment in Denmark and other Scandinavian countries. *International Review of Criminal Policy, 4*, 1–19.

Sturup, G. K. (1968). Treatment of sexual offenders in the Herstedvester, Denmark: The rapists. *Acta Psychiatrica Scandinavica, 44*(Supplementom 204), 1–63.

Sundberg, S., Barbaree, H. E., & Marshall, W. L. (1984). Anger and deviant sexual arousal. *Behavior Therapy, 15*, 287–294.

Sykes, C. J. (1992). *A nation of victims: The decay of the American character*. New York: St. Martin's Press.

Tangney, J. P. (1989, April). *Shame-proneness, guilt-proneness, and interpersonal processes*. Paper presented at the Biennial Meeting of the Society for Research in Child Development, Kansas City, MO.

Yates, E., Barbaree, H. E., & Marshall, W. L. (1984). Anger and deviant sexual arousal. *Behavior Therapy, 15*, 287–294.

11

FINDINGS AND RECOMMENDATIONS FROM CALIFORNIA'S EXPERIMENTAL TREATMENT PROGRAM

Janice K. Marques
David M. Day
California State Department of Mental Health

Craig Nelson
Mary Ann West
Atascadero State Hospital

The Sex Offender Treatment and Evaluation Project (SOTEP) is a controlled, longitudinal study of the effectiveness of an intensive cognitive–behavioral treatment program for rapists and child molesters. In the first part of this chapter, we describe the treatment program and how we are evaluating it and summarize some of our preliminary findings. In the second part, we propose, based on our experience in SOTEP, a number of recommendations about the design, implementation, and evaluation of sex offender treatment programs.

BACKGROUND

In 1981, the California State Legislature repealed the state's mentally disordered sex offender statutes and required new sex offenders to be sent to the Department of Corrections. Although this legislation eliminated the direct commitment of these offenders to state hospitals, it allowed the voluntary transfer of a small number of sex offenders to the Department of Mental Health for treatment during the last 2 years of their prison terms. The hospital program for these offenders was to be "established according to a valid experimental design

Preparation of this chapter was supported in part by National Institute of Mental Health Grant MH46391, awarded to Janice K. Marques and David M. Day. We want to thank Larry Potash for conducting the additional data analyses needed for this chapter. The opinions expressed in this paper are those of the authors and do not necessarily represent the policies of the California State Department of Mental Health.

in order that the most effective, newest and promising methods of treatment of sex offenders may be rigorously tested'' (California Laws, 1981).

In 1985, we started the Sex Offender Treatment and Evaluation Project (SOTEP) in order to determine if an innovative program at Atascadero State Hospital can significantly reduce recidivism among convicted sex offenders.

The key features of our project are: (a) an experimental design that includes random assignment of volunteers to either treatment or no treatment conditions; (b) an intensive cognitive–behavioral inpatient program designed specifically to prevent relapse among sex offenders; (c) a 1-year aftercare program designed to maintain treatment gains and reintegrate offenders into the community; and (d) a comprehensive evaluation of both in-treatment changes and long-term treatment effects (including a follow-up period in which recidivism rates for treated and untreated subjects are measured for at least 5 years).

METHOD

SOTEP's study sample includes three matched groups: (a) *Treatment group.* Sex offenders who volunteered to participate and were randomly selected for the treatment program at Atascadero. (b) *Volunteer control group.* Sex offenders in prison who volunteered but were assigned randomly to receive no treatment. (c) *Nonvolunteer control group.* Prisoners who qualified for the project, but chose not to participate. As this group is large and heterogeneous, some of our comparisons are made using a randomly selected subsample of nonvolunteers who were matched to the treatment group participants. SOTEP includes four study phases: selection, treatment, aftercare, and follow-up.

Selection Phase

SOTEP staff regularly visit 18 prisons that house sex offenders and review records to identify inmates who qualify. We have a number of selection criteria, the most important being that offenders must be convicted of rape or child molestation, and must be within 18–30 months of release. We also screen out offenders who are developmentally disabled or actively psychotic, have three or more prior felony convictions, or deny their crimes. We do not mean *minimize;* we mean *deny* any sexual contact with the victim. We accept offenders who ''can't remember'' or say it was not what the probation report indicated; we do not accept those who say they were framed. We do not do any further clinical screening to select subjects who are amenable to treatment.

Subjects who qualify are interviewed, and those who volunteer sign our consent form. Then, we match volunteers (on type of offense, criminal history, and age) and randomly assign one member of the matched pair to treatment and the other to the volunteer control group. A matched subsample of the nonvolunteer control group is selected later at random from the pool of inmates who learned of the project but did not choose to participate.

Treatment Phase

During this phase, members of the treatment group participate in an intensive 2-year treatment program at Atascadero State Hospital. The theoretical orientation of the program is relapse prevention (RP), a cognitive–behavioral treatment strategy developed in the field of addictive behaviors in the late 1970s (Marlatt & Gordon, 1980) and adapted shortly thereafter for use with sex offenders (Marques & Pithers, 1981). RP is a multimodal and prescriptive approach that is designed specifically to help clients maintain behavioral changes by anticipating and coping with the problem of relapse. As applied with SOTEP subjects, RP provides a comprehensive framework within which a variety of behavioral, cognitive, educational, and skill training approaches are used to teach the sex offender how to recognize and interrupt the chain of events leading to relapse or reoffense. The focus of both assessment and treatment procedures is on the specification and modification of the steps in this chain, from broad lifestyle factors and cognitive distortions to more circumscribed skill deficits and deviant sexual arousal patterns.

Because a detailed description of SOTEP's treatment program is available elsewhere (Marques, Day, Nelson, Miner, & West, 1991), only a brief summary is provided here. The primary treatment structure is the core relapse prevention (RP) group, which meets for three 90-minute sessions each week throughout the program. This highly structured group is the setting in which the offender's cognitive–behavioral offense chain is constructed and is used to integrate other program components into a system specifically designed to enhance control and prevent relapse for each individual offender.

In addition to this intensive RP training, treatment group subjects participate in a wide range of other treatment activities designed to modify various determinants of sexual offending. The project's specialty groups focus on the specific knowledge, attitudes, and skills that the offender needs to identify and cope with potential high-risk situations. All participants attend the following groups: sex education, human sexuality, relaxation training, stress and anger management, and social skills. A prerelease class designed to prepare the offender for "life on the streets" is also mandatory. Other specialty groups (e.g., substance abuse group) and individualized treatment components (e.g., behavior therapy) are provided by the project on a prescriptive basis. In order to maintain consistency and fidelity in the program, all treatment services (with the exception of individual psychotherapy) are provided according to highly structured treatment manuals.

The primary evaluation tasks during the treatment phase involve the measurement of treatment fidelity and in-treatment changes. This includes assessment of the effects of each component, as well as the effects of the overall program. For the core RP group, measures focus on whether the group is indeed teaching its members the RP model. Other treatment components are evaluated by analyzing the pre–post changes in variables relevant to the focus of intervention (e.g., social skills, stress management, deviant sexual arousal, etc.).

Overall effects of treatment are addressed by our pre–post assessment battery, which includes: (a) a variety of standardized measures of psychological functioning, personal responsibility, and attitudes related to offending and victims; (b) the SOTEP behavioral measures (Sex Offender Situational Competency Test and physiological assessment; (c) a program evaluation form completed anonymously by participants; and (d) clinician ratings of each subject's ability to apply the RP model and his likelihood of reoffending. In addition, just prior to their discharge from the hospital, treatment group members participate in a prerelease assessment, which includes an interview focused on the subject's expected postrelease situation; self-report measures (addressing deviant sexual interests, cognitive distortions, and perceptions about high-risk situations); and an introduction to the randomized response technique (RRT) (Warner, 1965). RRT, a statistically based technique designed to ascertain group differences while protecting the identity of individual subjects, is used to supplement official criminal records in determining offense rates.

Volunteer control group members receive no treatment services from the project during the treatment phase, but those who consent before their release participate in an assessment session that includes the same measures as does the session conducted with treatment group members. Subjects are paid to participate in this and all subsequent assessment sessions.

Recently, as a result of funding that we obtained from NIMH, SOTEP's prerelease assessment has been enhanced. First, to collect information on a larger sample of sex offenders, members of the nonvolunteer control group who consent are also asked to participate in prerelease assessment sessions. Second, the assessment procedures have been expanded to include additional measures of personal and social controls, coping styles, and commitment to abstinence. Hare's Psychopathy Checklist (Hare, 1991) also has been added to more fully describe the sample, identify characteristics that may interact with treatment, and determine the importance of psychopathy as a predictor of reoffense.

Aftercare Phase

California sex offenders are routinely placed on parole for a period of at least 1 year following their release from incarceration. For treatment group members, attending two sessions a week in the Sex Offender Aftercare Program (SOAP) is a condition of parole for the first year. SOAP services are provided on a contractual basis by clinicians who are trained individually by project staff to provide an extended version of the RP program that is tailored to meet the needs of the paroled offender. Sessions focus on "boosting" treatment effects (i.e., enhancing the participants' understanding of RP concepts, practicing the skills learned in the program, and testing nondeviant lifestyles). Depending on the treatment needs of the participant, aftercare also may include family interventions, drug testing, laboratory assessments of sexual arousal, and/or behavior therapy booster sessions.

Treatment progress is monitored during the aftercare phase by monthly contacts between project staff and SOAP providers. In addition, providers are obligated to notify the Department of Corrections in the event of treatment failure or violation of other conditions of parole. Members of the two control groups are also on parole during this period, and the parole may be revoked (i.e., returned to custody) if parole violations are detected.

Near the end of the 1-year aftercare period, SOTEP evaluation staff meet individually with subjects in the treatment and volunteer control groups to conduct a follow-up assessment. Due to our NIMH enhancement funds, nonvolunteer controls will also be assessed, and the content of the sessions for all groups has been expanded to collect more information on variables such as commitment to abstinence, personal and social controls, coping skills, self-efficacy, and deviant interests. Direct questions about the subjects' legal and illegal sexual behavior will be asked in this session. To encourage disclosure and protect subject identities, we applied for, and were granted, a Certificate of Confidentiality from the U.S. Department of Health and Human Services.

Follow-up Phase

This phase includes the aftercare phase and will continue for 5 years following the release of the last study participant. The treatment program is scheduled to end in 1995, therefore subject follow-up will continue until the year 2000. In this period, automated data on all three groups are gathered on a routine basis from the California Department of Justice, and arrangements are being made to secure data on out-of-state offenses from the U.S. Department of Justice. NIMH enhancement funds are also allowing us to complete up to four additional follow-up interviews with consenting subjects during their first 5 years at risk.

FINDINGS

Reoffense Data

The real test of our treatment is whether it succeeds in reducing recidivism. Although it is too early in this longitudinal study to report findings on long-term outcomes, we have completed a number of analyses of the reoffense data we have collected thus far. These include simple calculations of rearrest rates and the identification of some of the correlates of reoffending for study participants.

SOTEP staff routinely monitor automated rapsheet records maintained by California's Department of Justice for subjects' arrests and convictions for sex offenses, other violent offenses, drug possession and sales, property crimes, and violations of parole not further identified with respect to specific rule or law violation. The results presented here are based on these reports, but we must warn the reader that automated rapsheet data do not represent subjects' criminal behaviors accurately. As we noted earlier, our long-range plan is to base estimates of reoffense on additional sources of information. We are collecting official record data from the Department of Corrections, which include parole agent notes and reports, charge sheets, child abuse reports, parole board reviews, and court records. We are also asking subjects about their criminal behaviors by means of confidential self-reports secured directly from them and via the Randomized Response Technique.

A study we recently completed illustrates the importance of supplementing official record data. Our staff reviewed all of the SOTEP subjects' parole files ($N = 125$) stored by the Department of Corrections in the Northern California region. Evidence was found of 49 incidents involving law enforcement contacts. In 33 of these, there was some corresponding arrest report on subjects' rapsheets; in 16 cases (33%) there was not.

Perhaps the most striking finding in this study was the variety of offenses represented on rapsheets simply as "parole violations." Most of the events leading to parole revocation involved some form of absconding or charges of drug offenses, but also included were four instances of child molesters associating with minor children, two of child molesters annoying or propositioning children, and one of a rapist committing a new rape.

Although it is important to incorporate multiple sources of information on postrelease behavior in determining whether subjects have committed new offenses, we have not collected enough data to employ this approach for the present analyses. Because of our use of random assignment, we do not expect that examining only rapsheet criminal behaviors will introduce bias affecting comparisons across groups, but the lower rates of offending yielded by rapsheets may make difficult the identification of significant correlates.

Reoffense Rates

By the end of 1991, 95 treatment group subjects (76 child molesters and 19 rapists) had completed the program at Atascadero and had been released to aftercare. As is always the case in studies of sex offender treatment, we have had to cope with the problem of attrition. The subjects in our treatment program can be returned to prison either by withdrawing their consent or by being removed involuntarily because of serious rule violations in the hospital. This attrition has been managed by including in the treatment group those subjects who left the hospital and returned to prison after receiving at least 1 year in the inpatient phase of the program. The treatment group in Table 1, which includes 13 subjects who were returned to prison after at least 1 year of treatment, is composed of 83 child molesters and 25 rapists. The nine subjects (seven child molesters and two rapists) who left the program before completing 1 year of treatment are considered separately as the "ex-treatment group."

Table 1 presents the arrest rates for the matched SOTEP study groups (i.e., the treatment and ex-treatment groups, their volunteer controls, and the matched subsample of treatment refusers selected from the nonvolunteer control group). Arrests are shown for new sex offenses (including child molestation and rape), other violent offenses (including murder, assault, and robbery), and parole violations. The rates for the very small ex-treatment group were higher than those for other subjects in all three offense categories. With one exception, arrest rates for treated subjects were lower than those for untreated subjects. The exception was for the category of other violent offenses, in which the volunteer controls had the lowest arrest rate.

Statistical comparisons were made between treated subjects and each of the two control groups using survival analysis (Singer & Willett, 1991), a method that permits incorporation of time at risk information in analyses. As is the case with most statistics, the power of statistical tests using survival analysis increases as a function of sample size. The power of survival analysis is also dependent on the length of time at risk for subjects and the number of failures observed. Because these latter two characteristics are a problem for these data, an alpha level of .10 was used as a criterion for the significance of the tests made here.

Even using a relaxed criterion of significance, none of the differences between the reoffense rates presented in Table 1 was large enough to be statistically significant. However, there were significant results produced by a model controlling for type of offense and the interaction between it and the experimental group.

First, there was a main effect for the experimental group, with treated subjects having lower risk of new sex arrests than untreated volunteers. Rapists were at higher risk of new offenses than were child molesters overall, but this effect was confounded by the experimental group. Treated rapists were at lower risk to commit new sex offenses than were treated child molesters, whereas untreated rapists were at higher risk than were untreated child molesters.

Correlates of Reoffense for Rapists

At the present time, analyses of our treatment group data look quite promising in that prerelease measures of constructs we expect to be affected by our treatment model appear related to reoffense (new sex crimes). Survival models testing the effects on reoffense of deviant sexual arousal, as measured phallo-

TABLE 1   Arrest Rates for Matched SOTEP Study Groups

Variable	Treatment group	Ex-treatment group	Volunteer control group	Nonvolunteer control group
N	108	9	108	110
Time at risk (months)	34	44	37	33
Arrests for:				
Sex offense	4.6%	33.3%	7.4%	8.2%
Other violent offense	6.5%	11.1%	4.6%	7.3%
Parole violation	5.6%	33.3%	13.0%	10.0%

Note. Percentages for new arrests are unduplicated. For subjects with multiple arrests, sex offenses were considered first, other violent offenses next, and parole violations last.

metrically and by subscales of the Multiphasic Sex Inventory (Nichols & Molinder, 1984) showed significant positive relationships. We also found that cognitive distortions (measured by subscales of the Multiphasic Sex Inventory) significantly predicted reoffense. Two factors that had significant negative effects on reoffense were sensitivity to high-risk situations (measured by the High-Risk Situations Test) and performance on key measures of skills taught in the Core Relapse Prevention Groups (measured by clinician ratings). However, these findings concerned the entire treatment group. Because only 19 of these subjects were rapists, and none of them has committed a new sex offense, it is currently impossible to examine the effects of these variables separately by offense type.

Although the cohort of treated rapists is small, there are sufficient prerelease data in the combined treatment and volunteer control group to permit some verification of findings. Thirty-four rapists (20 treatment, 10 volunteer control, and 4 ex-treatment) have completed the Cognitive Distortions and Immaturity Scale of the Multiphasic Sex Inventory. The results indicate that this measure is significantly related to both new sex offenses and other violent offenses in that less distorted thinking was related to a lower risk for reoffense.

Twenty-seven rapists (13 treatment, 13 volunteer control, and 1 extreatment) have completed the High-Risk Situations Test, which was devised to measure awareness and recognition of factors that affect an offender's risk for reoffense. The 30 situations included on the test yield six 5-item scales: Negative Emotional States, Negative Physical States, Testing Control, Social Pressure, Enhancing Emotional States, and Interpersonal Conflict. Although no significant increases were found for risks for new sex offenses, four of the scales (Negative Emotional States, Social Pressure, Enhancing Emotional States, and Interpersonal Conflict) were related to increased risk for other violent reoffenses. These same four scales and the Testing Control Scale were also significantly related to increased risk for parole violations. The more situations subjects identified as potential risks for reoffense, the less likely they were to be arrested for a violent offense or to have their paroles violated. Such results tend to support an important tenet of our treatment model—that recognition and acknowledgment of specific risk factors are important steps in preventing reoffense.

Data collected at the time of subject recruitment were available on 214 rapists in the SOTEP database who had been released to the community. This group includes all of those who were eligible for the project, regardless of whether they volunteered. Nineteen variables were examined with respect to their effects on reoffending (see Table 2). Only age of the subject at the time of the instant offense was predictive of all three arrest outcomes (sex offense, other violent offense, and parole violation). As expected, younger subjects

TABLE 2 Multivariate Survival Analyses of Times to Reoffense for Sex Crimes, Violent Crimes, and Parole Violations as a Function of 19 Treatment, Personal History/Demographic, Criminal History, and Offense Characteristic Predictors Rapists Only

	Outcome		
Predictor	Sex offense	Other violent offense	Parole violation
Treatment variables			
Volunteered	$p < .12$ (+)	ns	ns
Completed treatment	$p < .10$ (−)	ns	$p < .01$ (+)
Length of time in treatment	ns	ns	$p < .01$ (−)
Personal history/demographic variables			
Alcoholism	ns	ns	ns
MDSO commitment	$p < .05$ (+)	ns	ns
Victim of physical abuse	ns	ns	ns
Victim of sexual abuse	$p < .05$ (+)	ns	ns
Employed at time of offense	ns	$p < .001$ (−)	$p < .001$ (−)
Age at time of offense	$p < .05$ (−)	$p < .05$ (−)	$p < .05$ (−)
IQ level	ns	$p < .05$ (−)	$p < .01$ (−)
Offense characteristics			
Injured victim	ns	$p < .10$ (−)	ns
Intoxicated at time of offense	ns	$p < .10$ (−)	$p < .10$ (−)
Use of a weapon	ns	ns	ns
Victim unknown to offender	ns	$p < .11$ (+)	ns
Victim verbally abused	ns	ns	ns
Criminal history variables			
Prior sex offense	ns	ns	ns
Prior felony offense	ns	$p < .10$ (+)	$p < .01$ (+)
Time served on sentence	ns	ns	$p < .001$ (−)
Loss of time in prison	ns	ns	ns

Note. +, the effect of the predictor is to increase the risk for reoffending; −, the effect is to decrease the risk; ns, not significant.

were at greater risk to reoffend. Contrary to expectation, no relationship was found for number of prior sex offenses and risk for any arrest outcome.

As is evident in Table 2, a different pattern of predictors emerges for each of the three types of reoffense outcomes. Subjects who completed treatment were less likely to be arrested for a new sex offense. Rapists who volunteered for treatment were more likely to sexually reoffend than those who did not. Within this group, those who volunteered but received no treatment were at greatest risk for a new sex crime arrest, followed by those who dropped out of treatment. Rapists who completed treatment had the lowest risk for reoffense.

Having an identified history of being a victim of childhood sexual abuse also increased the risk that the subject would later be arrested for a new sex crime, whereas having an identified history of physical abuse did not. In our sample the prevalence of documented child sexual abuse was low (3.9%), but this small group was 92% more likely to be arrested for a new sex offense, based on these data.

Although no relationship was found between any kind of reoffending and previous convictions for sex crimes, a history of previous treatment for sexual aggression as a Mentally Disordered Sex Offender (MDSO) was associated with a greater risk for a new sex crime arrest.

In addition to age at the time of the instant offense, several other factors were associated with being arrested for violent crimes other than a sex offense. Employment, intoxication, and acquaintance with the victim at the time of the instant offense all suggested a lower risk for a violent offense other than a sex crime. As expected, both a history of prior felony offenses and lower IQ levels were associated with increased risk.

In contrast to arrests for new sex offenses, completing treatment increased the rapists' risks for parole violation, and those who received no treatment were least likely to be revoked. However, this effect was moderated by length of treatment (subjects with longer periods of treatment were less likely to violate parole than were those with shorter treatment experiences). As was the case with the other violent offense outcome, employment or intoxication at the time of the offense, as well as higher IQs, reduced the risk for a parole violation. Finally, subjects who served longer sentences were less likely to violate their parole conditions.

These preliminary findings using survival analysis techniques emphasize that different risk factors may be associated with very different arrest outcomes. Therefore, combining different types of arrest outcomes, such as sex and other violent crimes, into one category (Rice, Harris, & Quinsey, 1990; Rice, Quinsey, & Harris, 1991) may tend to hide important relationships for predictors with varied arrest outcomes.

RECOMMENDATIONS FOR TREATMENT AND EVALUATION

Although it is too early in this longitudinal study to make policy recommendations based on our own evaluation data, we want to present some ideas about where the field of sex offender treatment is going and about what needs to be done. First, we discuss some general trends and suggestions related to the treatment of sex offenders; second, we present our recommendations about the direction that should be taken in evaluating sex offender treatment programs.

Treatment

Although the public controversy regarding sex offender rehabilitation continues, treatment providers have been moving toward a consensus regarding the essential components of state-of-the-art treatment for this population. First, it is generally accepted that the overall goal of treatment is one of management or control, not cure. This rejects the notion that sex offending is a circumscribed psychosexual disorder from which one will recover, and the expectation that successful treatment will eliminate the disorder. Instead, it is assumed that offenders must accept a lifelong responsibility for managing their sexual behavior, and that treatment is never "over."

In addition to emphasizing offender responsibility, current treatment programs tend to be much more comprehensive than those in the past. For example, it would be difficult to find a program that focuses on only one determinant (e.g., deviant sexual arousal), or includes only one modality (e.g., "garden variety" group therapy). Sex offender treatment has become a sophisticated clinical speciality that is dominated by multimodal assessment and treatment packages designed to measure and modify specific determinants of sex offending. Several common targets of treatment are: (a) deviant sexual interests; (b) cognitive distortions about offending; and (c) a broad range of skill deficits such as social incompetence, lack of empathy, and impaired anger or affect management (Laws, 1988; Marshall & Barbaree, 1990; Solicitor General of Canada, 1990).

Consistent with the idea that the goal of treatment is management (vs. cure), there has also been an increased emphasis on self-management skills for sex offenders. Although it was first proposed as a treatment for sex offenders just over 10 years ago (Marques & Pithers, 1981), the Relapse Prevention model (Marlatt & Gordon, 1980, 1985) has become very popular in the field of sex offender treatment. As the programs described in Laws' (1989) recent book demonstrated, RP can be applied either as a program's overall theoretical framework (as in our program) or as a specific component (as in the Florida program). In both cases, the emphasis of RP is on training the offender to recognize the chain of events and specific risk factors that have led to his sex crimes, and how to interrupt that chain of events to avoid reoffense.

Finally, there is a definite consensus regarding the importance of aftercare/ community supervision in sex offender treatment. Current outpatient programs have a heavy emphasis on supervision, and often include techniques more often seen in criminal justice than in psychotherapy settings, such as drug screening, electronic monitoring, unscheduled home visits, and polygraph examinations. Similarly, state-of-the-art institutional programs include strong aftercare components designed to facilitate community readjustment, deliver booster sessions to prolong treatment effects, and provide direct supervision over an extended posttreatment period (Maletzky, 1991; Marshall, Laws, & Barbaree, 1990).

While the above trends toward more sophisticated and comprehensive treatment are encouraging, our experience in SOTEP leads us to make the following additional points about what state-of-the-art treatment should include. First, as Quinsey (1991) put it: "to advance our knowledge, we must base intervention on theory so that when the intervention is tested, we simultaneously test the theory" (p. 3). In our view, a comprehensive program not only should be multimodal, but should be based on a clearly articulated treatment model that defines the targets of treatment and the changes that treatment should produce to reduce the likelihood of reoffense.

Due to the heterogeneity of the sex offender population, the program model should also provide assessment-driven treatment. That is, a comprehensive treatment program must address not only the common precursors of sexual aggression, but also the individual offender's particular combination of risk factors.

One important part of the treatment process involves getting the offender to recognize and understand the sequence of thoughts, feelings, and events that precede his sex crimes. For example, a rape is neither an isolated nor a discrete event. It is an endpoint of a long series or chain of events. Some of these events are external or environmental (e.g., presence of a potential victim, interpersonal conflict, etc.), whereas others are intrapersonal precursors (e.g., negative affective states such as anger or rage, intoxication, internal needs for power and control, etc.) (Marques & Nelson, 1989). Offenders must be able to identify the risk factors that increase the likelihood of their offending in the future. A technique used in SOTEP to assist offenders in recognizing and understanding this pattern is the construction of cognitive–behavioral chains leading to the offense (Nelson & Jackson, 1989). Once the offender understands his unique, idiosyncratic offense pattern, he must learn how to intervene or break into this offense pattern at its earliest sign. Each step in the cognitive–behavioral chain leading to offense can be examined for coping responses that would reduce the chances that he would reoffend. These coping responses must be planned, problem solved, and practiced (Steenman, Nelson, & Viesti, 1989).

Although the process of building a cognitive–behavioral offense chain seems rather straightforward, it can be a very difficult task for offenders, and some obviously do not succeed in interrupting the chain after release. Among rapists, those with high "criminal versatility" have an enormous number of situations that are high-risk for offending, and a wide variety of ways to relapse (including both sex and nonsex crimes). Situations involving power and control needs may be more complex and difficult to recognize than are those involving sexual attraction. Also, for rapists who are impulsive and have problems with affect management, the chain of events does not proceed slowly or systematically, but moves very quickly from a high-risk situation (e.g., anger, frustration) to a full-blown relapse. We suspect that the common factor of substance abuse in these offenders may contribute to this "crash and burn" phenomenon, but we do not yet have data to support this idea.

It has been observed previously (Marshall, Jones, Ward, Johnston, & Barbaree, 1991) that treatment, even comprehensive cognitive–behavioral programs, has been less effective with rapists, and that more research is needed to identify which offenders can best be treated. We agree with these authors and endorse their suggestion that "research should be directed at identifying what it is that current programs are missing rather than identifying who should or should not be treated" (p. 481). We recently began an in-depth study of reoffenders to learn more about the relapse process and treatment needs that are not being met.

Our final comments on treatment concern the delivery of treatment services. In contrast to the "sexual psychopath" era, more institutional programs are now in correctional than in mental health facilities. Although our program is provided in a secure state hospital, it is unlikely that California programs that follow our experiment will be hospital based. Operating a program within a JCAHO-accredited psychiatric facility is extremely expensive, and requires compliance with staffing patterns and practices that are more appropriate for mentally ill individuals than for most sex offenders.

It also seems unlikely that programs following ours will have as heavy an institutional component as SOTEP does; more emphasis will probably be on intensive transitional and community supervisory components. If so, care should be taken to include in the community programs individuals who have failed or dropped out of institutional treatment. That is, aftercare should not be provided only to program "graduates." Again, although our results are preliminary, treatment dropouts such as SOTEP's ex-treatment group appear to be high-risk offenders without community follow-up. Obviously, solid recommendations on such policy matters will not be made until later in our study.

Evaluation

Although there is evidence that cognitive–behavioral treatment programs have been effective with some sex offenders (Marshall et al., 1991), methodological problems continue to limit the conclusions we can draw from previous studies. In our view, every program is in fact "experimental," and should be designed with as much attention as possible to scientific rigor. New programs should be required to include strong evaluation components from the outset, so that attention can be paid to subject selection and group assignment, treatment fidelity and pre–post measures, management of attrition, and definitions of success/ failure. Because SOTEP represents this type of prospective study, we describe some of the features of our project that we believe are important.

First, our evaluation effort has enjoyed strong support from the state of California, and we have been able to obtain the resources needed for a major evaluation study to be successful. Also critical to the quality of the project was the decision, made at the beginning, to develop and maintain separate components for treatment and evaluation efforts. Although many of the investigators in the field have been trained in the clinical tradition, SOTEP's evaluation staff received their training in research and statistical design, and keep abreast of new developments in methods for handling longitudinal data, linear structural modeling, log linear analysis, and so on.

In addition to independent treatment and evaluation components, SOTEP was planned from the outset to have a valid research design. Indeed, such a design was mandated by the Legislature in the laws that established the program. Thus, all eligible offenders are assessed and tracked by project staff, random assignments of volunteers to treatment and control conditions are made, methods have been developed to control for critical features that may differentiate experimental groups from one another, attrition is minimized and monitored, and criteria to be employed in determining outcome have been specified.

We have also made efforts to clearly specify our treatment model, program structure and intensity, and the content of all treatment components. As was described earlier, pre–post measures are used for each treatment component, and an overall pre–post assessment battery is used to determine whether subjects are achieving in-treatment goals. In these efforts, we have not relied exclusively on available standardized tests (the workhorses of traditional clinical research), but have developed additional measures relevant to our relapse prevention framework, and have presented data here indicating their value in the prediction of reoffense. Our evaluation staff have expertise in issues concerning measurement, and have been able to operationalize the key concepts set forth in our treatment model, to develop and test new measures of these, and to modify and improve them as data concerning their reliability and validity are collected.

We have also revised and added assessment procedures as new data are collected that demonstrate the need. As SOTEP sample participants began leaving prison or treatment, it became clear to us that we were not measuring several constructs critical to their potential success or failure in abstaining from new offenses. To correct this problem, we sought and obtained funding from the NIMH to enhance our measures.

As our experience demonstrates, the conduct of a controlled, prospective treatment outcome study takes considerable resources and a great deal of experimenter patience. Because our project is limited to treating 46 individuals at a time, and requires at least 5 years of follow-up data to be collected on all subjects, we cannot expect a significant treatment effect to emerge quickly. This is especially true because our major indicators of reoffense—official records—are known to provide underestimates of actual crimes. As should be clear from our project description earlier, we have a number of suggestions for what evaluators should do while they are waiting for a treatment effect to emerge. First, as was discussed in our Findings section, important in-treatment changes should be measured. Are subjects achieving the goals of the program and showing changes in variables evaluators have reason to believe are related to recidivism? Such measures provide some immediate information on how the program is working, and will also be useful in developing prediction models later.

Second, we suggest conducting more sensitive analyses of the available data on reoffense. Simple comparisons of reoffense rates tend to be uninformative without supporting information concerning statistical significance. Also, many of the statistical procedures (e.g., chi square, linear discriminant analysis) used in sex offender research require equivalent times at risk for study groups, a requirement rarely met in treatment outcome studies. Similarly, the usefulness of linear regression methods is limited, because the outcome to be predicted is often a binary variable, reoffense, which requires the use of nonlinear models (Aldrich & Nelson, 1984).

In our experience, it is important that the dimension of time be taken into account. First of all, events predictive of reoffending tend to occur at different rates over time for different types of offenders. In addition, status on measures of performance, attitudes, beliefs, and interests may show changes over time, which would prove enlightening about the course of reoffending. The probability, or risk, of reoffense may not be constant over time. Subjects may be less likely to offend immediately after release from prison, due to parole supervision, and the risk of their reoffending may increase as they become acclimated to life on the street. On the other hand, successful adjustment over a prolonged period of time at risk may be associated with decreases in the probability of reoffense.

We have been operating on the assumption that the best method for testing hypotheses about the effects of treatment on sex offenders is survival analysis (Singer & Willett, 1991; Willett & Singer, 1991). This method permits both nonparametric and parametric models to be developed that allow comparisons among groups, development of prediction models, and use of covariates for variables whose values either remain constant or change over time.

In addition to measuring in-treatment changes and conducting more sensitive analyses of available outcome data, we suggest that evaluators work with different definitions of, and measures of, recidivism. As our study of parole files presented earlier in this chapter reveals, much information about reoffending is lost if one relies on rapsheet data alone. Multiple data sources should be used, and efforts should be made to obtain descriptions of offenses before they are processed in the criminal justice system. Also, we suggest including nonsex crimes (especially those against persons) in some outcome analyses to get a fuller picture of how subjects are doing in the community. Research on the variety of crimes committed by sex offenders (Weinrott & Saylor, 1991) has supported this suggestion.

Much of the outcome research with sex offenders has asked a simple question ("Does treatment work?"), and has used a simple definition of success/failure (e.g., failure = rearrest for sex crime). We suggest that the question is more complicated; perhaps, "What treatment works, for what kind of offender, in what type of setting, and with what definition of success?" We also suggest that there are shades of treatment success/failure that are missed by the use of a single, dichotomous reoffense variable. If we really believe that there is no cure for the disorder of sex offending, and that offenders must assume a lifelong commitment to self-management, we must expect that even strong treatment effects will tend to dissipate over time. A treatment may not eliminate reoffending, but may achieve a goal of delay and containment of reoffending. Again, length of time to reoffense must be considered in outcome research, and efforts should be made to determine the number and severity of crimes as well. Knowing that treatment produced significant interruptions in intense and destructive criminal careers would be an important finding indeed.

Although our comments here clearly indicate that rigorous outcome studies such as ours are crucial in the field of sex offender treatment, we want to end on a cautionary note about the importance of any single study, regardless of its rigor. One study is just that: one attempt to measure the effects of a particular intervention on a particular sample of offenders. As Breiling (1991) suggested, each study must be considered in the larger context of other similar efforts. However, if enough well-designed and documented studies are done, it may be possible to use meta-analytic procedures to combine their results statistically. Such analyses would produce more meaningful estimates of treatment effects in various settings and with various types of offenders.

REFERENCES

Aldrich, J. H., & Nelson, F. D. (1984). *Linear probability, logit, and probit models*. Beverly Hills, CA: Sage.

Breiling, J. (1991). Comments on evaluating the effectiveness of mental health programs for dangerous clients. *Proceedings of the Second Annual Conference on State Mental Health Agency Services Research* (pp. 124–127). Alexandria, VA: National Association of State Mental Health Program Directors Research Institute.

California Laws. (1981). Chapter 928, codified as *California Penal Code* Sections 1364 and 1365.

Hare, R. D. (1990). *Manual for the revised psychopathy checklist.* Toronto: Multi-Health Systems. Unpublished.

Laws, D. R. (1988). Introductory comments. In R. Prentky & V. Quinsey (Eds.), *Human sexual aggression: Current perspectives* (Vol. 528, pp. 203–204). New York: Annals of the New York Academy of Sciences.

Laws, D. R. (Ed.). (1989). *Relapse prevention with sex offenders.* New York: Guilford.

Maletzky, B. M. (1991). *Treating the sexual offender.* Newbury Park, CA: Sage.

Marlatt, G. A., & Gordon, J. R. (1980). Determinants of relapse: Implications for the maintenance of behavior change. In P. O. Davidson & S. M. Davidson (Eds.), *Behavioral medicine: Changing health lifestyles* (pp. 410–452). New York: Brunner/Mazel.

Marlatt, G. A., & Gordon, J. R. (Eds.). (1985). *Relapse prevention: Maintenance strategies in the treatment of addictive behaviors.* New York: Guilford.

Marques, J. K., Day, D. M., Nelson, C., Miner, M. H., & West, M. A. (1991). *The Sex Offender Treatment and Evaluation Project: Fourth report to the Legislature in response to PC 1365.* Sacramento: California State Department of Mental Health.

Marques, J. K., & Nelson, C. (1989). Elements of high-risk situations. In D. R. Laws (Ed.), *Relapse prevention with sex offenders* (pp. 35–46). New York: Guilford.

Marques, J. K., & Pithers, W. D. (1981, November). *Relapse prevention with sex offenders.* Paper presented at the International Conference on the Treatment of Addictive Behaviors, Grand Canyon, Arizona.

Marshall, W. L., & Barbaree, H. E. (1990). Outcome of comprehensive cognitive–behavioral treatment programs. In W. L. Marshall, D. R. Laws, & H. E. Barbaree (Eds.), *Handbook of sexual assault: Issues, theories, and treatment of the offender* (pp. 363–385). New York: Plenum.

Marshall, W. L., Jones, R., Ward, T., Johnston, P., & Barbaree, H. E. (1991). Treatment outcome with sex offenders. *Clinical Psychology Review, 11,* 465–485.

Marshall, W. L., Laws, D. R., & Barbaree, H. E. (1990). Present status and future directions. In W. L. Marshall, D. R. Laws, & H. E. Barbaree (Eds.), *Handbook of sexual assault: Issues, theories, and treatment of the offender* (pp. 389–395). New York: Plenum.

Nelson, C., & Jackson, P. (1989). High-risk recognition: The cognitive–behavioral chain. In D. R. Laws (Ed.), *Relapse prevention with sex offenders* (pp. 167–177). New York: Guilford.

Nichols, H. R., & Molinder, I. (1984). *The multiphasic sex inventory manual.*

Available from Nichols and Molinder, 437 Bowes Drive, Tacoma, WA 98466. (Unpublished)

Quinsey, V. L. (1991). Approaches to treating adult offenders. In C. D. Milloy & R. Wilkes (Eds.), *Successful interventions with sex offenders: Learning what works* (pp. 2–3). Olympia, WA: Washington State Institute for Public Policy.

Rice, M. E., Harris, G. T., & Quinsey, V. L. (1990). A followup of rapists assessed in a maximum security psychiatric facility. *Journal of Interpersonal Violence, 5,* 435–448.

Rice, M. E., Quinsey, V. L., & Harris, G. T. (1991). Sexual recidivism among child molesters released from a maximum security facility. *Journal of Consulting and Clinical Psychology, 59,* 381–386.

Singer, J. D., & Willett, J. B. (1991). Modeling the days of our lives: Using survival analysis when designing and analyzing longitudinal studies of duration and the time of events. *Psychological Bulletin, 110,* 268–290.

Solicitor General of Canada. (1990). *The management and treatment of sex offenders.* Report of the Working Group: Sex Offender Treatment Review. Ottawa, Ontario: Minister of Supply and Services Canada.

Steenman, H., Nelson, C., & Viesti, C. (1989). Developing coping strategies for high-risk situations. In D. R. Laws (Ed.), *Relapse prevention with sex offenders* (pp. 178–187). New York: Guilford.

Warner, S. W. (1965). Randomized response: A survey technique for eliminating evasive answer bias. *Journal of the American Statistical Association, 60,* 63–69.

Weinrott, M. R., & Saylor, M. (1991). Self-report of crimes committed by sex offenders. *Journal of Interpersonal Violence, 6,* 286–300.

Willett, J. B., & Singer, J. D. (1991). How long did it take . . . ?: Using survival analysis in psychological research. In L. M. Collins & J. L. Horn (Eds.), *Best methods for the analysis of change: Recent advances, unanswered questions, future directions* (pp. 309–326). Washington, DC: American Psychological Association.

12

JUVENILES WHO COMMIT SEXUAL OFFENSES: A CRITICAL REVIEW OF RESEARCH

Judith V. Becker
Arizona Health Sciences Center

Cathi D. Harris
Bruce D. Sales
University of Arizona

Sexual offenses historically have been, and continue to be, a problem facing our society. At the present time, the majority of clinical and research information relevant to sexual offending centers around the adult perpetrator, grossly neglecting the adolescent offender. The reasons for this are broad, ranging from the idea that all juvenile sexual behavior is "exploratory" in nature, to not wanting to label the adolescent as being sexually deviant.

This neglect is unfortunate. Although the exact number of sexual offenses committed by juveniles in unknown, in 1983 the Uniform Crime Report indicated that 20% of all reported forcible rapes were committed by individuals under the age of 18. This breaks down to 50 arrests of forcible rape per 100,000 adolescent males. This statistic may be only the tip of the proverbial iceberg, because it accounts only for rape and does not consider other sexual offenses. Adolescents also engage in other types of "hands-on" offenses, such as frottage, fondling, and child molestation, along with "hands-off" offenses, such as voyeurism and exhibitionism (Davis & Leitenberg, 1987).

The need to study juvenile sex offending is enhanced further by the fact that if a sex offender is left untreated he or she may go on to commit further sexual offenses. Abel, Mittelman, and Becker (1985) found that of more than 400 adult sex offenders interviewed, 58% self-reported the onset of their deviant sexual interest patterns began prior to the age of 18. Given these data, it is safe to say that juveniles contribute significantly to the number of sex offenses committed today.

The purpose of this chapter is to review critically the empirical literature relevant to the juvenile sex offender. Our goal is not only to present a review of the research findings, but also to identify the limitations in the current research and suggest areas where further research should be conducted.

To find all of the relevant studies, a 10-year search on the MedLine and PsychLit databases was performed using the key words and phrases: juvenile/adolescent sex offending, juvenile/adolescent sexual offenders, and juvenile/adolescent offending. In addition, a small number of articles was taken from years prior to 1982. These articles were selected because they have been cited extensively in other juvenile offender literature.

This process resulted in 73 articles being identified. Forty-three (59% of the total sample) related to the characteristics of juvenile sex offenders. Of these, 43 articles (12% of the total sample) descriptively covered offender and offense characteristics without statistical information presented; 29 (40% of the total sample) covered offender and offense characteristic topics using a sample population, but did not have a control comparison group; the remaining 5 articles (7% of the total sample) studied offender and offense characteristics by comparing a sample offender population with a random sample of either juvenile offenders who had not committed sexual offenses or juveniles from the general population.

Treatment issues were covered in 23 (31.5%) of the articles. The majority of the treatment articles (15; 21% of the total sample) had no sample population, therefore no statistical data were provided. They were just descriptive of treatment facilities and programs. Although the remainder of the articles (8; 11% of the total sample) employed a sample population, there was no control group used.

The final 7 articles (10% of the total sample) related to miscellaneous issues, such as characteristics of the parents (e.g., the mothers of sexual offenders), adolescent sexual behavior, and sexual knowledge in general.

CATEGORIZING OFFENSES

It is generally considered acceptable to break down sexual offenses into three categories: hands-off offenses, hands-on offenses, and pedophilic offenses. This classification system has been derived from the adult literature, and is used widely by adolescent researchers. The first group is referred to as the hands-off offenses and includes voyeurism, exhibitionism, and obscene phone calls. In a study conducted by Saunders, Awad, and White (1986), approximately 36% of their sample of 63 adolescent sex offenders committed these nonviolent sexual offenses. The victims of these offenses quite often are the perpetrator's peers and adults (Davis & Leitenberg, 1987).

The second category, the hands-on offenses, includes fondling, sexual assaults, rape, and attempted rape. These offenses usually entail physical force and may also involve the use of a weapon. They are usually perpetrated against female strangers who are the same age or older than the perpetrator (Lewis,

Shankok, & Pincus, 1979). Generally speaking, victims of age 12 or more are considered peer age, although the age may vary depending on the researcher. In a study of 35 sex offenders identified from a group of violent delinquents, 79% committed forcible rape and 13% committed sexual assaults (Fagan & Wexler, 1986).

The third and final group, pedophilic offenses or child molestation, involves offenses against victims 4 or more years younger than the offender (Deisher, Wenet, Paperny, Clark, & Fehrenbach, 1982); in addition, the victim often knows the offender and might possibly be a relative (Saunders et al., 1986). Although males and females are likely to suffer from child molestation, as the age of the victim falls there is an increase in the number of male victims (Davis & Leitenberg, 1987). It is here in the pedophilic offenses that the highest degree of coercion is found. Moreover, no age is immune to sexual victimization; victims of sexual offenses range in age from 4 to 60 years old (Lewis et al., 1979).

DEVELOPMENT OF SEXUAL DEVIANCE

Although the typologies for characterizing offenses and offenders may be helpful for assessment and treatment purposes, they do not address the etiology of the behavior. Currently, two models exist in the literature on the development of sexual deviance. Ryan, Lane, Davis, and Isaac's model (1987) identified the "sexual assault cycle." This model was derived from the cognitive–behavioral dysfunction cycle, and involves six steps. It begins with the adolescent offender having a negative self-image, which results in an increased probability of maladaptive coping strategies when confronted with negative responses to him- or herself (negative self-image stage). The negative self-image also leads the individual to predict a negative reaction from others (prediction rejection stage). To protect against this anticipated rejection, the adolescent will become socially isolated and withdrawn (isolation stage) and begin to fantasize to compensate for his or her feelings of lack of control or powerlessness (fantasy stage). The fantasies may provide the opportunity to visualize the offense (planning stage). Finally, the sexual offense is carried out physically, leading to more negative self-imaging and thoughts of rejection (sexual offense stage). As can be seen, this is a vicious repetitive cycle.

Why some individuals respond to negative self-imaging in a sexually aggressive manner and the majority of juveniles do not has not been addressed in the literature to date. However, if the interaction between individual and environmental characteristics discussed later in the chapter can be proven empirically to be etiological factors, this issue can be revisited with favorable results.

Becker and Kaplan's model (1988) developed from the idea that the first sexual offense results from a combination of individual characteristics, such as lack of social and assertive skills and history of nonsexual deviance; family variables, including family relationships; and social–environmental variables, such as social isolation and antisocial behavior. (More detailed information on these characteristics is provided later.) Following the commission of the first sex crime, the juvenile can embark down three possible paths: (a) the dead end path, where he or she commits no further crimes; (b) the delinquency path, where the individual commits not only other sex offenses, but also engages in general nonsex offenses and deviant behaviors; and (c) the sexual interest pattern path, where the adolescent continues to commit sex crimes and often develops a paraphiliac arousal pattern.

It is important to note that neither of these models have been derived empirically, nor have they been validated empirically. The cycle by Ryan et al. (1987) evolved from a treatment premise. The basic assumption is that to prevent further offending, offenders must have a framework on which to analyze their thoughts and feelings so that they can self-monitor and modify their behavior prior to offending. The Becker-Kaplan (1988) model was derived through clinical observation of those characteristics shared by juvenile sex offenders.

CHARACTERISTICS OF OFFENDERS AND THEIR ENVIRONMENTS

Although Becker and Kaplan's (1988) model was not based on empirical research, there is some research that is relevant. As in Becker and Kaplan's (1988) model, the common characteristics found in these studies can be broken down into three areas: characteristics of the individual, the family environment, and the social environment.

Individual Characteristics

Many studies have drawn the general conclusion that the greatest number of offenders are caucasian males (Schram, Milloy, & Rowe, 1991). This conclusion is most likely due to the large percentage of caucasians in our society. Indeed, when the percent of the population is taken into account, no one race or socioeconomic class commits a significantly larger number of offenses (Hsu & Starzynski, 1990; Schram et al., 1991).

The literature identifies certain individual characteristics that are prevalent among these individuals, the first being the lack of social and assertive skills (Awad & Saunders, 1989; Fagan & Wexler, 1986; Katz, 1990; Shoor, Speed, & Bartelt, 1986). Here the individual may find it hard to associate with both adults and peers alike, which in turn leads to social isolation, one of the social environmental variables. Also, a history of nonsexual delinquency is seen. Fehrenbach, Smith, Monastersky, and Deisher (1986) found that in a sample population of 293 male adolescent sex offenders, 44% committed nonsexual offenses prior to their first sexual offense. Low academic performance (Awad & Saunders, 1989; 1991; Fagan & Wexler, 1986; Schram et al., 1991) is another characteristic that is prevalent among juvenile offenders. For example, in a study conducted by Awad and Saunders (1989), 83% of their sample population had serious learning problems, 48% had diagnosed learning disabilities, whereas a number of the sample evidenced truancy and general chronic academic and behavior problems in school. A fourth common characteristic is lack of impulse control. A study of 262 male adolescents, who were committed for less violent and less aggressive sexual offenses (Smith, Monastersky, & Deisher, 1987), showed that approximately 50% of the common variance was explained by the propensity to act out impulsively. The average adolescent sex offender also was found to have below average skills in anger control. Becker, Kaplan, Tenke, and Tartaglini (1991) identified depression as being a shared characteristic. They conducted a study of 246 male adolescent sex offenders, and found that 42% of their subjects suffered from major depression as measured by the Beck Depression Inventory. The mean score of the sex offenders on the BDI was 14.3, a figure that is two tiers higher than a random sample of adolescents as reported by Kaplan, Hong, and Weinhold (1984). Finally, lack of proper sex education is demonstrated. Kaplan, Becker, and Cunningham-Rathner (1988) investigated the characteristics of parents of adolescent incest perpetrators. The findings indicated that 62% of the 27 parents or parent surrogates gave no sex education to their adolescents. This finding provides a possible explanation to the thought distortions and deviant sexual fantasies and arousal patterns experienced by juvenile sex offenders.

However, these characteristics are not unique to juvenile sex offenders. Two studies that compare juvenile sexual offenders to other violent and nonviolent juvenile offender populations have been conducted (Lewis et al., 1979; Tarter, Hegedus, Alterman, & Katz-Garris, 1983). Tarter et al. (1983) found that in a sample of 28 nonviolent offenders, 31 violent offenders, and 14 sex offenders, there were no significant differences regarding neuropsychological, intellectual, or psychological capacities. Lewis et al. (1979) reported similar findings. Their sample of 17 violent juvenile sex offenders did not differ significantly from a comparison sample of 61 violent juvenile nonsex offenders on neurological, psychological, or psychoeducational characteristics.

It is possible that these studies focused only on conduct disorder characteristics, which are common among all groups of juvenile offenders. Also, the assessment tools may not be sensitive enough to discriminate between groups or to pick up sexual pathologies.

Characteristics of the Family Environment

The family environment also contains features that are common among the young sexual offenders. The first of these features is an unstable home environment (Smith & Israel, 1987). This can involve distant relationships or no relationship at all with siblings and parents. An unusual, unhealthy home situation, such as a parent having a sexual pathology or the child viewing sexual interactions between the parental figures whether they are biological parents or parent surrogates (Smith & Israel, 1987), is another common element. The juvenile witnessing family violence between a parent and a child, or more often between two parental figures (Davis & Leitenberg, 1987), is also identified. The last family characteristic is the juvenile's prior experience of being abused. In a study conducted by Johnson (1988), 66% of a sample of 47 juvenile sex offender males, with a mean age of 9.7 years, had been victimized either physically (19%) or sexually (49%) prior to committing their first offense. Interestingly, only one child reported being both physically and sexually abused.

There is disagreement within the literature about whether the separation of a child from his or her parents or parental separations is an etiological variable for juvenile sex offending. Kaplan, Becker, and Martinez (1990) compared the mothers of adolescent incest perpetrators with nonincest sexual offenders and found that the majority of the incest perpetrators had a mother that was not living with a partner.

Characteristics of the Social Environment

One of the most commonly looked at etiological variables falls within the social environmental area—social isolation. In Awad and Saunders' study (1989), 62% of their sample of 49 male adolescent sex offenders was considered socially isolated. These juveniles were unable to establish or maintain close relationships with peers, although they typically got along very well with children who were at least 4 or 5 years younger. Awad and Saunders (1991) also found that of their sample of 49 juvenile sex offenders, 63% had a history of antisocial behavior that coincided with or predated the commission of the charged offense.

Moreover, although research has suggested that these characteristics describe the young sex offender, it should not be assumed that they present a profile of the adolescent sex offender, because there is no definite set of characteristics that a juvenile must have to be labelled as a sex offender. In addition, this literature is limited in that there is no empirical evidence as to how these variables interact with one another, both in regard to explaining the etiology of juvenile sex offending or in predicting amenability to treatment or recidivism. This limitation is unfortunate, because a more definitive description of the correlates and predictors of juvenile sex offending would facilitate assessment and therapy.

ASSESSMENT

As with any clinically deviant population, it is important to have the ability to clinically assess individuals to determine if they are part of that population. Although a discussion of the full clinical protocol for such an assessment is beyond the scope of this chapter, this section examines the content, reliability, and validity of the Forensic Assessment Instruments (FAI) that are used in assessing the adolescent sex offender.

The Adolescent Cognition Scale

The Adolescent Cognition scale is a revised version of the earlier Abel-Becker Cognition scale, which was designed to assess if the offender has any distorted cognitions regarding sexual behaviors (Abel & Becker, 1984). The test consists of 32 true/false items that the juvenile is asked to rate as being true or false. An example of a statement would be, "Some people are shy about asking for sex so they really want you to force them." The test–retest reliability for this instrument was found to be only marginal, and it does not discriminate between offender and nonsex offenders' attitudes (Hunter, Becker, & Kaplan, in press).

The Adolescent Sexual Interest Cardsort (ASIC)

The ASIC is a self-report measure of sexual interest that was designed to determine the presence of any deviant sexual interest patterns the juvenile may have (Abel, 1979). This measure gives the individual the opportunity to disclose his or her true feelings without having to do so in a face-to-face interview. The juvenile is asked to rate, on a three-point scale, his or her arousal to 64 items that describe sexual scenarios. For example, "I am holding a 12-year-old down. She is helpless as I rub my penis between her legs." The test–retest reliability on this instrument appears to be poor (Becker & Kaplan, 1988). However, this may be a result of the ethical requirement to provide feedback following initial assessment regarding certain sexual acts that are considered inappropriate. Therefore, researchers may be seeing a reactive response to negative feedback from the clinician. Also, to date there has been no research conducted on comparison samples of nonsexual offenders or nonoffender populations. There are no reported validity data.

The Math Tech Sex Test

This test assesses the juvenile's sexual knowledge (Kirby, 1984). The juvenile is asked to respond to 34 sexual knowledge questions, along with 70 value and attitude questions. The scores obtained on this test can be compared to a number of normed samples on nonoffending adolescents. Unfortunately, we are unable to locate any information relating to the reliability and validity of this FAI.

Plethysmography

Plethysmography is used widely in the assessment of alleged juvenile sex offenders, because it provides a direct measurement of the juveniles' psychophysiological arousal response to different stimuli (Becker & Kaplan, 1988). By the use of a strain gauge, the juveniles' arousal in response to sexually explicit situations presented on audiotape can be measured. There are no reliability or validity studies reported in the literature. One reason for this is that no researcher has ever been able to conduct measurements on a random sample of nonoffending juveniles (Becker, Hunter, Stein, & Kaplan, 1989; Becker & Kaplan, 1988; Becker, Kaplan, & Tenke, 1992).

Prediction of Recidivism

Despite its potential importance, there is no FAI that can discriminate between those juveniles who are likely to reoffend sexually or nonsexually. Smith and Monastersky (1986) conducted a study that assessed the ability of a community-based treatment program's personnel to accurately predict the likelihood of offenders to recidivate. A set of 36 variables (e.g., initial offense characteristics, historical characteristics, and how the clinician viewed the effectiveness of the treatment) was used in predicting reoffending behavior. They found that the hit rate of predictions was not much higher than chance alone. Overprediction usually occurred when the clinician was asked to predict whether the offender would commit a nonsex or sex offense.

TREATMENT

Two of the goals of assessment are to improve our ability to predict amenability to treatment and predict recidivism. Interestingly, Davis and Leitenberg (1987) found low recidivism rates in their review of follow-up studies of juvenile sex offenders conducted in the 1940s and 1950s—10% and 3%, respectively. These studies were of comparable length and subject number, but no systematic treatment programs were specified.

By 1982, there were only 22 identified treatment programs in the United States for juvenile offenders (Knopp, 1982). However, at the present time, there are over 600, with 80% of them being community based. These programs range from individual therapy to Youth Wilderness Programs, which are designed to promote self-discipline (Roberts & Camasso, 1991). Although there are diverse approaches to treatment, the majority of the programs center around the same treatment goals: developing social and assertive skills, developing victim empathy and nondeviant sexual interests, and teaching sex education. In addition, most programs also have designed sessions in cognitive restructuring and how to identify the precursors to deviant behavior for proper self-monitoring interventions. Despite these commonalities, there is an emphasis in the literature regarding two approaches to treatment: cognitive–behavioral and multisystemic.

Cognitive–Behavioral Therapy

A study conducted by Sapp and Vaughn (1990) inquired into the types of treatment that treatment programs use and which they would like to use. Their results indicated that most state-operated correctional institutions prefer behavioral approaches. In a survey conducted in 1988, Knopp found that out of 574 juvenile sex offender providers who responded to the survey, 63% utilized a cognitive–behavioral model and 62% a psychosocioeducational model.

A behavioral approach specifically tailored for juvenile sex offenders was described by Becker, Kaplan, and Kavoussi (1988). There are seven components in their cognitive–behavior therapy program that take place each week: (a) eight 30-minute sessions of verbal satiation, (b) four 75-minute group sessions focusing on cognitive restructuring, (c) one 75-minute session explaining covert sensitization to provide the offender with the skills needed to disrupt the cycle of coming in contact with his or her victim, (d) four 75-minute sessions of social skills training, (e) four 75-minute sessions of anger control, (f) two 75-minute sessions of relapse prevention, and (g) sex education and value clarification training; Becker et al. (1992) did not specify the number or length of sessions for this last component. Becker et al. (1988) have not investigated recidivism rates among their treated population, but have looked at the overall change in deviant sexual arousal. This change was measured using the erection response to both deviant and nondeviant sexual stimuli pre- and posttreatment. Following their cognitive–behavioral treatment program, subjects demonstrated a significant decrease in sexual arousal to inappropriate stimuli.

Multisystemic Treatment

The multisystemic approach (Borduin, Henggeler, Blaske, & Stein, in press) to treatment takes into consideration that any one or a number of factors can contribute to the juveniles offending. Because of the interaction of these factors, it is important to focus on all of these issues to intervene in the offending process. The areas of focus are different depending on the clinical assessment and what areas are found to be deficient. However, in general, the areas of cognitive processes, family relations, peer relations, and school performance are addressed.

Borduin et al. (in press) investigated the difference between their proposed multisystemic therapy and individual therapy on the recidivism rates of juvenile sex offenders. Individual therapy consisted of 45 hours of therapy in which counseling focused on personal, family, and academic issues. The follow-up period ranged from 21 to 49 months, with an average period being 37 months or a little over 3 years. The results for the multisystemic therapy were encouraging—12.5% sexual recidivism compared with 75% sexual recidivism for the individual therapy.

Schram et al. (1991) looked at the reoffending behavior of 197 male adolescent sex offenders 5–10 years following their release from an offender specific treatment program. The mean follow-up period was 6.8 years. Twenty-four offenders (12%) were arrested for alleged new sex crimes in the follow-up period. Of these 24, 20 (10% of the sample) were convicted of new sex offenses. On the other hand, 94 adolescents (48% of the total sample) were convicted of nonsex offenses. Thus, the juvenile sex offenders were much more likely to commit nonsex offenses if they were going to recidivate. The total percentage of juveniles who committed no new offenses, either sex or nonsex, was 37%. Moreover, although these treatments hold great promise, treatment staff are satisfied if the time between offenses can be lengthened and the seriousness of the offenses can be reduced. In short, although the hope is to cure, the aim is to control (Sapp & Vaughn, 1990).

CHARACTERISTICS OF RECIDIVISM

When a juvenile is going to recidivate, what characteristics are predictive? Smith and Monastersky (1986) addressed this question in a study of 112 juvenile sex offenders. Five factors were found that affected reoffense rates: (a) understanding the exploitativeness of the sex offense—the greater the understanding, the lower the likelihood of reoffending nonsexually; (b) identifying personal strengths—the lower the ability, the greater the likelihood of reoffending nonsexually; (c) noting unhealthy attitudes regarding sexuality—the less healthy the attitude (for example, not understanding one's own sexuality and proper sexual activities), the less likely to reoffend both sexually and nonsexually; (d) understanding the seriousness of the initial offense (rape as opposed to voyeurism)—the more serious the initial offense, the less likely the individual is to reoffend; and (e) identifying a lack of willingness to discuss and explore the offense in a nondefensive manner—the greater the lack, the greater the likelihood of sexually reoffending.

Schram et al. (1991) identified four different factors. Sexual recidivists were far more likely to: (a) have deviant sexual arousal patterns, (b) demonstrate a history of truancy, (c) have identified thinking errors/cognitive distortions, and (d) have had at least one prior conviction for a sexual offense. These authors also found that juveniles who recidivate share many of the same characteristics (e.g., threat or use of force, lack of victim empathy, and lack of remorse for offense), whether their recidivism be for sexual or nonsexual offenses.

CONCLUSION

Although there is increasing research on the juvenile sexual offender, there are still many areas that remain to be considered. Out of the two proposed models of adolescent sex offending, the Becker-Kaplan (1988) model addressed the research issues most commonly studied: the characteristics of the juvenile sex offender, their social environment, and their family environment. However, this model awaits empirical validation. Because of this, there is a methodological limitation to calling the variables that fall under these factors etiological to sex offending behavior.

The sexual assault cycle proposed by Ryan et al. (1987) appears to be good in theory, but here again lacks empirical validation. At this point, there is no literature as to its implementation or efficacy. The sexual assault cycle approach, if valid though, could lead to effective treatment. In addition to further studies of these models, research needs to continue on offender characteristics. To date, researchers have been unable to develop a way in which to discriminate between juvenile sex offenders and nonsex offending juveniles. The suggestion in the literature has been that many of the same characteristics are shared between offenders, whether they be sexual or nonsex offenders. This commonality may be an artifact of the characteristics studied. For example, it is likely that if adolescent cognitive distortions, deviant sexual interest patterns, and sexual knowledge were studied, there would be significant differences between the characteristics of juvenile sexual offenders, nonsexual offenders, and normal juveniles. Further research should be conducted in this area, because it may lead to the validation of existing FAIs as well as to the development of new instruments.

Finally, research must focus on treatment outcome. Because effective treatment lowers recidivism rates, it is in the best interest of everyone for the clinician to select the treatment program that is most effective. Yet there is a dearth of such research. In addition, there are not studies of individuals who have completed treatment compared with those who have not. Some may argue that it would be unethical for researchers to withhold treatment from an offending population. We would argue the opposite. Until treatment outcome research clearly demonstrates the value of these treatments, researchers and clinicians are not withholding treatments of known effectiveness. Further research should look at treated individuals in comparison with those who offended but who receive no treatment; to do so is socially responsible and ethical (Freedman, 1987).

REFERENCES

Abel, G. (1979). Assessment and treatment of sex offenders. Unpublished manuscript.

Abel, G., & Becker, J. V. (1984). *Adult Cognition Scale.* Research document available from G. Abel, Behavioral Medicine Laboratory, Atlanta, GA.

Abel, G., Mittelman, M., & Becker, J., (1985). Sex offenders: Results of assessment and recommendations for treatment. *Clinical Criminology: Current Concepts,* 191–205.

Awad, G. A., & Saunders, E. B. (1989). Adolescent child molesters: Clinical observations. *Child Psychiatry and Human Development, 19,* 195–206.

Awad, G. A., & Saunders, E. B. (1991). Male adolescent sexual assaulters; Clinical observations. *Journal of Interpersonal Violence, 6,* 446–460.

Becker, J. V., Cunningham-Rathner, J., & Kaplan, M. S. (1986). Adolescent sexual offenders. *Journal of Interpersonal Violence, 1,* 431–445.

Becker, J. V., Hunter, J. A., Stein, R. M., & Kaplan, M. S. (1989). Factors associated with erection in adolescent sex offenders. *Journal of Psychopathology and Behavioral Assessment, 11,* 353–363.

Becker, J. V., & Kaplan, M. S. (1988). The assessment of sexual offenders. *Advances in Behavioral Assessment of Children and Families, 4,* 97–118.

Becker, J. V., Kaplan, M., & Kavoussi, R. (1988). Measuring the effectiveness of treatment for the aggressive adolescent sexual offender. In R. A. Prentky & V. L. Quinsey (Eds.), *Human sexual aggression: Current perspectives* (pp. 215–222). New York: New York Academy of Science.

Becker, J. V., Kaplan, M. S., & Tenke, C. E. (1992). The relationship of abuse history, denial and erectile response: Profiles of adolescent sexual perpetrators. *Behavior Therapy, 23,* 87–97.

Becker, J. V., Kaplan, M. S., Tenke, C. E., & Tartaglini, A. (1991). The incidence of depressive symptomatology in juvenile sex offenders with a history of abuse. *Child Abuse and Neglect, 15,* 531–536.

Borduin, C. M., Henggeler, S. W., Blaske, D. M., & Stein, R. J. (in press). Multisystemic treatment of adolescent sexual offenders. *International Journal of Offender Therapy and Comparative Criminology.*

Davis, G. E., & Leitenberg, H. (1987). Adolescent sex offenders. *Psychological Bulletin, 101,* 417–427.

Deisher, R. W., Wenet, G. A., Paperny, D. M., Clark, T. F., & Fehrenbach, P. A. (1982). Adolescent sexual offense behavior. *Journal of Adolescent Health Care, 2,* 280–286.

Fagan, J., & Wexler, S. (1986). Explanations of sexual assault among violent delinquents. *Journal of Adolescent Research, 3,* 363–385.

Fehrenbach, P. A., Smith, W., Monastersky, C., & Deisher, R. W. (1986). Adolescent sexual offenders: Offender and offense characteristics. *American Journal of Orthopsychiatry, 56,* 225–233.

Freedman, B. (1987, July). Equipoise and ethics of clinical research. *New England Journal of Medicine, 317*(3), 141–145.

Grisso, T. (1986). *Evaluating competencies: Forensic assessments and instruments.* New York and London: Plenum.

Hsu, L. K. G., & Starzynski, J. (1990). Adolescent rapists and adolescent child sexual assaulters. *International Journal of Offender Therapy and Comparative Criminology, 34,* 23–30.

Hunter, J., Becker, J., & Kaplan, M. (in press). The Reliability and Discriminative Utility of the Adolescent Cognitions Scale for Juvenile Sexual Offenders.

Johnson, T. C. (1988). Child perpetrators—children who molest other children: Preliminary findings. *Child Abuse and Neglect, 12,* 219–229.

Kaplan, M. S., Becker, J. V., & Cunningham-Rathner, J. (1988). Characteristics of parents of adolescent incest perpetrators: Preliminary findings. *Journal of Family Violence, 3,* 183–191.

Kaplan, M. S., Becker, J. V., & Martinez, D. F. (1990). A comparison of mothers of adolescent incest vs. non-incest perpetrators. *Journal of Family Violence, 5,* 209–214.

Kaplan, M. S., Becker, J. V., & Tenke, C. E. (1991). Assessment of sexual knowledge and attitudes in an adolescent sex offender population. *Journal of Sex Education and Therapy, 17,* 217–225.

Kaplan, S., Hong, G., & Weinhold, C. (1984). Epidemiology of depressive symptomatology in adolescents. *Journal of the Academy of Child Psychiatry, 23,* 91–98.

Katz, R. C. (1990). Psychological adjustment in adolescent child molesters. *Child Abuse and Neglect, 14,* 567–575.

Kirby, D. (1984). *Sexuality education: An evaluation of programs and their effects.* Santa Cruz, CA: Network Publishing.

Knopp, F. (1982). *Remedial intervention in adolescent sex offenses: Nine program descriptions.* Orwell, VT: Safter Society Press.

Lewis, D. O., Shankok, S. S., & Pincus, J. H. (1979). Juvenile male sex assaulters. *American Journal of Psychiatry, 136,* 1194–1196.

Lewis, D. O., Shankok, S. S., Pincus, J. H., & Glaser, G. H. (in press). Violent juvenile delinquents: Psychiatric, neurological, psychological and abuse factors. *Journal of American Child Psychiatry.*

Matson, J. L., Exveldt-Dawson, K., & Kazdin, A. (1983). Evaluating social skills with youngsters. *Journal of Clinical Child Psychology, 12,* 174–180.

Roberts, A. R., & Camasso, M. J. (in press). Juvenile offenders treatment programs and cost benefit analysis. *Juvenile and Family Court Journal.*

Ryan, G., Lane, S., Davis, J., & Isaac, C. (1987). Juvenile sex offenders: Development and correction. *Child Abuse and Neglect, 11,* 385–395.

Sapp, A. D., & Vaughn, M. S. (1990). Juvenile sex offender treatment at state-operated correctional institutions. *International Journal of Offender Therapy and Comparative Criminology, 34,* 131–146.

Saunders, E. B., & Awad, G. A. (1988). Assessment, management, and treatment: Planning for male adolescent sexual offenders. *American Journal of Orthopsychiatry, 58,* 571–579.

Saunders, E. B., Awad, G. A., & White, G. (1986). Male adolescent sexual offenders: The offender and the offense. *Canadian Journal of Psychiatry, 31,* 542–549.

Schram, D. D., Milloy, C. D., & Rowe, W. E. (1991). Juvenile sex offenders: A follow-up study of reoffense behavior. Unpublished manuscript.

Shoor, M., Speed, M. H., & Bartelt, C. (1986). Syndrome of the adolescent child molester. *American Journal of Psychiatry, 122,* 783–789.

Smith, H., & Israel, E. (1987). Sibling incest: A study of the dynamics of 25 cases. *Child Abuse and Neglect, 11,* 101–108.

Smith, W. R., & Monastersky, C. (1986). Assessing juvenile sexual offenders' risk for reoffending. *Criminal Justice and Behavior, 13,* 115–140.

Smith, W. R., Monastersky, C., & Deisher, R. M. (1987). MMPI-based personality types among juvenile sexual offenders. *Journal of Clinical Psychology, 43,* 422–430.

Tarter, R. E., Hegedus, A. M., Alterman, A. I., & Katz-Garris, L. (1983). Cognitive capacities of juvenile violent, nonviolent, and sexual offenders. *The Journal of Nervous and Mental Disease, 171,* 564–567.

13

CONCLUSION: COMPLEMENTARY APPROACHES TO SEXUAL AGGRESSION

Gordon C. Nagayama Hall, Richard Hirschman,
Andrea Fox Boardman, Denise D. Shondrick, Kathleen P. Stafford,
Victoria Codispoti, Gerald Heinbaugh, Steven Neuhaus,
and David Krenrick

Although sexual aggressors are part of a heterogeneous population, there is a considerable amount of overlap in the motivational determinants of sexually aggressive behavior. Across samples of sexually aggressive men, some sexually aggressive acts are considered primarily paraphilic and others primarily violent. A radio bandwidth model with channels of varying strength may be a useful way to conceptualize the various motivational variables of sexual aggression in different samples.

The multiple determinants of sexually aggressive behavior have received differing emphases in existing theoretical models. Although evolutionary considerations are not in the mainstream of most contemporary theories and research, Ellis (chapter 3) and Malamuth et al. (chapter 5) have included evolutionary variables as a context for sexually aggressive behavior. However, as with some other vestiges of human evolution, such as the appendix, sexual aggression no longer has an adaptive function. Although neurohormonal variables explain some of the variance in aggressive behavior in general, they fail to explain much of the variance in sexually aggressive behavior (Gladue, 1990; Hall, 1990; Prentky, 1985). It appears that a minority of sexually aggressive men may have abnormal hormonal levels, or excessively high levels of sexual drive, as reflected in sexual arousal patterns. Moreover, hormonal and sexual arousal patterns may be influenced by behavior and the environment (Barbaree & Marshall, 1991; Gladue, Boechler, & McCaul, 1989). Nevertheless, any comprehensive model of sexually aggressive behavior should account for biological etiologies.

There are several motivational variables associated with sexually aggressive behavior that have been studied fairly extensively and have been identified across samples of sexual aggressors, as presented in this volume. Among these variables are deviant sexual arousal and fantasies, cognitive distortions or attitudes, hostile masculinity, empathy and intimacy deficits, lifestyle impulsivity and psychopathy, needs for dominance and control, and social skills deficits. Developmental factors associated with sexual aggression are family and social environment, childhood sexual abuse, childhood physical abuse or neglect, caregiver instability, and institutionalization as a juvenile. Interactive models of these variables explain more of the variance in sexually aggressive behavior than do additive models (Malamuth, 1986). However, the complexity of interactive models may become unwieldy for research and applied purposes. A major task that faces theorists and researchers is to develop a model that is comprehensive, yet sufficiently parsimonious for research and clinical applications.

Ideally, treatment approaches should focus on major etiological variables of sexual aggression. Although many programs have components to treat most of the motivational variables discussed earlier, many treatment programs proceed without an emphasis on etiology. It is possible that the relatively poor effectiveness of treatment programs with sexual aggressors is at least partially a function of a lack of theories to guide treatment efforts toward the most critical motivational factors (Hall & Hirschman, 1991; Hall, Shondrick, & Hirschman, 1993).

Existing treatment programs for sexual aggressors have been more effective with child molesters than with sexual aggressors against women (Maletzky, 1991; Marshall, Jones, Ward, Johnston, & Barbaree, 1991). This differential effectiveness may be partially a function of the prominence of deviant sexual arousal among child molesters. Various behavioral methods have been developed that are effective in reducing deviant sexual arousal. However, deviant sexual arousal may be characteristic of a minority of men who are sexually aggressive against women. The relative ineffectiveness of treatment programs for rapists may be a result of their being too closely modeled after treatment programs for child molesters (Marshall, chapter 9). Moreover, rapists and child molesters typically are combined in groups that use a single set of treatment procedures, some of which may not be particularly relevant to rapists (e.g., assertiveness training; avoiding situations with potential victims, which is difficult for rapists because potential victims are almost everywhere).

The treatment approaches of Marshall (chapter 9), Pithers (chapter 10), and Marques et al. (chapter 11) are comprehensive in that they address many of the important motivational variables in sexual aggression and emphasize the importance of follow-up. A sexual aggressor is not cured at the end of his formal meetings with a therapist before he has had the opportunity to reenter the environment in which he had been sexually aggressive. Ideally, follow-up by persons in the environment, such as the probation system and significant others, and, ultimately, self-monitoring by the client, and extended treatment beyond the formal therapy sessions may be necessary for better outcomes. The outcome data provided by Marques et al. provide initial evidence of the effectiveness of these treatment methods with sexual aggressors against women.

In the same fashion in which treatment has been extended prospectively beyond formal therapy sessions, a retrospective extension of the important components of treatment programs for sexual aggressors also appears to be a viable method of prevention. The treatments reviewed by Becker, Harris, and Sales (chapter 12) may prevent juvenile sexual aggressors from continuing their sexually aggressive behavior into adulthood. More generally, increased empathy, improved intimacy, and reduced hostility toward women are skills from which males of all ages may benefit. Because such skills appear to be important in preventing relapse among sexual aggressors, it is logical that the same skills may be effective in preventing sexually aggressive behavior before it occurs. To coin a term, this approach might be considered *prelapse* prevention. However, most prevention efforts have been directed at women and children who are the potential victims of sexual aggression. Although these efforts are critical in terms of empowering women and children, equal effort should be devoted to the men who are ultimately responsible for perpetrating sexual aggression (Hall, 1983). Moreover, because there are no lobbying groups in society for perpetrators as there are for victims, it is incumbent on clinicians and researchers to advocate the benefits of prevention efforts with potential perpetrators (Marshall, chapter 8).

Sexual aggression prevention programs may be difficult to implement with men. Although innovative efforts with men in college fraternities and athletic teams exist (Walsh, 1990), it seems unlikely that men will volunteer en masse for such programs. Thus, it may be most practical to implement such programs at an early point in a young male's education. An existing educational program that teaches and rewards nonaggressive and noncompetitive behavior is the cooperative learning approach (Johnson & Johnson, 1989). Success in this approach is contingent on cooperative efforts within a group of students. Thus, students are required to learn and develop social skills that may reduce aggressive tendencies, and presumably sexually aggressive tendencies as well. Another potentially promising approach would be education regarding sexual aggression at the high school or college level (Linz, Fuson, & Donnerstein, 1990; Linz, Wilson, & Donnerstein, 1992). Hopefully, such education will change attitudes toward sexual aggression and ultimately reduce sexually aggressive behavior. However, prevention efforts should be designed and evaluated carefully, rather than being implemented without consideration of impact, as has been the case in some child sexual abuse prevention programs (Berrick & Gilbert, 1991; Miller-Perrin & Wurtele, 1988; Reppucci & Haugaard, 1989).

We view the approaches to sexual aggression in this volume as complementary, rather than competing. No single approach accounts for all the variance in sexually aggressive behavior, and different approaches may be more relevant for different populations of sexually aggressive men. A combination of approaches may be necessary for optimal understanding, treatment, and prevention of sexually aggressive behavior. We hope that the approaches offered in this volume provide a framework and impetus for much needed future research and clinical innovations in an effort to understand, treat, and prevent sexually aggressive behavior.

REFERENCES

Barbaree, H. E., & Marshall, W. L. (1991). The role of male sexual arousal in rape: Six models. *Journal of Consulting and Clinical Psychology, 59,* 621–630.

Berrick, J. D., & Gilbert, N. (1991). *With the best of intentions: The child sexual abuse prevention movement.* New York: Guilford.

Gladue, B. A. (1990). Hormones and neuroendocrine factors in atypical human sexual behavior. In J. Feierman (Ed.), *Pedophilia: Biosocial dimensions* (pp. 274–298). New York: Aldine de Gruyter.

Gladue, B. A., Boechler, M., & McCaul, K. (1989). Hormonal response to competition in human males. *Aggressive Behavior, 15,* 409–422.

Hall, G. C. N. (1990). Prediction of sexual aggression. *Clinical Psychology Review, 10,* 229–245.

Hall, G. C. N., & Hirschman, R. (1991). Toward a theory of sexual aggression: A quadripartite model. *Journal of Consulting and Clinical Psychology, 59,* 662–669.

Hall, G. C. N., Shondrick, D. D., & Hirschman, R. (1993). Conceptually-derived treatments for sexual aggressors. *Professional Psychology: Research and Practice, 24,* 62–69.

Hall, J. D. (1983). The mind that burns in each body: Women, rape, and racial violence. In A. Snitow, C. Stansell, & S. Thompson (Eds.), *Powers of desire: The politics of sexuality* (pp. 328–349). New York: Monthly Review Press.

Johnson, D. W., & Johnson, R. T. (1989). *Cooperation and competition: Theory and research.* Edina, MN: Interaction Book Co.

Linz, D., Fuson, I. A., & Donnerstein, E. (1990). Mitigating the negative effects of sexually violent mass communications through preexposure briefings. *Communication Research, 17,* 641–674.

Linz, D., Wilson, B. J., & Donnerstein, E. (1992). Sexual violence in the mass media: Legal solutions, warnings, and mitigation through education. *Journal of Social Issues, 48,* 145–171.

Malamuth, N. M. (1986). Predictors of naturalistic sexual aggression. *Journal of Personality and Social Psychology, 50,* 953–962.

Maletzky, B. M. (1991). *Treating the sex offender.* Newbury Park, CA: Sage.

Marshall, W. L., Jones, R., Ward, T., Johnston, P., & Barbaree, H. E. (1991).

Treatment outcome with sex offenders. *Clinical Psychology Review, 11,* 465–485.

Miller-Perrin, C. L., & Wurtele, S. K. (1988). The child sexual abuse prevention movement: A critical analysis of primary and secondary approaches. *Clinical Psychology Review, 8,* 313–329.

Prentky, R. A. (1985). The neurochemistry and neuroendocrinology of sexual aggression. In D. P. Farrington & J. Gunn (Eds.), *Aggression and dangerousness* (pp. 7–55). New York: Wiley.

Reppucci, N., & Haugaard, J. J. (1989). Prevention of child sexual abuse: Myth or reality. *American Psychologist, 44,* 1266–1275.

Walsh, C. (1990, April). *FARE: Fraternity acquaintance rape education.* Paper presented at the meeting of the Southeastern Psychological Association, Atlanta, Georgia.

INDEX